Globalization and Europe

D0246067

The Open University

Globalization and Europe

jazz 60
Warszawa 27-30·X·1960
ZRZESZENIE STUDENTÓW POLSKICH

EDITED BY Mark
Pittaway

This publication forms part of an Open University course AA300 *Europe: Culture and Identities in a Contested Continent*. Details of this and other Open University courses can be obtained from the Course Information and Advice Centre, PO Box 724, The Open University, Milton Keynes MK7 6ZS, United Kingdom; tel. +44 (0)1908 653231; e-mail general-enquiries@open.ac.uk

Alternatively, you may visit the Open University website at http://www.open.ac.uk where you can learn more about the wide range of courses and packs offered at all levels by The Open University.

To purchase a selection of Open University course materials visit the webshop at www.ouw.co.uk, or contact Open University Worldwide, Michael Young Building, Walton Hall, Milton Keynes MK7 6AA, United Kingdom for a brochure. Tel. +44 (0)1908 858785; fax +44 (0)1908 858787; e-mail ouwenq@open.ac.uk

The Open University
Walton Hall, Milton Keynes
MK7 6AA

First published 2003

Copyright © 2003 The Open University

Reprinted 2009

All rights reserved. No part of this publication may be reproduced, stored in a retrieval system, transmitted or utilized in any form or by any means, electronic, mechanical, photocopying, recording or otherwise, without written permission from the publisher or a licence from the Copyright Licensing Agency Ltd. Details of such licences (for reprographic reproduction) may be obtained from the Copyright Licensing Agency Ltd of 90 Tottenham Court Road, London W1T 4LP.

Edited, designed and typeset by The Open University

Printed in the United Kingdom by TJ International Ltd, Padstow.

Colour plates origination by Interscan Graphics, Malaysia

Colour plates printed in the United Kingdom by Nicholson & Bass Ltd.

ISBN 0 7492 96127

1.1

The paper used in this publication contains pulp sourced from forests independently certified to the Forest Stewardship Council (FSC) principles and criteria. Chain of custody certification allows the pulp from these forests to be tracked to the end use (see www.fsc-uk.org).

Mixed Sources
Product group from well-managed forests and other controlled sources
www.fsc.org Cert no. SGS-COC-2482
© 1996 Forest Stewardship Council
FSC

Contents

Contributors

Tim Benton, Professor of Art History, the Open University

Marion Bowman, Senior Lecturer in Religious Studies, the Open University

Colin Chant, Senior Lecturer in the History of Science, Technology and Medicine, the Open University

David Crowley, Tutor in the History of Design, Royal College of Art

Mark Pittaway, Lecturer in European Studies, History Department, the Open University

Hugh Starkey, Senior Lecturer, Centre for Citizenship Studies in Education, University of Leicester

Readings

The readings that appear in this book are extracts from the following works.

Chapter 1

Judit Bodnár, *Fin de Millénaire Budapest: Metamorphoses of Urban Life*

Caroline Humphrey, 'Creating a culture of disillusionment: consumption in Moscow, a chronicle of changing times'

Sidney W. Mintz, *Sweetness and Power: the Place of Sugar in Modern History*

Raphael Samuel, *Theatres of Memory*, vol. 1: *Past and Present in Contemporary Culture*

Chapter 2

Altiero Spinelli, the Ventotene manifesto, 'Towards a Free and United Europe'

Resolutions and conclusions of the Congress of Europe, The Hague, May 1948

Statute of the Council of Europe

European Convention on Human Rights and Fundamental Freedoms

Chapter 3

Simon James, *The Atlantic Celts: Ancient People or Modern Invention?*

Malcolm Chapman, *The Celts: the Construction of a Myth*

Marion Löffler, *'A Book of Mad Celts': John Wickens and the Celtic Congress of Caernarfon 1904*

Chapter 5

Jonathan Zatlin, 'The vehicle of desire: the Trabant, the Wartburg, and the end of the GDR'

Chapter 6

Harrison E. Salisbury, 'Nixon and Khruschev argue in public as US exhibit opens; accuse each other of threats' *New York Times*

Stanisław Komornicki, 'Jak urządzić nowe mieszkanie: artykuł dyskusyjny', *Stolica*

Victor Buchli, 'Khrushchev, Modernism, and the fight against *petit-bourgeois* consciousness in the Soviet home' *Journal of Design History.*

Introduction

MARK PITTAWAY

Globalization and Europe explores the issues that are fundamental to understanding shifting identities in contemporary Europe. It has often been argued that pressures of globalization are fundamentally challenging the basis for distinct European identities. These pressures, identified by commentators, range from the globalization of finance, production and trade to the growing scope and power of international organizations and notions of international law; from the increasing influence of transnational mass media to patterns of migration that cross continents. This book takes a critical look at the impact of such phenomena on the identities that exist in Europe today. It is organized around a discussion of the impact of particular global processes on local patterns of identity formation. Much commentary assumes the novelty of globalization, associating it with changes in the international economy that have occurred over the past twenty-five years. This book argues that European identities (and identities within Europe) have, in fact, interacted with global process for at least two hundred and fifty years. The chapters in this book suggest that patterns of European colonialism and imperialism, for example, should be included in discussions of contemporary globalization in order to situate more recent changes in Europe in their proper historical context.

The book consists of a series of case studies that aim to show how various global processes over the course of the past two and a half centuries have interacted with particular local identities. In doing this they reveal several important points. First, they show that there are and have been a large number of different projects that have developed either as part of, or in response to, various global processes. These range from the transformation of finance, production and trade to European integration, or from the attempts of various states to shape consumer cultures in order to preserve cultural distinctiveness and tradition in the face of pressures that have threatened to eradicate cultural diversity. Secondly, they stress that while economic processes on a global level have been fundamental to the reshaping of identities in modern Europe, such processes are not exclusively economic. The development of mass consumer cultures – one of the most striking manifestations of early twenty-first century globalization – is as much a cultural and social, as an economic phenomenon. The global discourse of human rights, furthermore, is without doubt the manifestation of a political process, in which European bodies have played a part. Thirdly, these case studies point out that the result of global processes has not been the eradication of cultural distinctiveness within Europe and still less the replacement of European with 'global' identities. Instead European identities, whether these are the pan-continental identities associated with the European Union and the Council of Europe, or regional and local identities embodied in the Open-Air Museum Movement, have been constructed and reconstructed as a result of engagement with these processes.

The case studies focus on how these shifts in identities have been reflected in culture. Culture is taken to mean here, in Cristina Chimisso's definition, 'the totality of symbols and artefacts produced by human beings .... Modes of thinking, feeling and behaving .... values, customs, traditions and norms' (Chimisso, 2003, p. 14). The range of cultural identities through which the authors explore these themes is therefore very broad, from Scandinavian and central European open-air museums to postwar Polish domestic interiors, from Euro Disney to the artefactual expressions of contemporary Celtic identities in Scotland, Ireland and Wales, from the cultural values attached to the motor car in the two postwar German states to the attempts of the Council of Europe to project a European identity by harnessing the global discourse of human rights. The importance attached to the material and visual culture in which many of these identities are embodied is reflected in the inclusion of two visual essays that are attached to two of the essays that make up the book. The first deals with changing forms of Celtic artistic expression, while the second traces the history of Europe's Open-Air Museums Movement by exploring the museums themselves. The chapters in this book approach these issues from an interdisciplinary perspective, recognizing that their own disciplines alone are insufficient to explore the questions that surround the interaction between global processes and identities in Europe.

Chapter 1, 'European identities in a globalized world', provides a theoretical discussion and analysis of the issues involved in exploring the interaction between global process and identities in Europe, providing a framework for the other chapters. I analyse this interaction through a case study of the export of capitalist, western (European and North American) consumer cultures to the former socialist states in central and eastern Europe during the 1990s. I examine how these cultures have been received in central and eastern Europe, and probe the issues of identity that are illuminated by their reception. Then I shift focus in order to situate contemporary patterns of 'globalization' in their broader historical context, and conclude with an examination of how growing international cultural exchange has resulted in a search in many European societies for particular roots. I discuss a variety of texts, including extracts from the work of an urban sociologist, Judit Bodnár, the arguments of two anthropologists discussing different contexts, Caroline Humphrey and Sidney Mintz, and one historian, Raphael Samuel.

In Chapter 2, 'The Council of Europe: defining and defending a European identity', Hugh Starkey analyses the attempts of the Council of Europe to promote a vision of a common European identity, appropriating global discourses of democracy and human rights in order to forge a pan-continental notion of belonging. Starkey sets this attempt within the historical context of Europe at the end of the Second World War. He explains the Council of Europe's attempts to project a new identity as being rooted in a reaction to the devastation wrought by the Second World War. Starkey discusses a number of legal and political texts that are essential to exploring the origins and the practice of the Council of Europe. First, he examines the Ventotene manifesto, before moving on to consider the economic and social, political and cultural resolutions of the Congress of Europe, the congress's message to Europeans, the Statute of the Council of Europe and extracts from the European Convention on Human Rights.

Chapter 3, 'From Keltoi to cybercelts: continuity and change in Celtic identities', investigates shifting Celtic identity in contemporary Europe. Marion Bowman examines the development of Celtic identities in both their historical and transnational context. In considering the articulation of Celtic identities in France, Ireland, Scotland and Wales she is able to show that there are 'different versions of Celticity and complex histories behind them'. Her historical examination of modern Celtic identities, shows that they are and have been in a constant process of construction and reconstruction, usefully illustrating how certain identities have been affected by global processes within contemporary Europe. In her chapter she discusses extracts from the work of academic analysts of Celtic identity like Malcom Chapman, Marion Löffler and the archaeologist Simon James. This chapter is also accompanied by a visual essay entitled 'Celtic arts: images and imagination'.

In her discussion of Celticity Bowman focuses to some extent on how artefacts – in other words, material culture – can both embody and reflect debates surrounding identity. Material culture, in the form of architecture, is the focus of Chapter 4, 'Architecture and identities: from the Open-Air Museum Movement to Mickey Mouse'. Tim Benton examines Europe's open-air museums, beginning with those founded in the late nineteenth century with the intention of preserving the 'authentic' rural cultures of many European regions, at a time when ways of life were threatened by the relentless march of industrialization. He ends his discussion with an examination of Euro Disney, Paris, a case study of the fluidity of culture in an age of globalization, where 'authentic' European cultural artefacts have been reproduced in American cinema and then sold back to Europe through the theme park. Benton shows how the Open-Air Museum Movement embodies the construction and reconstruction of local identities over a century and a half. His texts are of course the museums themselves, which are represented by a range of colour and black and white photographs.

The focus on the intersection of everyday material culture and identity is retained and developed in Chapter 5, 'Cars, contexts and identities: the Volkswagen and the Trabant'. Colin Chant discusses the intersection between material culture and national identities in the context of east and west Germany during the cold war. In doing so he raises issues of the impact of mass consumerism in postwar Europe and the effect of the spread of consumer culture on identities in Europe. Though his essay contains an extract by the historian Jonathan Zatlin, the cultural artefacts he discusses are the cars themselves.

The reception of mass consumerism in postwar Europe is a theme that is developed by the historian of design David Crowley, in Chapter 6, 'Making the socialist home in postwar eastern Europe'. Crowley's focus is on how socialist regimes in postwar central and eastern Europe sought to import 'western' models of mass consumerism to boost their legitimacy. He considers how these models influenced the design of central and eastern European homes, how those designs impacted on the lives of the citizens of socialist states and the consequences this reception had for the legitimacy of the regimes themselves. While his chapter is centrally concerned with discussing the design of postwar central and eastern European homes, it is supplemented with readings drawn from an article originally published in the *New York Times*, articles from contemporary Polish periodicals and an academic article by the anthropologist Victor Buchli.

This is the last of four books in the series *Europe: Culture and Identities in a Contested Continent*. They form the main texts of an Open University level 3 course of the same name.

Reference

Chimisso, C. (2003) *Exploring European Identities*, Milton Keynes, The Open University.

1

European identities in a globalized world

MARK PITTAWAY

Introduction

Austria, Belgium, Finland, France, Germany, Greece, Ireland, Italy, Luxembourg, the Netherlands, Portugal and Spain.

On 1 January 2002 **twelve** of the fifteen member states of the European Union adopted a new single currency – the euro   as their legal tender. This heralded the end of an era in which each of these states had possessed their own national currencies. With this act the twelve countries bound their economic futures in a direct way to the European Union. It was the culmination of a process of economic and monetary union that had, at least in part, been conceived as a specifically European response to the globalization of finance and trade during the final quarter of the twentieth century. The deregulation of global financial markets and trade regimes was coupled with the revolutionary spread of new information and communication technologies. Consequently

> world exports were worth twice as much in real terms in 1993 than twenty years earlier, while daily turnover on the foreign exchange markets had exploded from $200 million in the mid-1980s to $1.2 trillion in 1995.

(Reynolds, 2000, p. 652)

In this global economic context the introduction of the euro represented a plank of a programme that was designed to make the European Union a global economic power in its own right, with the power and influence over market forces to protect the fundamental economic interests of its member states.

It was argued that the globalization of finance and trade would have important cultural implications, resulting in the homogenization of everyday culture, at least in the wealthy consumer societies of North America, western Europe and Australasia. In turn this would lead to a 'consciousness of the world as a whole' (Robertson, 1992, p. 8). The euro was in part a response to the globalization of finance and the

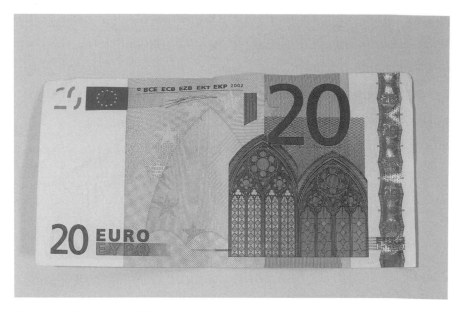

Figure 1.1   Front of 20 euro note. Photo: Trip/Helen Rogers ©
European Central Bank

Figure 1.2   Back of a 20 euro note. Photo: Trip/Helen Rogers ©
European Central Bank

consequent domination of the European economy by the German economy. At the same time the new currency represented an attempt to lay the foundations of a European cultural identity; in Manuel Castells's term 'a legitimizing identity' (Castells, 1997, p. 8) for the European Union that would buttress its claim to be a global power in its own right.

Money not only forms a means of exchange but is a central part of everyday material culture; for this reason currency reveals much about identity and how it can be expressed by cultural artefacts. National currencies, in particular, have been used to legitimize national identities. The pound, the currency of the United Kingdom, carries an image of the head of the sovereign in order to make the link between monarch, state and currency, though the addition of this image to English banknotes occurred only in 1960. Other national currencies have reached into actual or mythologized national pasts to decorate coins or banknotes.

EXERCISE

Please look at Figures 1.1 and 1.2. What identity or identities are being projected in the design of the 20 euro banknote depicted here? By what means are these identities constructed?

DISCUSSION

This banknote is clearly attempting to both project and legitimize a European identity. It sets out to achieve this first with reference to a geographic identity – see the representation of Europe as geographical space in the bottom right hand corner on the back of the note. This representation is itself interesting, for it excludes most of Russia and most of Turkey – although Turkey is a current applicant to and possible future member of the European Union. Secondly, the note's reference to a European architectural heritage makes a claim to a European identity that is historically rooted. Presumably because a 'history' based on events or cultural figures might be controversial or divisive, a less potentially controversial approach has been adopted. Neither the windows depicted on the front of the banknote nor the bridge shown on the reverse are specific sites; to have used images of actual places might have provoked unnecessary controversy about the inclusion of one member state's 'national' monuments and the exclusion of others. The idea is therefore to represent generic architectural features that are to some extent to be found in all European states.

The euro is both simultaneously and paradoxically an attempt to appropriate economic forces that are breaking down state borders and homogenizing identities in order to legitimize a European identity. It is not the only project that has sought to create a specifically European identity through the appropriation of global forces. In Chapter 2 of this volume, 'The Council of Europe: defining and defending a European identity', Hugh Starkey discusses the attempts of another European institution, the Council of Europe, to generate a European identity using the global political discourse of human rights. Both projects, the introduction of the euro and of the council, can be said to seek to supplant national identities and replace them with a broader, all-encompassing European identity.

It has, however, been the project to create a single European currency that has generated most controversy in setting European identities against national ones during the end of the twentieth and the beginning of the twenty-first centuries. Concerns about the future of national identity in a Europe with a single currency have played a role in the mobilization of anti-EU sentiment across the continent. This was evident in referenda on the Maastricht Treaty (which included the creation of a single currency as one of its central planks) held in France in 1992 and in Denmark in 1992 and 1993. It was a key concern of eurosceptics in the United Kingdom throughout the period and a central question in Germany where the deutschmark, introduced in 1949, was a key symbol of the postwar economic miracle that had served to stabilize cold war West Germany. Most significant, concern about national sovereignty and identity was central in Denmark's rejection of the single currency in a further referendum in September 2000.

In part the political controversy that surrounded the introduction of the euro was a product of the very real conflict within European societies that its creation engendered. Member governments of the EU prepared for the introduction of the currency by pursuing policies that accepted the power of financial markets in a globalized economic environment. These policies, designed to create 'convergence' between states, meant budget cuts, especially to social welfare plans, and strict counter-inflationary programmes that led to low growth and high unemployment. In a few countries, like France in 1995, such policies provoked open protest. Everywhere they led to considerable discontent.

Resistance to the euro, however, has been as much about defending national identities against the *assumed* threat that projects to create all-encompassing European identities are seen to pose. In Europe, perhaps to a greater extent than anywhere else, nation-states have played a central role in defining political citizenship and shaping cultural identities. Nation-states have been challenged not only by the European project but also by the globalization of economic life, which has limited their ability to maintain domestic social contracts. Because the challenges to national identities and to nation-states coincided in the 1990s, resistance to European integration was fuelled by a feeling that national identities are threatened by impersonal forces. In the United Kingdom, according to one observer writing in 2001, 'the issue' of the euro was 'about cultural identity' (Tripathi, 2001). A debate over a currency was in reality one over national identity cast as a 'resistance identity' to a European project that had an ambiguous relationship to global economic forces.

This brief and cursory discussion suggests that the cultural reactions to global economic forces are complex, and highly dependent on the societies and identities that they interact with. It further suggests caution about the arguments made by many observers about the shifts in economic forces and other factors, such as cheap travel, which have produced homogeneous, 'global' identities. The anthropologist Jonathan Friedman has proposed that we distinguish analytically between 'globalization' as a process which he argues is essentially about 'global awarenesses' (Friedman, 1994, p. 198), and global systems, phenomena like the world economy. This leads him to argue that 'the question of identification is properly a question of global systems and not of globalization' (Friedman, 1994, p. 200). In short, when locating European identities in a globalized world we are looking for the effects of concrete global forces for example the operation of the world economy, global ideas about consumption or the notion of human rights – on the construction of identities that are local in nature. The sociologist Manuel Castells has gone further; for him, global forces in the form of what he terms 'the network society' are forcing people to shape 'project identities' that stem from 'the reconstruction of defensive identities around communal principles' (Castells, 1997, p. 11). In other words, the globalization of societies has produced a reaction, as people have sought to resist the process by 'defending' identities they perceive to be threatened.

All of the chapters contained in this volume explore the formation of identities in Europe in relation to defined global forces. In this first chapter I want to introduce you to some of the issues that you will encounter in more depth later, through a discussion of how global processes are remaking and have remade cultural identities in Europe. I cannot in the space available to me here provide a comprehensive treatment of this subject; rather, I shall focus on the following issues.

- Global economic forces manifest themselves in everyday culture, through phenomena such as forms of consumerism.

- The intrusion of such forces into everyday life means that cultural identities both reshape and are reshaped by local contexts.

- These local contexts are highly variable and the reactions to such forces differ according to that context.

- The interaction of global forces and local contexts have been ongoing in Europe for much of the last 250 years.

- What we know as 'globalization' is only the most recent manifestation of that phenomenon.

- Finally, European identities, based on religion, language, history and geography, are again being reconstructed as a result.

This chapter, therefore, echoes many of the themes introduced in the previous three books of this series (Chimisso, 2003; Pittaway, 2003; Emsley, 2003) and sets them in the context of the way global forces are remaking and have remade identities across the continent. By the end of your work with this chapter you should have gained some appreciation of the diverse ways in which global forces are remaking identities throughout Europe, and how this process has been influenced by and in turn influences the development of cultural identities. My focus is not on abstract global processes, but in the spirit of this book, which is based primarily on concrete cultural artefacts, I shall concentrate on how global processes and the effect they have on cultural identities are and have been manifested in everyday life and culture.

Consumerism as a case study: global process and cultural identities

In order to help you think about some of the issues that were raised in abstract form in my introduction I want to introduce you to a concrete case. It has been widely argued that the development of postmodern mass consumerism in the last two decades and the cultural forms associated with it – in the shape of hypermarkets or shopping malls, or even the development of transnational brand identities – represent one of the most ubiquitous manifestations of the globalization of economic processes (Klein, 2000; Miller, 1998; Zukhin, 1995). In post-socialist central and eastern Europe which, prior to the 1990s, had consumer economies that were relatively closed to the outside world and were often riddled with shortages, the impact of the introduction of global forms of capitalist consumerism has been striking. Indeed it has been one of the central symbols of the globalization of the economies of the region as policies of privatization and trade liberalization have forced their introduction into the capitalist world market. At the same time the political landscape of the region has been transformed by the expression of reconstructed national identities. Such expressions of identity have not only been a reaction to the experience of the recent socialist past but have been fuelled by the everyday experience of the globalization of economic life.

The first reading in this chapter was written by the Hungarian-born, urban sociologist Judit Bodnár. It describes the introduction of the shopping mall to the Hungarian capital, Budapest, during the mid 1990s. While both the geographical and temporal contexts of the reading are highly specific, the extract raises issues that have become familiar in other contexts. At a deeper level it speaks to concerns about the links between the globalization of economies on the one hand, and local cultures and identities on the other.

In Defense of Shopping: Secluding Public Space in the Mall

In terms of their aesthetics as well as their relationship to globalization, shopping malls are a counterpoint to art movie theatres. Instead of using commercial revenues to subsidize art (as Budapest Film has done), malls incorporate all manifestations of art into the overarching logic of commerce. Their spectacular spread is linked to global finance and culture quite directly, as the process is represented in public speech.

What is called in the Hungarian press a 'European-quality shopping mall' was constructed in Budapest right next to a socialist-modernist 'shopping center' in the middle of a large housing estate with outlets of the supermarket chain Kaiser's, the construction materials chain Bauwellt, and McDonald's. An 'American-type' service center, for some reason called Europark Kispest – financed mostly by American capital – has emerged on the outskirts of Pest at a major subway and train station whose aesthetic was already strikingly reminiscent of similar establishments on the working-class margins of Vienna. In 1995, a most grandiose and symbolically important project was conceived and begun, a combined 'administrative-shopping-entertainment center for the family,' the Pole Center. The $100 million establishment is housed in a redesigned former Soviet Army garrison in District XV. The progenitors and financiers of the enterprise are North American businessmen and Hungarian émigrés Peter Munk, Béla W. Fejér, Andrew Sarlos, and Otto Blau – the developer of the World Financial Center in New York – along with revered Hungarian entrepreneur Sándor Demján, who gained recognition and millions by establishing the East Bloc's first, cooperatively owned, supermarket in a busy traffic center of Budapest in the early 1980s. The Pole Center was designed as the prototype for an additional twenty-five multifunctional centers to be erected all over eastern Europe. Following the success of Pole Center, the Pole Holding Company announced the opening of additional malls in twelve to fifteen Hungarian towns, 'creating 700 new jobs' at each.

The Pole Center is touted as a place that is all-around 'American.' The public has even been told that the separation of ownership and management 'followed the American practice.' The only 'Hungarian feature' of the establishment is that it accommodates a traditional farmers' market. Apart from its grand opening, Pole center has made it to the national news only once, precisely for its 'American' character. The announcement that the center would be open on May Day – a national holiday – evoked strong sentiments from the public: the protests of unions and other interest groups were joined by criticism from the Ministry of Labor, which declared that working on a holiday is unlawful and that it would fine any stores that opened.

The second major mall, Danube Plaza ... is in a traditional industrial district of the city – a location chosen mostly because of the convenient availability of a major subway line and as a major contribution to the ongoing effort to 'upgrade' that neighborhood into a minor commercial center. Another recently opened shopping mall, built by the same Israeli developers as Danube Plaza, has been named Csepel Plaza, after the district and island of Budapest where it is located; its name is synonymous with that of Csepel Iron- and Metal Works, the symbol of socialist industrialization ... Apart from stores, Csepel Plaza includes a multiplex cinema and a video arcade.

Records are to be superseded, by definition. Hardly had the Pole Center opened as the number one site in Budapest before multinational and local capital and expertise realigned to promote the 'construction of the century,' the West End City Center, the scale of which is indeed unmatched since the fin de siècle. The U.S.$200 million project was launched by the cooperation of the same Sándor Demján and Peter Munk who had pooled resources for the Pole. The area, as suggested by the name, acquired its present layout with the construction of the wrought-iron structure of the Western Station – very much in line with the style of the Eiffel Tower, in fact, designed and erected by the company of Jean Eiffel in 1877. The station is an important switch point on the Pest side of the main ring whose transportation function was later supplemented and reinforced by a new subway line. The small square facing the iron-and-glass hall of the station gave place to a new department store in the 1980s that changed the character of the neighboring shopping streets. At that time the square was called Marx Square, and allegedly one entry in the competition to name the supermarket suggested 'Karl Marx World Department Store.' The store opened, but under a different name: Skála Metró. Its fame quickly declined with the status of the area, which in 1992 became revernacularized quite appropriately as Western Square. The new West End City Center, which involves the reconstruction of an area of 110,000 square meters, will not be simply another 'town center'; the developers' ambition is to make it Budapest's new downtown (Szalai, 1998). The wide-open space that drives constructions of this size to the outskirts of cities is created in this particular inner-city environment by covering the train tracks. Planned to debut at the turn of the millennium, the urban spectacle – 'splendid as Piccadilly Circus but more exciting' – will offer a mixture of old and new themes: a main concourse wider than the Champs Elysées, wax figures in the manner of Madame Tussaud's, a scale replica of Niagara Falls, and a 'world cinema' projecting life-size images from six cities of the world (Szalai, 1998). One of the developers – the largest in North America – who is building the new city claims, 'Budapest is the most exciting investment site in Europe' (quoted in Szalai, 1998).

The new city is built in the form of shopping malls. Malls are a novelty in the local culture of shopping. They radiate a clearly Western, thus 'more advanced,' lifestyle and a general sense of abundance to consumers whose appetites had been whet for quite a long time by a socialist shortage economy. This partly explains the lack of popular resistance to malls, something that could lead through social and political conflicts to the emergence of more creative forms of shopping culture. Ironically, it is not the Hungarian press but the Western media that note the poverty of localization strategies. With respect to shopping malls and megastores in Budapest, even the *Financial Times*, overall hardly a bastion of resistance to the power of capital, observes:

[Figure 1]   Danube Plaza (Photo: Judit Bodnár)

Budapest does not learn from western examples. ... There are a lot of developers in the Hungarian capital today that could not work at home for reasons of environmental and urban planning considerations. Local municipalities short of resources are eager to sell off their real estate, thinking ahead for a mere 3 months, which could cost them a lot later.

One of the few instances of registered resistance came from traditional market vendors, who occasionally protested the removal of their old market-places: competition and higher stall fees tend to make their operation infeasible. Another genre of resistance has also been reported; an ecological group went to court claiming that the increased traffic due to the construction of the new megastore of a French chain would reduce the quality of life for two hundred thousand residents and pollute the environment. The lack of support for the protest on the part of the local government took the steam out of the initiative. The attitude of the local government was influenced by the $5 million it received for the land sale; in an unconscious response to pollution and health concerns, the government planned to invest it in a new health center. In February 1998, Budapest held its first conference on shopping malls. Experts in attendance saw malls as an unambiguous result of 'the spread of global and multinational trends,' noted the poverty of mall architecture ('The outer look is not very sophisticated ... and the interior design is only slightly better'), and warned about the explosive contrast of enormous consumption and poverty.

For five years, the list of investments of more than $10 million in Budapest has included almost exclusively shopping, trade, or business centers and, occasionally, housing parks. In other words, multifunctional service centers (malls) fill the space for communal development projects. Such ambitions are captured in the straightforward language of the media, which refer to them as 'new town centers.' Malls are interesting not so much as new shopping places, but as a new genre of public space that has made a forceful appearance in Hungary. As such, they are becoming part of public culture. They figured very prominently in the narrative of a horrible crime story for the first time as public places (where one goes for the sake of company).

In late fall 1997, the Hungarian public was shaken by the brutal murder of a cab driver. What led to an uproar was not the murder itself but the fact that it was committed by two fourteen-year-old schoolgirls who were caught almost immediately and who told the shocked police that they did it in order to get the driver's car (although they were hesitant whether the new car, a Ford, was as good as the old one, a Mercedes, that he – the two girls' friend for a few weeks by then – replaced on the day of the murder) and show it off to their friends at Danube Plaza, where they hang out. In fact, they were caught while driving to Danube Plaza, in a routine traffic check. The only firsthand information released about the two perpetrators to the Hungarian public was an investigative reporter's interview with the two girls' friends, whom she found in front of the multiplex cinema at Danube Plaza. This narrative indicates how quickly the shopping mall as public space has been vernacularized by youth culture in a bundle of images intimately linked to cars. Although Danube Plaza is on a major subway line, it is mostly frequented by people who feel safe leaving their fancy cars in the mall's garage instead of on the streets, let alone taking the subway. This ghastly story also plays into the symbols used by conservative politicians who refer to the new, foreign-owned shopping malls as present-day equivalents of the Soviet tanks of 1956, stationed at the edge of Budapest.

References

Szalai, Anna (1998) 'Az évszázad építkezése a Nyugatinál', *Népszabadság*, 28 October.

(Bodnár, 2001, pp. 145–9)

EXERCISE

Please read the extract now and take notes, organizing them around answers to the following questions.

1   How were Budapest's new shopping malls represented to the city's population when they were opened during the mid 1990s?

2   What forms of resistance existed to the construction of the malls? How successful was this resistance?

3   What social problems does Bodnár argue can be linked to the spread of shopping malls across the city?

4   More abstractly, what kinds of identity are embodied in either the public use of shopping malls or opposition to them? Your answer to this question may repeat some of your earlier answers, though it should almost certainly expand on them.

DISCUSSION

1   The new shopping malls were represented as either a 'European-quality shopping mall', or an 'American-type' shopping experience. In a relatively poor, peripheral country, once part of the Soviet sphere of influence and now undergoing painful and radical market transformation, the very use of the term 'European' was extremely powerful. It suggested that the spread of shopping malls was indicative of the 'progress' Hungary was assumed to be making in burying its past as, economically, part of the Soviet bloc. Certainly the image of the shopping mall as 'European' helped legitimize the nature of the experience it offered in the eyes of ordinary Hungarian consumers. The notion of the 'American-type' shopping experience in the reading seems to carry different and more ambiguous meanings, in that it was associated in part with an attempt by powerful multinational corporations to violate the local labour legislation.

2   Numerous examples of fragmented opposition to aspects of the introduction of western-style shopping malls to Budapest are given in the reading. The protest of trade unions against the attempts of the malls' owners to ignore the May Day public holiday – a time when unions and left-wing parties still organize all-day programmes in most major cities that are attended by thousands of people – is one form of opposition. Limited opposition by Hungary's small environmentalist movement is another. Most notably , the 'resistance' of market traders is mentioned, as the vendors worried about the effect of new kinds of shopping experience on their trade.

3   Bodnár can be situated as a critic of shopping malls; for her they represent the colonization of urban space by multinational capital. Though Bodnár notes what she describes as 'the lack of popular resistance to malls' among the Hungarian population at the time they were introduced into the country, she is fiercely critical of them. She regards the malls as the result of an obsession of impoverished local authorities with the privatization of land, rather than any real considerations of rational planning to improve amenities. They have created a new form of public space out of privatized consumption which has generated new kinds of anti-social behaviour – Bodnár describes one notorious and extreme case of criminal behaviour, a murder, as an example. Furthermore she sees the shopping centres as promoting a culture based on privately owned motorized transport, necessarily excluding those dependent on public transport (though this point is not totally borne out by most of the malls she discusses, which are well served by public transport, it is truer of a generation of shopping centres built on the outer edges of the city close to the motorway exits).

4   This is in many ways the most difficult and interesting of the questions that I asked you to consider in relation to this extract. The owners and developers of the malls themselves are seeking to market their shopping centres by projecting an identity on to the consumers who actually shop there. These consumers have 'European' or 'American' shopping habits, rhetorically defined as more advanced and sophisticated than might be implied by the simply 'Hungarian' consumer patterns of shopping in the 'traditional farmers' market' at the Pole centre, or the 'socialist' consumer patterns of going to the Skála Metró. In this very task of marketing the malls their owners are projecting a local version of a broader identity of consumer in a global economy: one designed to appeal to ordinary Hungarians, whose certainties have been shaken by the economic consequences of the 'transition' from 'socialism' to 'Europe'.

The malls are associated with a remaking of Hungarian youth culture and the reshaping of identities associated with terms such as 'teenager' and 'young person'. While certain aspects of western European youth culture – rock music and discos, for example – had penetrated the Iron Curtain in the years prior to 1989 (Kürti, 2002, pp. 180–214), the mall was one of the spaces that allowed the development of a new, explicitly consumerist youth culture during the 1990s. This was not only a response to the development of malls and the multiplex cinemas and indoor skating rinks that some of them contain, but was linked to other cultural consequences of Hungary's integration into the capitalist global economy – the arrival of commercial radio stations and cable television, for instance, which became widely available due to the transformation of the 1990s.

The shopping malls and the debates surrounding them have provided a space for identities to be articulated within Hungarian society that are resistant to globalizing forces. Political identities on both left and right are mentioned by Bodnár. On the left, the unions have attempted to defend the sanctity of the May Day holiday against the attempts of mall owners to erode labour legislation that protected it. Among sections of the nationalist right, 'foreign-owned shopping malls' have been equated with 'Soviet tanks'. The use of these powerful symbols is suggestive of a perceived threat to national values and identities from the cultural artefacts peddled by foreign businesses, as well as a more concrete material threat to Hungarian shopkeepers driven out of business by foreign competition.

Lastly, of course, there are the identities of market traders and small shopkeepers – occupational identities – that are articulated in opposition to the shopping malls. These occupational identities have often been coupled with political identities, especially certain right-wing political identities, that have sought to stress the role of the Hungarian entrepreneur and the Hungarian small-scale producer as central parts of 'the backbone of the nation'.

In short, I hope that working with this reading has helped give you an appreciation of how globalizing pressures manifest themselves in the development of identities that are most definitely local in that they are determined by their immediate context. Appeals made by global multinationals offering 'European' shopping experiences, for example, reflect the concerns of Hungarians about their ambiguous relationship to notions of Europe, exacerbated by their forty-year membership of the Soviet bloc. Furthermore, such pressures and their effects on patterns of consumption have almost completely remade the identities adopted by Hungarian youth. They have also generated identities that can be described as resistant; in the cases discussed above these are based on class, politics, nation and occupation.

Budapest's shopping malls, as described by Bodnár, are merely one manifestation of how these pressures have reshaped Hungarian society at the turn of the century and are continuing to reshape it. The shifts in identities that have accompanied Hungary's 'globalization' have been the products of the circumstances of the country's integration into the global economy during the 1990s and its incomplete political integration into European institutions. At the end of the 1980s, despite limited market reform, the economy of Hungary was dominated by the state which enjoyed a monopoly over foreign trade, commercial banking and much of industry. Private sector elements (where they existed) were relatively marginal.

As a result of economic transformation, by 1997 enterprises owned by foreign multinationals accounted for 65 per cent of all economic activity in the country (Árva and Diczházi, 1998, p. 263). Political change meant a substantial easing of travel restrictions for Hungarians wishing to travel, work or study abroad. The arrival of multinational corporations created a substantial demand for those with western business experience and competence in English, which the domestic labour market proved incapable of satisfying. This led to the establishment of a significant expatriate community (until the mid 1990s one commercial radio station in Budapest broadcast a daily English-language magazine programme). The spread of cable television in the cities and satellite television in rural areas broke the monopoly of the local state broadcaster, not only allowing local television stations to arise, but creating an audience inside Hungary for stations like the music-video-based MTV and German-language providers such as SAT1. The problematic commercialization of the banking sector, the spread of automatic teller machines, the widespread introduction of cash-card-based accounts from 1994 onwards, and the later spread of credit cards all reshaped aspects of daily life.

The introduction of market mechanisms has created new forms of consumerism that not all Hungarians have been able to share equally. The 'globalization' of the economy, particularly in the first half of the 1990s, was accompanied by serious social problems. Unemployment rose from virtually nothing in 1989 to peak at 12.2 per cent in 1993. Moreover by 1994 some 35 per cent of the total population was estimated as living below the officially established poverty line, while income differentials had increased enormously (Ékes and Ernst, 1995, p. 99). Social welfare measures were ruthlessly cut back during the middle of the decade as high inflation further eroded fixed incomes. While the economy recovered from 1996 onwards, increasing inequality and severe poverty among large sections of the population remained problems.

The identities expressed and discussed in the first reading, dealing with Budapest's shopping malls, should therefore be considered in the broader context of the encroachment of global economic forces into the domestic economy and the radical remaking of Hungarian society that has resulted. Social polarization has fed a nostalgia for the comfort of the later years of state socialism among large sections of the population. The arrival of foreign multinationals in many sectors has provoked opposition from those seeking to defend Hungarian ownership of sectors of the economy. To some extent these attitudes have come to be shared not only by those who have emerged as 'losers' from the 'globalization' of the country's economy but also by some of the members of the 'new' middle classes able to enjoy the 'European-quality' shopping experiences offered by foreign multinationals in the retailing sector.

The Hungarian experience of 'globalization' echoes many of the issues raised in western European societies in dealing with similar phenomena. Moreover, it is not the only one to be considered here. As perceptions of the borders of Europe were remade by the political and economic changes of the 1990s, the 'globalization' of other central and eastern European economies and the introduction of forms of western mass consumerism produced other kinds of reaction that underline the importance of local context when considering the impact of global economic forces. The second reading is an extract from an essay entitled 'Creating a culture of disillusionment: consumption in Moscow, a chronicle of changing times', written by the British-born anthropologist Caroline Humphrey. In the extract Humphrey focuses on the attitudes of middle-class Muscovites to consumption at a time when the experience of consumption in Moscow was being remade by the new Russian state's attempts to 'globalize' the country's economy during the early 1990s.

An Ethnography of Consumption in Moscow, 1993

In the Soviet period, the people of Moscow bought basic goods mostly in state shops and, if they were relatively well off, in the few state-run markets, where vegetables and fruit were sold by collective farms and peasants at higher prices. Besides this, there was an extensive system of allocation of difficult-to-obtain goods through the workplace, sometimes paid for 'by order' and sometimes distributed free as a bonus (Humphrey, 1991). Meanwhile, of course, people sought every means – the black market, networks of acquaintances, barter and exchange magazines, patrons and back doors of all kinds (*blat*) – to get hold of other things they needed.

In Moscow in the spring of 1993, there were not only the state stores and official markets of old but also private and foreign shops, kiosks, street peddlers, informal markets, and huge weekly fairs, such as the arts and crafts fair at Izmailovo Park. However, all this did not make shopping in Moscow like shopping in London,

Paris, or Rome. Somehow, the sovereignty of the Western shopper, enticed to wander and inspect, to titillate desire, to take pleasure in the whole process – that is, shopping promoted as a leisure activity – had not occurred and seemed indeed far from Russian reality.

In Soviet times, there used to be an underlying sense that for the most part goods were not really bought by choice but were allocated. This intensified during the first years of economic collapse (1989–91) before the freeing of prices. During those years there was an increase in workplace orders and state distributions to various needy and honored social groups, and rationing was introduced in many places for basic goods such as meat, flour, or butter. Thus, even though the Soviet consumer formally engaged in buying – went to a shop, decided what to purchase, and paid money for it – the ways people talked about this revealed that at some level they realized that they were at the receiving end of a state-planned system of distribution. People said that goods were there to buy because 'they' (the authorities) had given them out. 'What are they giving (*daiut*) in GUM today?' people would ask. In slang 'they' threw out (*vybrosili*) or chucked out (*vykidyvali*) the goods to the people.[1] This was recognition that shops and markets were lower-priority parts of the same system as the specially distributed package of luxuries of officials and the nameless, closely curtained buildings that contained foreign currency stores. Voinovich (1985, 113) wrote ironically, 'With socialism, as everyone knows, there can be no *uravnilovka* (egalitarianism, a pejorative term in the late Soviet times – C H). From each according to ability, to each according to rank. Even Marx said that. Or Lenin. Or maybe I dreamed it up myself, I can't remember when.'

In working-class Moscow in the spring of 1993 the stark signs of the distributory era 'Bread,' 'Footwear,' 'Meat' – were still virtually the only labels a shop was likely to have. Most of them, private or not, did not bother with anything much in the way of window displays (though they were not as downright misleading as they used to be: in the old days, if you saw something in a shop window it was almost a guarantee that it could not be bought inside). Strangely, rather than private shops approximating some Western model, and state shops being forced by competition to emulate them, almost the reverse was the case. State stores remained unchanged, and private shops, which were often only state ones

---

[1] The expression gave rise to an inevitable anecdote: an American goes up to a queue and asks what is being sold. People tell him, 'They're selling (throwing out) boots!' He has a look and says 'Yes, in America they throw those out too' (Voinovich 1985, 42).

taken over by the collective of workers, were usually indistinguishable from them in any outward way. Only locals could tell if a given ruble grocery was in private hands (though the prices were higher). It is true that private and foreign shops selling in dollars were somewhat different, since hardly anyone could afford to buy at them;[2] but here, too, minimal effort was made to make the goods attractive. Decorated Italian sweaters jostled with Swedish fridges, lace underwear with salami, whisky, or videos. The idea was simple: these things are foreign; bring your dollars and pay up. Inside state shops for basic goods, in contrast, there were crowds, and the salespeople, as of yore, had precedence. The shoppers were subjected to the triple queuing system, as irritable shoulder-to-shoulder masses shuffled in three lines to order the goods, pay for them, and collect them.

In its way, the Soviet state shop was a microcosm of what Bukovskii called the 'hidden civil war,' and essentially this system continued into the spring of 1993. As befits the idea that the state managed this microcosm to its own Olympian benefit, the manager remained invisible in a separate room and the cashier's desk was often elevated on a stand, so buyers had to pass money up to someone sitting at shoulder height. This made it feel as though one was petitioning to be allowed to pay. The cashier might refuse to accept anything but the exact sum, or alternatively might throw down (literally) some sweets as change. The shoppers cursed or agitatedly counted through their packets of multifarious banknotes. In the ordering queue something of the distributive mentality remained, partly because prepackaging of goods in units a shopper might want to buy was still a rarity. So when buying butter or cheese, for example, the purchaser named a weight and the shop worker cut a certain amount off a huge block with a spatula and weighed it, often with a bored and careless look, so the buyer had to glare or remonstrate that it was too little, and then a bit more would be added, all with the facial expression, 'This is as much as you deserve.' Frequently shoppers were turned away if they had not brought their own wrapping paper. In the case of meat, people could reach the top of the queue only to find that the shop worker refused to give a good piece unless some scrawny, dried-up bits were taken too. So mistrustful of one another were the two sides that payment by check (were such things to exist) was unthinkable. In 1993, a few large stores introduced their own 'credit cards,' and some people were attracted by such a seemingly Western modernity. But not only did purchasers have to buy the

---

[2] Dollar sales were officially eliminated at the beginning of 1994.

cards by paying up to their 'credit limit' in advance, they soon found that the goods in these stores were regularly more highly priced that outside. Shoppers were not really surprised to be disillusioned, and queuing continued, though during the year it changed its goals.

The queue, heaving involuntarily forward and looking with gimlet eyes at each transaction, could not be said to be supportive of the shopper at the head. An almost palpable vexation arose if someone 'bought too much,' and it was almost as bad if they 'wasted time' by querying the weighing, or insisted on picking and choosing between good and rotten fruit, or made a mistake in their sums and arrived from the cashier's queue with a chit that did not exactly correspond with the price/weight of the items. Of course, queues varied: in neighborhood shops people often kept places for friends or jumped the queue by prior arrangement with the shop worker (this was grimly borne by those behind). In the fashionable Western franchises in central Moscow, it was more a case of each for himself and physical elbowing into a more advantageous position.

The Russian queue was not simply a social presence but was also a social principle, one that regulated social entitlements in time. It enshrined the social and psychological idea of consumption through state distribution. As Voinovich (1985, 42) wrote, and it is still true, 'Queues are various. They can be for a few minutes, overnight, for several days. People stay in the queues for cars or apartments for years.' Russians fleeing from Tajikistan report that the Dushanbe riots of 1991 were caused by the rumor that Armenian refugees had been allotted places at the head of the queue for apartments. The preservation of the queue for flats in the metropolis was the main reason given by the Russian Federal Migration Service for their support for the residence-permit system, despite its 'undemocratic' nature and the fact that it served to exclude their clients (refugees) from all major cities (Baiduzhii, 1993).

How did this change during 1993? On one hand, the system of consumption through the allocation of benefits if anything increased. On the other, the old Soviet-type queuing, where the availability of scar[c]e goods rather than price was what mattered, has to a great extent been replaced by the desperate search for cheap goods.

One reason why allocated benefits have increased relative to money wages is the newly introduced income tax (Hansen 1993, 92). Wage increases over government-regulated levels are subject to punitive taxes of up to 60 percent, a measure to control inflation. But social welfare benefits are exempt from taxation. Many state organizations and companies therefore choose to give workers raises in the form of vouchers or coupons, calling them something like 'subsidy for food.' A recent study of living conditions in a northern province of Russia (Hansen, 1993) showed the benefits to be: free/subsidized transport (27 percent), vouchers for purchase of consumer durables (7 percent), humanitarian aid from Western countries (7 percent), free meal at the workplace (6 percent), food orders for families with many children (2 percent), food orders for invalids and veterans (15 percent), and food orders through the workplace (35 percent). This essentially continues an old practice of the Soviet state, but it is now supplemented by the distribution of imported goods which companies can obtain by purchase or barter for their own locally generated profits.

This system may take the edge off subsistence shopping for some employed people, but it leaves the unemployed and the dispossessed in a desperate situation. Furthermore, state wages do not keep pace with inflation, and many loss-making factories, though they do not dismiss their workers, close down for months on end without pay. During 1993 large numbers of state and collective farms were unable to pay wages for as much as six months. Russians divided their 'money' into *nalichnye* (cash in hand) and *beznalichnye* (notional money owed). There is a terrible shortage of cash.[3] Thus the glittering goods are mostly things people are unable to buy, and the Soviet search for scarce goods has been replaced by combing the city for cheap basic products.

However, this is exactly what the market is not providing. There are many reasons, perhaps the main one being that state shops (and even privatized state shops) still to a great extent rely on their old suppliers, and these are the doddering collective farms and ramshackle factories which themselves have problems with supplies. Here, however, I focus on the activities of entrepreneurs, which are another major factor. Entrepreneurs in Russia, not surprisingly, started out by trading the most profitable goods, luxury items not found in the Soviet economy. This explains the historical appearance first of foreign liqueurs, 'designer' jeans, expensive flashy jackets, and so forth, in the Russian marketplace. People rushed to buy them in 1990–92, but now they are beyond the pockets of ordinary workers. Only a few Western goods have penetrated everyday consumption, notably Mars bars and Snickers

---

[3]   Cash is worth up to 20 percent more than the equivalent sum in *beznalichnye*.

('Karl Mars and Friedrich Snickers'). In 1993, entrepreneurs started to import American and European foods (Norwegian salami, American butter, and so forth), which have appeared in state and private shops. But the prices are still too high, and today, if you see a crowd of people, you know the queue is for cheap Russian produce – the very opposite of the situation a few years ago.[4]

A friend of mine 'in business' said that if a certain item sells well, her reaction is not to get in more of the goods but to raise the price. Muscovite shoppers describe how you may hear that something (soap, tights, cassettes) is cheaper in one quarter of the city than another, but it never makes sense to trek over there to get it, because by the time you get there the price will have gone up. It is clear how pricing tricks work locally: there is a row of kiosks all selling the same items. One has a lower price for something. Thinking they have got a bargain people eagerly buy it. The kiosk holders are in league and divide up the profits. In fact, local Mafias ensure that prices are never truly lowered.

The purchaser thus encounters a different kind of anxiety from the queue: a threatening kind of lawlessness. The kiosks which cluster around railway stations and the entrances to the Metro sell a range of profitable goods: Western cigarettes, cans of drink, electronic equipment, Italian shoes, CDs, briefcases, tights, and obscure (but always the same) liqueurs. Near the kiosks sit the peddlers, with their trays of local cigarettes, ice cream, Mars bars, or apples. But roundabout, sometimes hidden, but often sitting openly alongside, are the minders. There is not a single old woman selling Marlboros and matches who does not have her allotted stretch of pavement and pay her protector for the right. One kiosk cannot lower prices or the owner would immediately be beaten up by the others or by the minders. If a customer spots a fraud and complains about it aloud, a number of leather-jacketed men are likely to appear instantaneously at his or her elbow. They do not hesitate to threaten or even beat ordinary women shoppers.

People shop at the kiosks with their threatening entourages even though they know they are being 'cheated.' They know a good proportion of the price is going to the minders and the higher-level Mafia, not to speak of the 'good-for-nothing' young kiosk

---

[4]   During 1993 Moscow benefited from the disastrous situation in the Ukraine and Belorussia. The total collapse of these economies and currencies made even the ruble an attractive proposition, and peasants from these countries came to sell their produce at railway stations and roadsides.

holders themselves. The goods are suspected of being counterfeit and defective. A kiosk worker I knew, a Russian dropout student, worked for Chinese merchants, and she realized she was hired to do the face-to-face selling because foreign traders are so resented. I heard people liken them to cockroaches. Where this differs from negative attitudes to ethnic groups as traders elsewhere in the world is the cynicism in every relationship down the line. All sides cheated one another: the owners underpaid the sellers, the purchasers tried to steal, the buyers were given defective goods, and the sellers hid some of the takings from the owner. Massive takings nevertheless ended up with the main Chinese trader (early 1990s), but my friend was almost sorry for him because, since banks took high taxes, he had to sit day and night by his trunk of rapidly devaluing money.[5]

As for the street peddlers, Muscovites know exactly how they operate. Often they are old people who have fallen on hard times, and almost all are women. They get to know the managers of large shops located in inconvenient places. Having paid a bribe, they are able to buy up quantities of the goods before other shoppers get access. They then take the goods (say, cans of beer or flowers) to strategic spots where people are in a hurry and are prepared to pay far more than the usual price.[6] Sometimes goods change hands through several traders before they reach the streets. A money-conscious Muscovite would not buy from these peddlers but would prefer to do without or to make the trek to the original shop and pay the lower price. Nevertheless, passersby, being certain the women must have been driven to it, are horrified at the plight of the elderly street-sellers, who stand meekly in rows, with their prowling minders nearby.

As the structure of the Soviet Union collapsed, two things happened: there was a phenomenal growth in the number and type of economic transactions, and the old system of laws became obsolete. New laws hurriedly passed have failed to keep pace with the economic life of the streets, and the growth of some kind of 'protection' for transactions was inevitable. This has become so pervasive that the authorities, colluding with at least some parts of

[5] Banks and money-changing kiosks sprang up during 1993, but ordinary people avoided using them. Not only were deposits taxed, but the state sometimes forbade withdrawals point blank.

[6] In March 1993 a single rose at the Orangery nursery in northern Moscow cost 125 rubles; in flower shops the price was around 300; street traders charged 1,000 rubles.

the Mafia, have so far only ventured to attack relatively powerless outsiders (traders from the erstwhile 'younger brother' peoples of the Caucasus and Central Asia).

The following newspaper report is noteworthy because it links such anti-foreign drives with new consumer reactions. In October 1993 the mayor of Moscow, Iurii Luzhkov, justified the use of the state of emergency as a way of expelling from the city several thousand Armenian, Georgian, and Azerbaijani traders without residence permits.

> Mr. Luzhkov ... said that after the state of emergency ended, he would probably introduce an entry visa regime to prevent those expelled from returning to Moscow. As for the markets, they might offer fewer 'exotic fruits' in future, but 'honest traders from Tambov, Lipetsk, Briansk, and other [Russian] towns will arrive with good products and will sell traditional Russian food.'

> If Mr. Luzhkov carries out his threat, Muscovites will face a diet of potatoes, beetroot, cabbage, and pickled cabbage. But they don't care. Because some Caucasians are involved in crime, they blame them all and welcome the police action. 'It's just a pity this state of emergency can't be permanent,' said Vera Vladimirovna, a pensioner looking for something affordable on the few stalls left at the Chernomuzhkinskaia Market.

> (Womack, 1993)

Sometimes at a market one can see heaps of unsold meat. It is not just that many people cannot afford it, a large number refrain from consuming altogether as far as possible. They prefer to save or invest, for reasons that will be explored below.

It is interesting to try to discover what people do actually buy. Some information is available from large-scale, all-Russian statistics, although it is not clear how these were gathered, In 1991–92 Russians spent between 30 and 40 percent of their incomes on food, 40–50 percent on nonfood manufactures, around 12–15 percent on services, and 8–10 percent on alcohol. In 1992–93 the amount spent on food rose to 40–50 percent, payments for manufactures and services declined, and alcohol remained the same (Struktura, 1993). A probably more reliable survey in 1992 in the Kola Peninsula suggested that householders spent between 70 percent and 82 percent of their budget on food (Hansen, 1993, 99).

I close this section with a description of the budget of a Moscow middle-class family with whom I stayed during March–April 1993. I wish to use this to make two points: first, to show how consumption even in the middle class was largely devoted to basic necessities; and second, to indicate the kind of bouleversement that people are living through, since only six months later, such a consumption pattern became impossible. The family in the spring of 1993 regarded itself as not particularly well-off, less so, for example, than that of an experienced factory worker. Their income for the month from March 15 to April 15 was 70,100 rubles.[7] In December 1992, a Russian economist from the Ministry of Labor estimated that the 'threshold of survival' of such a family (three adults and a child) would be around 16,100 rubles a month, while the 'poverty line' would stand at around 40,000 rubles a month (Valiuzhenich, 1993).[8] Extrapolating this by the 70 percent price increase between then and March 16, 1993 (Goriacheva, 1993), we can estimate that the family's income of 70,100 rubles was around the official 'poverty line,' though well above the survival rate. The family's food for the month cost 25,955 rubles; payment[s] for services (including transport and one-time payments for school repair and a foreign passport) were 14,319; nonfood manufactures were 5,121; and alcohol was 550. The total spent was 45,695 rubles. Potatoes, bread, cabbage, pickled cabbage, and beetroot indeed figured prominently in the budget, though the family was also able to afford meat, fish, eggs, and cheese. Fearful of total economic collapse, the household also kept stockpiles of food like flour, tea, noodles, and sugar, and these were being gradually used up as such Russian goods became more and more difficult to obtain.[9]

---

[7] This was made up of a man's salary of 33,000, a grown-up daughter's income of 12,000, the wife's pension of 15,000, and two smaller state benefits for a school-age daughter who was in bad health.

[8] This was calculated using the minimum of buyable foods estimated necessary for survival for adult men, adult women, the elderly, and children per day. The portions did not represent the actual diet of any studied group of people but theoretical dietary requirements. Added to this were sums for heating, rent, and other expenses and the absolute minimum of products required for sanitation and health. The costs of clothing, furniture, footwear, television, and similar goods were not included, as 'unfortunately the situation today is such that it is necessary to make do on existing reserves of these things' (Valiuzhenich 1993, 3).

[9] Hansen (1993, 95) notes that over 60 percent of households in the Kola Peninsula kept stockpiles in 1992, and that these included not only food but also medicines, clothing, footwear, and consumable durables. A majority of his respondents said they drew constantly from their stockpiles and expected them sooner or later to be exhausted.

We should note that the budget was provided by the wife and assumed to cover the whole family. This is a characteristic Russian assumption regarding the household, according to which it is the wife who has to make do.[10] In fact, the housewife's budget did not take into account certain expenditures of the husband and older daughter. I have estimated these to include around 8,600 rubles for cigarettes, 1,000 for vodka, some 1,000 for newspapers, and around 5,000 for dressmaking. The family's total expenditure would therefore have been at least 61,295 for the month. Any savings were put toward [the] purchase of a dacha outside town.

Although the family did not spend their entire income, they felt hard-pressed. Steep inflation was perceptible even during the month. The housewife, the main shopper, went to great efforts to find products that were good bargains. She was dependent on the fact that it was possible to buy good bread cheaply (bread is subsidized, and people buy it even several times a day from numerous local bakers). Very little was spent on clothing, and nothing on books, cinemas, or music. What is most noticeable about this budget is that, with the exception of one piece of imported butter, nothing in it was foreign. 'American butter' was regretted and bought only because 'our fatherland's butter' was sold out. The cigarettes were Russian, and so were a door lock and pair of child's skis. It was as though the global influx of goods to Moscow had never taken place.

Before discussing the thinking behind this kind of consumption, I should explain that its Russianness is no longer an option. Even the state and collectively owned shops are now full of imported products, and to the amazement of Muscovites these are packaged in convenient units and in such a way that they can be preserved longer. But people told me they would rather go without, or restrict their food to a few repetitive items, than buy foreign produce. However, they do not have much choice. The Caucasian and Central Asian traders with their fruits and kebabs continue to be kept out of Moscow. Unless you can grow produce yourself or

[10] As Bukovskii has written (1981, 99), 'It is not in the Russian character to economize. "Eh, the devil!" concludes the husband, "We've never lived well and now is not the time to start." Somehow or other it seems they do manage. Our families are maintained by women, and all their economy consists of buying cheap products.' This gender difference in consumption is an issue I have not been able to develop in this paper, though it is highly important. With the new emphasis on subsistence production (such as potatoes) even among urban families, the expectations of women are even more burdensome.

have relatives on a farm, it is a case of imports or nothing, and these tightly packaged foods many Russians find 'doubtful' and 'likely to cause illness.'

Deceit

From the 1920s onward, the Communist Party's propaganda sections put forward Soviet styles for people to emulate. These included styles of clothing, house interiors, food, and etiquettes of behavior that were designed to express the classless, health-conscious, labor-oriented direction that society should take. In the Khrushchev era (1950s–1960s), an important change took place. Rather than representing goals for the future, the propaganda images were presented as if they really existed. At first, these images were deceitful because they were utterly unattainable – all items represented either were absent from Soviet shops or so expensive as to be beyond ordinary people's most extravagant hopes. But later, as these very goods became available for the middle class, it became apparent that the range of products was so limited as to enforce an involuntary homogeneity on all consumption.

Thus there was another aspect to the feeling of being involved in a gigantic deception. This derived from the growing sense during the 1970s–1980s of being removed, by being entombed in the

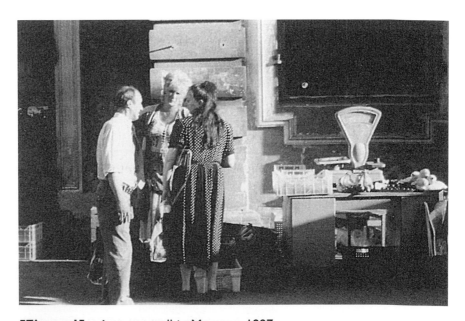

[Figure 1]   A street stall in Moscow, 1997

Soviet Union, from another more real but curtained-off history, that is, from the history of the world. Soviet citizens were told that they were at the forefront in every sphere, they led the world, but disorienting glimpses on television, and above all foreigners themselves, seemed like evidence that this might not be so.

So propaganda images were widely seen as a deceit, even though they aroused consumer desire. Furthermore, as Verdery (1992) has perceptively observed, this desire was constituted as a 'right,' since material plenty was an essential measure of the advancement of the Soviet socialist system. Quoting a Romanian friend, Verdery wrote: 'What everyone strives to do is to figure out how not to have frustration be too costly: not to want something so much that being denied it will devastate you. The test of character becomes managing to accept yet another denial without being undone by it.' Verdery continues,

> Socialism intensified this experience ... for the regimes themselves paradoxically abetted the emphasis on consumption. First, organized shortage made procuring something – anything – a major triumph. Second, even as the regimes prevented people from consuming by not making goods available, they insisted that under socialism the standard of living would constantly improve ... Socialism ... aroused desire without? [sic] focalizing it, and kept it alive by deprivation. That is, in socialism desire floated free in endless search of goods people saw as their right.

> ... The arousal and frustration on consumer desire and East Europeans' consequent resistance to their regimes led them to build their social identities specifically *through consuming.* Acquiring consumption goods and objects conferred an identity that set one off from socialism. To acquire objects became a way of constituting your selfhood against a regime you despised. (Verdery, 1992, 25–26)

Russia under the Soviet regime was more pervasively subject to hegemonic propaganda than Eastern Europe, and this ensured that Western goods were not merely representative but constitutive of social identity (see, for example, Friedman 1990, 318). Ordinary people would hide things, such as tape recorders, of obviously Western provenance, since they were associated with resistance to the regime. The *soccer fans, hippies, punks, rockers,* and other counterculture groups in Moscow in the 1970s–1980s used English for their graffiti, wore approximations of Western fashions and hairstyles, and conceptualized their way of life by 'English' terms:

flety ('flats,' or crash-pads), *grin* ('green,' dollars), *askat'* ('to beg/ ask'), and so forth (Brushnell, 1990, 116–117). Just looking like a *khippi* was enough to provoke the authorities. Many were dispatched to short terms in the *kreiza* (loony bin) just for their appearance (Brushnell, 1990, 115).

There is a crucial difference between Eastern European countries, discussed by Verdery, and Russia. In the former, the Soviet system was easily seen as alien, whereas in Russia it had to be acknowledged as 'ours.' Consequently the experience of deception was both internalized and globalized, as though that was the way things were in the world in general. So 'the West,' too, was read as some kind of mirage or trick. Both Bukovskii and Voinovich describe this reaction of the Soviet visitor first faced with the unimaginable plenty of the West, the 'pointless' diversity, the objects 'of whose use we know nothing, even old people can't remember them' (Bukovskii 1981, 82). Voinovich recounts how an elderly Russian came to visit his daughter who had emigrated to Germany; she took him into a shop. He looked around and frowned, 'No,' he said. 'Take me to a real shop. This must be a special one for foreigners. Show me one for ordinary people' (Voinovich, 1985, 44). Bukovskii (1981, 82) describes the same feeling of the visitor to the West: all these things must be for show (*na pokaz*), as in a Soviet shop window, and of course, no one will buy them. That is why there are no queues and such huge quantities of goods lie around unsold. Real goods must be procured with difficulty (*dobyvat'*), unearthed (*otkopit'*), or obtained on the side (*nalevo*), from under the counter, or from such crafty places as are known only to the dedicated.

A first reaction to 'the West' was to buy everything in sight. A second was depression and inertia, 'too good is also no good,' and the feeling that it was impossible to find anything unique in these jungles of wealth. 'I stood before a counter with twenty-four kinds of salad oil, and I couldn't choose one, I only got tired. What is oil, after all? One can live without it' (Bukovskii, 1981, 83). It seems to me that these reactions are not irrelevant to the stages of the opening of Moscow to global goods in the early 1990s. Muscovites now are tired, having experienced the 'deception' they were expecting. 'Sophisticated Western equipment is not for us,' people often say, suspecting it to contain some hidden drawback or delicate mechanism which will prevent it from functioning in Russian conditions. My Russian friend, whose budget is given above, had rushed to buy a magnificent German washing machine. It does not work. Nobody quite knows why, but not many efforts are devoted to finding out. 'We should have realized,' sighs my friend. Now the machine stands there, taking up a lot of space in the bathroom, and everything is washed in a 'reliable but rough' Soviet contraption or by hand. Likewise, glossily packaged produce like salami is suspect. Why encase it in such brightness? People say, 'At least with our Russian sausage we won't be eating all those chemicals.'

This feeling that Western goods are in some way a sham, contaminated, or somehow inassimilable and unsuited for Russian life has transformed the politicization of consumption noted by Verdery for the late Soviet period. Now, for many people at least, Western goods are no longer a goal in themselves, and they have lost much glamour. Above all, using Western consumer goods no longer confers a defiant social identity against the regime. Rather, they are associated with the new businessmen created by the Yeltsin government's economic reforms. Their suspect nature is compounded by their contiguity with shady dealings and what is guessed to be an insubstantial, dangerously risky kind of existence. Hundreds of thousands of Muscovites have been turning in another direction; they are forgoing Western consumer goods for the sake of more down-to-earth values: plots of land, dachas, or, if they have country relatives to look after them, cows, chickens, and pigs.

Prices for vegetable plots and small farms have grown enormously, and in the more desirable, unpolluted environs of Moscow they are now always quoted in dollars. It is possible to build a dacha, plant a few trees there, and sell the whole thing a year later for a large profit. Thus both entrepreneurs and ordinary workers invest in land, but they do so for different reasons. Even in 1991 over 30 percent of Muscovites owned a dacha (Hansen, 1993, 100), and since then the country cottage has become even more a part of city life. The produce of the plot is important to subsistence, but the dacha also has a symbolic value. It represents space, repose, 'Russianness.' The dacha may be no more than a hut, and the journey to get there may involve several wearisome and expensive trains and buses with a walk at the other end, but people say it is worth the effort, since in the country they can recreate a familiar, 'age-old' security lacking in Moscow. All this requires effort, saving, self-denial, and forethought. Sudden huge drops and gains in income have torn apart relationships, but the situation has also welded together families in new, strained dependencies. Saving is a survival strategy, and there is almost a frenzy to produce safety against the unpredictability of chaos. This pulls people back from 'the market' and turns them inward to networks of security. The dacha is one of these, and combining a city job and even a moderately productive plot is not something anyone can do on their own.

References

Baiduzhii, A. (1993) 'Tat'iana Regent: Rossiia ne mozhet vypolnit' svoi obiazatel'stva v otnoshenii bezhentsev' (Tat'iana Regent: Russia cannot fulfill her obligations with regard to refugees), *Nezavisimaia gazeta*, 23 April, p. 6.

Bukovskii, V. (1981) *Pis' ma russkogo puteshestvennika* (Letters of a Russian traveller), New York, Chalidze Publications.

Bushnell, J. (1990) *Moscow Graffiti: Language and Subculture*, Boston, MA, Unwin Hyman.

Friedman, J. (1990) 'Being in the world: globalization and localization', in M. Featherstone (ed.) *Global Culture: Nationalism, Globalization and Modernity*, London, Sage, pp. 311–28.

Goriacheva, I. (1993) 'Stoimost' produktov s nachala goda vyrosla na 70 protsentov', *Izvestiia*, 24 March.

Hansen, E. (1993) 'Living conditions on the Kola Peninsula' FAFO-SOTECO Report, no. 155. FAFO-SOTECO, Oslo.

Humphrey, C. (1991) '"Icebergs", Barter and the Mafia in Provincial Russia', *Anthropology Today*, vol. 7, no.2, pp.8–13.

Struktura (Unauthored) (1993) 'Struktura potrebitel'skikh rashkhodov i sluzhashchikh na chlena sem'I', *Argumenty i Fakty*, no.12, p. 649.

Valiuzhenich, G. (1993) 'Porog vyzhivaemosti' *Argumenty i Fakty*, no. 4, p. 3.

Verdery, K. (1992) *The Transition from Socialism: Anthropology and Eastern Europe. Lewis Henry Morgan Lectures, University of Rochester.* Cambridge University Press, Cambridge.

Voinovich, V. (1985) *Antisovetskii sovetskii soiuz* (The Anti-Soviet Soviet Union) Ann Arbor, Ardis.

Womack, H. (1993) 'Moscow Expels Traders', *The Times*, 13 October, p. 7.

(Humphrey, 2002, pp. 44–56)

EXERCISE

As you re-read the extract I should like you to take notes, organizing them around answers to the following questions.

1   How, according to Humphrey's account, did the experience of shopping in Moscow differ from 'shopping in London, Paris, or Rome' in spring 1993?

2   How did the changes of the early 1990s reshape the experience of shopping in Moscow and the nature of the goods available?

3   What is the attitude to western consumer goods held by the middle-class Moscow housewife whose shopping habits are described in the extract?

4   How does Humphrey account for these attitudes?

DISCUSSION

1   At a fundamental level the experience of shopping in Moscow was different because the notion of 'shopping promoted as a leisure activity', common in western Europe at the time, 'seemed indeed far from Russian reality'. In Humphrey's account shops and kiosks that sold foreign goods were on the fringes of most Muscovites' experiences of consumption. In part this was because of the relative expense of the goods sold in them, or because their owners required payment in hard currency which was out of the reach of much of the population. For most Muscovites the experience of shopping continued to be shaped by the retail practices of the Soviet era, which did not regard shoppers as consumers in any western European sense of the word.

2   The liberalization of the economy in the early 1990s did bring about the arrival of new kinds of shop, selling different goods. The shops stocking foreign goods sold for dollars, and the kiosks offering goods at high prices, are examples which have already been mentioned. For reasons given above they failed to transform the experience of shopping for ordinary Muscovites. More fundamental was the impact of unemployment, the introduction of income tax and cuts in price subsidies. These measures had a number of different effects. Tax changes and income controls restricted the ability of employers to pay money wages, thus increasing the practice of payment in kind. Those without employment or employed in the type of enterprise able to pay in kind were seriously impoverished as prices rose and incomes failed to keep up. The Russian state's attempts, therefore, to 'globalize' the country's economy resulted not in the spread of 'global' consumption patterns, but in the impoverishment of a large section of the population.

3   The Moscow housewife and her family have a strong preference for Russian goods. In the language used to justify the choices made in the use of the family budget, national identities are

articulated strongly. 'Our fatherland's butter' is preferred to foreign butter imported from the United States. This might be seen as an example of consumption habits being influenced by 'the defensive identities' described by sociologist Manuel Castells.

4   Humphrey regards this as the legacy of the attitudes of ordinary Russians to the consumerist propaganda of the Soviet state, which at times advertised goods that did not actually exist (Kelly, 1998). They reacted to the gap between propaganda and reality by mistrusting goods, expecting to find a marked divergence between the image and the reality. This perception 'was both internalized and globalized', according to Humphrey. Consequently the image of abundance associated with western goods and products was distrusted. With the advent of the 1990s, Russian goods, as things that are known and tangible, have come to be preferred to the 'exotic' other.

The picture that is presented by Humphrey of the arrival of western goods and the impact of the attempted 'globalization' of Russia's economy on consumption patterns in Moscow is radically different to that advanced by Bodnár in her discussion of the reception of western shopping malls in post-socialist Budapest. This underlines the importance of local context in shaping the experience of globalizing forces. It furthermore suggests the highly particular nature of the identities that are shaped in such contexts.

EXERCISE

Before we move on I should like you to think about some of the differences between the experience of Moscow described by Humphrey and that of Budapest described by Bodnár. I have given you some of the economic and historical context to the arrival of the shopping mall in the Hungarian capital during the mid 1990s. Humphrey has given you some of the context necessary to understand the economic background to the phenomena that she discusses in the second reading. I want you to consider the similarities and differences between the experiences of the two cities as presented in the readings, and to think – provisionally of course – about how you might account for the differences.

DISCUSSION

I don't expect you to have definitive answers to these questions, but I hope that you noted or recognized some of the following points. First of all, though the differences are clearly the most striking there are some similarities too. In both contexts the arrival of visibly 'foreign' goods or consumption patterns elicited a defensive response that was rooted in Russian and Hungarian national identities respectively. This was weaker in the Hungarian case, associated with those who held nationalist political views or were small producers. In the Russian experience Humphrey argues that the response was much more general, rooted in both poverty and a culture of distrust of the promise of unfamiliar consumer goods. Yet in both instances the power of national identities in shaping some forms of resistance to the encroachment of global cultural forms in the sphere of consumption is striking.

Another similarity you might have noticed is the reality of class differences in determining access to material goods. Yet I hope that you noted that the extracts suggest a marked economic difference between Russia and Hungary. In 1993 Hungary, with a per capita gross domestic product of $3,380, was a significantly wealthier society than Russia, with a per capita GDP of only $2,340 (Johnson, 1996, p. 285). Hungary's economic transition, though rocky, has been less problematic than Russia's. You might have further noted the differences between the two countries' experiences under socialist dictatorship. From Bodnár's discussion of the Skála Metró store, you may have correctly deduced that Hungary had something of a functioning consumer-based economy prior to 1989, to a much greater degree than did Russia.

The most interesting difference that influenced consumer attitudes is the role that specifically Russian and Hungarian identities played in determining local responses to global consumption patterns. Hungary perceived itself to be naturally a part of 'Europe' and was therefore ready to accept western goods as part of a process of 'joining Europe'; witness the way in which Budapest's shopping malls were marketed to the local population. Russians saw themselves as more separate, in large part because the Soviet system and the goods it produced were seen as domestic creations.

Your work with the two readings and with this section in general should have given you an appreciation of the point that global, or even 'globalizing', processes do not produce uniform or homogeneous cultural identities. The extracts reveal something of the cultural consequences of attempts to integrate states that lie in Europe's fluid borderland into the global economy of the 1990s. They also point to the fact that this is always an incomplete, uneven and highly contested process.

What's new about 'globalization'?

Our discussion so far has qualified the applicability of the definition of 'globalization' as a process by which identities have become homogenized to the realities of contemporary Europe. Globalization has implicitly been defined as a process that describes the rise of transnational forces that operate on a global scale and thus affect all 'local' societies, and local identities, in highly particular ways. The discussion has centred on the globalization of transnational economic forces, highlighting the spread of certain forms of consumerism, to examine the interactions between globalizing processes and local identities. Following the literary scholar Crystal Bartolovich, we could expand our list of globalizing processes to include:

> the global, computer-aided circulation of credit, capital, currency and information, the movements of Diaspora populations, the intermixing of commodified fragments of different cultures, the beaming of media images simultaneously into vastly separated households, the escalation in awareness of environmental threats which refuse to respect state borders, the availability (and increased use) of swift means of transportation and communication, the stocking of store shelves with commodities whose routes of production read like the itineraries of a world tour.
>
> (Bartolovich, 2000, p. 127)

This list, which would be broadly representative of the lists of most commentators on globalization, suggests the novelty of the phenomenon, as does our discussion above of the impact of globalizing processes on the consumer economies of two central and eastern European cities. Certainly some of the processes listed are relatively new, but it is also true that globalizing processes in themselves are not so new, and have been shaping cultural identities within Europe for some time. It is therefore worth posing the question of how new globalization as a process actually is, and above all what precisely is new about it. I shall use this section to try to sketch the outline of a highly provisional answer to these questions in order to provide you with a framework for thinking about these issues. They are raised to some extent, though in different ways, by all of the chapters in this book.

You should begin thinking about some of these issues by turning to the third reading. It is an extract from the introduction to anthropologist Sidney W. Mintz's book *Sweetness and Power: the Place of Sugar in Modern History*, first published in 1985. In the book Mintz examines the development of sugar as a commodity and seeks to use it to reveal the links between changing tastes in European colonial states and the realities of plantation production in the Caribbean. It is very much about the links between global economic processes and aspects of everyday culture – in this case, food. The reading should also take us back from discussions of global/globalizing processes at the beginning of the twenty-first century, to those from another period.

Sweetness and power: the place of sugar in modern history

Most people in the Caribbean region, descendants of the aboriginal Amerind population and of settlers who came from Europe, Africa, and Asia, have been rural and agricultural. Working among them usually means working in the countryside; getting interested in them means getting interested in what they produce by their labor. Because I worked among these people – learning what they were like, what their lives were made into by the conditions they lived under – I inevitably wanted to know more about sugar and rum and coffee and chocolate. Caribbean people have always been entangled with a wider world, for the region has, since 1492, been caught up in skeins of imperial control, spun in Amsterdam, London, Paris, Madrid, and other European and North American centers of world power. Someone working inside the rural sectors of those little island societies would inevitably be inclined, I think, to view such networks of control and dependence from the Caribbean vantage point: to look up and out from local life, so to speak, rather than down and into it. But this insider's view has some of the same disadvantages as the firmly European perspective of an earlier generation of observers for whom the greater part of the dependent, outer, non-European world was in most ways a remote, poorly known, and imperfect extension of Europe itself. A view that excludes the linkage between metropolis and colony by choosing one perspective and ignoring the other is necessarily incomplete.

Working in Caribbean societies at the ground level, one is led to ask in just what ways beyond the obvious ones the outer world and the European world became interconnected, interlocked even; what forces beyond the nakedly military and economic ones maintained this intimate interdependence; and how benefits flowed, relative to the ways power was exercised. Asking such questions takes on a specific meaning when one also wants to know in particular about the histories of the products that colonies supply to metropolises. In the Caribbean case, such products have long been, and largely still are, tropical foods: spices (such as ginger, allspice, nutmeg, and mace); beverage bases (coffee and

This engraving by William Blake, *Europe Supported by Africa and America,* was commissioned by J. G. Stedman for the finis page of his book *Narrative of a Five Years' Expedition, Against the Revolted Negroes of Surinam* (London: J. Johnson & J. Edwards, 1796). (Photo courtesy of Richard and Sally Price)

chocolate); and, above all, sugar and rum. At one time, dyes (such as indigo and annatto and fustic) were important; various starches, starch foods, and bases (such as cassava, from which tapioca is made, arrowroot, sago, and various species of *Zamia*) have also figured in the export trade; and a few industrial staples (like sisal) and essential oils (like vetiver) have mattered; bauxite, asphalt, and oil still do. Even some fruits, such as bananas, pineapples, and coconuts, have counted in the world market from time to time.

But for the Caribbean region as a whole, the steady demand overall and for most epochs has been for sugar, and even if it is now threatened by yet other sweeteners, it seems likely to continue to hold its own. Though the story of European sugar consumption has not been tied solely to the Caribbean, and consumption has risen steadily worldwide, without regard to where the sugar comes from, the Caribbean has figured importantly in the picture for centuries.

Once one begins to wonder where the tropical products go, who uses them, for what, and how much they are prepared to pay for them – what they will forgo, and at what price, in order to have them – one is asking questions about the market. But then one is also asking questions about the metropolitan homeland, the center of power, not about the dependent colony, the object and target of power. And once one attempts to put consumption together with production, to fit colony to metropolis, there is a tendency for one or the other – the 'hub' or the 'outer rim' – to slip out of focus. As one looks at Europe the better to understand the colonies as producers and Europe as consumer, or vice versa, the other side of the relationship seems less clear. While the relationships between colonies and metropolis are in the most immediate sense entirely obvious, in another sense they are mystifying ...

I learned that although sugar cane was flanked by other harvests – coffee, cacao (chocolate), indigo, tobacco, and so on – it surpassed them all in importance and outlasted them. Indeed, the world production of sugar has never fallen for more than an occasional decade at a time during five centuries; perhaps the worst drop of all came with the Haitian Revolution of 1791–1803 and the disappearance of the world's biggest colonial producer; and even that sudden and serious imbalance was very soon redressed. But how remote this all seemed from the talk of gold and souls – the more familiar refrains of historians (particularly historians of the Hispanic achievement) recounting the saga of European expansion to the New World! Even the religious education of the enslaved Africans and indentured Europeans who came to the Caribbean with sugar cane and the other plantation crops (a far cry from Christianity and uplift for the Indians, the theme of Spanish imperial policy with which the conventional accounts were then filled) was of no interest to anyone.

I gave no serious thought to why the demand for sugar should have risen so rapidly and so continuously for so many centuries, or even to why sweetness might be a desirable taste. I suppose I thought the answers to such questions were self-evident – who doesn't like sweetness? Now it seems to me [that] my lack of curiosity was obtuse; I was taking demand for granted. And not just 'demand' in the abstract; world sugar production shows the most remarkable upward production curve of any major food on the world market over the course of several centuries, and it is continuing upward still. Only when I began to learn more Caribbean history and more about particular relationships between planters in the colonies and bankers, entrepreneurs, and different groups of consumers in the metropolises, did I begin to puzzle over what 'demand' really was, to what extent it could be regarded as 'natural,' what is meant by words like 'taste' and 'preference' and even 'good.'

Soon after my fieldwork in Puerto Rico, I had a chance for a summer of study in Jamaica, where I lived in a small highland village that, having been established by the Baptist Missionary Society on the eve of emancipation as a home for newly freed church members, was still occupied – almost 125 years later – by the descendants of those freedmen. Though the agriculture in the highlands was mostly carried out on small landholdings and did not consist of plantation crops, we could look down from the lofty village heights on the verdant north coast and the brilliant green checkerboards of the cane plantations there. These, like the plantations on Puerto Rico's south coast, produced great quantities of cane for the eventual manufacture of granulated white sugar; here, too, the final refining was done elsewhere – in the metropolis, and not in the colony.

When I began to observe small-scale retailing in the busy market place of a nearby town, however, I saw for the first time a coarse, less refined sugar that harked back to earlier centuries, when haciendas along Puerto Rico's south coast, swallowed up after the invasion by giant North American corporations, had also once produced it. In the Brown's Town Market of St. Ann Parish, Jamaica, one or two mule-drawn wagons would arrive each market day carrying loads of hard brown sugar in 'loaves,' or 'heads,' produced in traditional fashion by sugar makers using ancient grinding and boiling equipment. Such sugar, which contained considerable quantities of molasses (and some impurities), was hardened in ceramic molds or cones from which the more liquid molasses was drained, leaving behind the dark-brown, crystalline loaf. It was consumed solely by poor, mostly rural Jamaicans. It is of course common to find that the poorest people in less developed societies are in many regards the most 'traditional.' A product that the poor eat, both because they are accustomed to it and because they have no choice, will be praised by the rich, who will hardly ever eat it.

I encountered such sugar once more in Haiti, a few years later. Again, it was produced on small holdings, ground and processed by ancient machinery, and consumed by the poor. In Haiti, where nearly everyone is poor, nearly everyone ate this sort of sugar. The loaves in Haiti were shaped differently: rather like small logs, wrapped in banana leaf, and called in Creole *rapadou* (in Spanish, *raspadura*). Since that time, I have learned that such sugars exist throughout much of the rest of the world, including India, where they were probably first produced, perhaps as much as two thousand years ago.

There are great differences between families using ancient wooden machinery and iron cauldrons to boil up a quantity of sugar to sell to their neighbors in picturesque loaves, and the massed men and machinery employed in producing thousands of tons of sugar cane (and, eventually, of sugar) on modern plantations for export elsewhere. Such contrasts are an integral feature of Caribbean history. They occur not only between islands or between historical periods, but even within single societies (as in the case of Jamaica or Haiti) at the same time. The production of brown sugar in small quantities, remnant of an earlier technical and social era, though it is of declining economic importance will no doubt continue indefinitely, since it has cultural and sentimental meaning, probably for producers as well as consumers. Caribbean sugar industries have changed with the times, and they represent, in their evolution from antecedent forms, interesting stages in the world history of modern society.

I have explained that my first fieldwork in Puerto Rico was in a village of cane workers. This was nearly my first experience outside the continental United States, and though I had been raised in the country, it was my first lengthy encounter with a community where nearly everyone made a living from the soil. These people were not farmers, for whom the production of agricultural commodities was a business; nor were they peasants, tillers of soil they owned or could treat as their own, as part of a distinctive way of life. They were agricultural laborers who owned neither land nor any productive property, and who had to sell their labor to eat. They were wage earners who lived like factory workers, who worked in factories in the field, and just about everything they needed and used they bought from stores. Nearly all of it came from somewhere else: cloth and clothing, shoes, writing pads, rice, olive oil, building materials, medicine. Almost without exception, what they consumed someone else had produced.

The chemical and mechanical transformations by which substances are bent to human use and become unrecognizable to those who know them in nature have marked our relationship to nature for almost as long as we have been human. Indeed, some would say that it is those very transformations that define our humanity. But the division of labor by which such transformations are realized can impart additional mystery to the technical processes. When the locus of manufacture and that of use are separated in time and space, when the makers and the users are as little known to each other as are the processes of manufacture and use themselves, the mystery will deepen. An anecdote may make the point.

My beloved companion and teacher in the field, the late Charles Rosario, received his preparatory education in the United States. When his fellow students learned that he came from Puerto Rico, they immediately assumed that his father (who was a sociologist at the University of Puerto Rico) was a *hacendado* – that is, a wealthy owner of endless acres of tropical land. They asked Charlie to bring them some distinctive souvenir of plantation life when he returned from the island at the summer's end; what they would relish most, they said, was a machete. Eager to please his new friends, Charlie told me, he examined countless machetes in the island stores. But he was dismayed to discover that they were all manufactured in Connecticut – indeed, at a factory only a few hours' drive from the New England school he and his friends were attending.

As I became more and more interested in the history of the Caribbean region and its products, I began to learn about the plantations that were its most distinctive and characteristic economic form. Such plantations were first created in the New World during the early years of the sixteenth century and were staffed for the most part with enslaved Africans. Much changed, they were still there when I first went to Puerto Rico, thirty years ago; so were the descendants of those slaves and, as I later learned and saw elsewhere, the descendants of Portuguese, Javanese, Chinese, and Indian contract laborers, and many other varieties of human being whose ancestors [had] been brought to the region to grow, cut, and grind sugar cane.

I began to join this information to my modest knowledge of Europe itself. Why Europe? Because these island plantations had been the invention of Europe, overseas experiments of Europe, many of them successful (as far as the Europeans were concerned); and the history of European societies had in certain ways paralleled that of the plantation. One could look around and see sugar-cane plantations and coffee, cacao, and tobacco haciendas, and so, too, one could imagine those Europeans who had thought it promising to create them, to invest in their creation, and to import vast numbers of people in chains from elsewhere to work them. These last would be, if not slaves, then men who sold their labor because they had nothing else to sell; who would probably produce things of which they were not the principal consumers; who would consume things they had not produced, and in the process earn profit for others elsewhere.

It seemed to me that the mysteriousness that accompanied my seeing, at one and the same time, cane growing in the fields and white sugar in my cup, should also accompany the sight of molten metal or, better, raw iron ore, on the one hand, and a perfectly wrought pair of manacles or leg irons, on the other. The mystery was not simply one of technical transformation, impressive as that is, but also the mystery of people unknown to one another being linked through space and time – and not just by politics and economics, but along a particular chain of connection maintained by their production.

The tropical substances whose production I observed in Puerto Rico were foods of a curious kind. Most are stimulants; some are intoxicating; tobacco tends to suppress hunger, whereas sugar provides calories in unusually digestible form but not much else. Of all of these substances, sugar has always been the most important. It is the epitome of a historical process at least as old as Europe's thrustings outside itself in search of new worlds. I hope to explain what sugar reveals about a wider world, entailing as it does a lengthy history of changing relationships among peoples, societies, and substances.

The study of sugar goes back very far in history, even in European history. Yet much about it remains obscure, even enigmatic. How and why sugar has risen to such prevailing importance among European peoples to whom it had at one time been hardly known is still not altogether clear. A single source of satisfaction – sucrose extracted from the sugar cane – for what appears to be a widespread, perhaps even universal, human liking for sweetness became established in European taste preferences at a time when

European power, military might, and economic initiative were transforming the world. That source linked Europe and many colonial areas from the fifteenth century onward, the passage of centuries only underlining its importance even while politics changed. And, conversely, what the metropolises produced the colonies consumed. The desire for sweet substances spread and increased steadily; many different products were employed to satisfy it, and cane sugar's importance therefore varied from time to time.

Since sugar seems to satisfy a particular desire (it also seems, in so doing, to awaken that desire yet anew), one needs to understand just what makes demand work: how and why it increases under what conditions. One cannot simply assume that everyone has an infinite desire for sweetness, any more than one can assume the same about a desire for comfort or wealth or power. In order to examine these questions in a specific historical context, I will look at the history of sugar consumption in Great Britain especially between 1650, when sugar began to be fairly common, and 1900, by which time it had entered firmly into the diet of every working family. But this will require some prior examination of the production of the sugar that ended up on English tables in the tea, the jam, the biscuits and cakes and sweets. Because we do not know precisely how sugar was introduced to large segments of Britain's national population – at what rates, by what means, or under exactly what conditions – some speculation is unavoidable. But it is nevertheless possible to show how some people and groups unfamiliar with sugar (and other newly imported ingestibles) gradually became users of it – even, quite rapidly, daily users ...

I attempt to open the subject of the anthropology of food and eating, as part of an anthropology of modern life. This leads me to a discussion of sweetness, as opposed to sweet substances. Sweetness is a taste – what Hobbes called a 'Quality' – and the sugars, sucrose (which is won principally from the cane and the sugar beet) among them, are substances that excite the sensation of sweetness. Since any normal human being can apparently experience sweetness, and since all the societies we know of recognize it, something about sweetness must be linked to our character as a species. Yet the liking for sweet things is of highly variable intensity. Hence, an explanation of why some peoples eat lots of sweet things and others hardly any cannot rely on the idea of the species-wide characteristic. How, then, does a particular people become firmly habituated to a large, regular, and dependable supply of sweetness?

Whereas fruit and honey were major sources of sweetness for the English people before about 1650, they do not seem to have figured significantly in the English diet. Sugar made from the juice of the cane had reached England in small quantities by about 1100 A.D.; during the next five centuries, the amounts of cane sugar available doubtless increased, slowly and irregularly ... I look at the production of sugar as the West began to consume more and more of it. From 1650 onward, sugar began to change from a luxury and a rarity into a commonplace and a necessity in many nations, England among them; with a few significant exceptions, this increased consumption after 1650 accompanied the 'development' of the West. It was, I believe, the second (or possibly the first, if one discounts tobacco) so-called luxury transformed in this fashion, epitomizing the productive thrust and emerging intent of world capitalism, which centered at first upon the Netherlands and England. I therefore also focus on the possessions that supplied the United Kingdom with sugar, molasses, and rum: on their system of plantation production, and the forms of labor exaction by which such products were made available. I hope to show the special significance of a colonial product like sugar in the growth of world capitalism.

Thereafter ... I discuss the consumption of sugar. My aim is, first, to show how production and consumption were so closely bound together that each may be said partly to have determined the other, and, second, to show that consumption must be explained in terms of what people did and thought: sugar penetrated social behavior and, in being put to new uses and taking on new meanings, was transformed from curiosity and luxury into commonplace and necessity. The relationship between production and consumption may even be paralleled by the relationship between use and meaning. I don't think meanings inhere in substances naturally or inevitably. Rather, I believe that meaning arises out of use, as people use substances in social relationships.

Outside forces often determine what is available to be endowed with meaning. If the users themselves do not so much determine what is available to be used as add meanings to what is available, what does that say about meaning? At what point does the prerogative to bestow meaning move from the consumers to the sellers? Or could it be that the power to bestow meaning always accompanies the power to determine availabilities? What do such questions – and their answers – mean for our understanding of the operation of modern society, and for our understanding of freedom and individualism? ...

I try to say something about why things happened as they did, and I attempt some treatment of circumstance, conjuncture, and cause. Finally ... I offer a few suggestions about where sugar, and the study of sugar in modern society, may be going. I have suggested that anthropology is showing some uncertainty about its own future. An anthropology of modern life and of food and eating, for example, cannot ignore fieldwork or do without it. My hope is that I have identified problems of significance concerning which fieldwork might eventually yield results useful for both theory and policy.

(Mintz, 1986, pp. xv–xvii, xx–xxv, xxvii–xxx)

EXERCISE

I should like you to read the extract through carefully, taking notes which you should organize around answers to the following questions.

1   What factors, according to Mintz, have shaped the interconnections between European states and the Caribbean?

2   What economic forces does Mintz suggest led to the development of sugar plantations in the Caribbean?

3   How would you summarize Mintz's argument as presented in the last part of the reading?

DISCUSSION

1   Mintz recognizes the facts of crude colonial domination over Caribbean societies, whether military or economic. His argument is that the economic relation between Europe and the Caribbean is shaped at a deeper level by the products that flowed from the region to Amsterdam, Paris or London. While he lists a range of products as important to this relationship, his focus is on the flow of sugar.

2   Mintz's suggestion is that the Caribbean plantation was both created and extended by European investors who sought to respond to rising demand for sugar in their home states. This he sees in part as the result of falling prices in those states; something that presumably was one consequence of plantation-based production. A substantial element of this process, he suggests, can be described as cultural. With the introduction of sugar as a product to European markets tastes changed, increasing demand for sugar. In short, he argues for the importance of consumer demand in Great Britain particularly,

and Europe in general, as a driving force in the economic transformation of the Caribbean.

3 His argument is that taste is historically variable and therefore a cultural phenomenon. Mintz suggests that tastes change with the growing availability of goods. This is a matter of economics. As the production of sugar increased from 1650 onwards, it changed 'from a luxury and a rarity into a commonplace and a necessity in many nations'. It became a kind of early example of mass consumer goods in Europe, and thus transformed trade and economic relations between the European states that consumed sugar and those colonies – in the Caribbean – that produced it. According to Mintz, 'production and consumption were so closely bound together that each may be said partly to have determined the other'.

Mintz's temporal focus is on the period of the emergence of a European-centred world economy. This was a time when, as Stuart Woolf has pointed out, 'Europe's development of its economic relations with the extra-European world was without precedent'. Furthermore, this shift in relations was tied to growing commercial exploitation of colonial possessions by European powers; 'the motor of growth of the eighteenth century European economy was integrally tied to the colonies, and was reflected in the dynamism of the ports' (Woolf, 1992, p. 75). Mintz's discussion underlines how the growth of trade stemming from Europe's new 'economic relations with the extra-European world' (as Woolf has it) produced new patterns of consumption that reshaped material cultures in northwestern European societies, such as Britain, the Netherlands and France (see Brewer and Porter, 1993; McKendrick et al., 1982; Schama, 1987). The growth of trade led not only to the increased consumption of goods, like tobacco and sugar, that were produced in Europe's colonial possessions, but to new forms of consumption of luxury goods in general. New identities were articulated through these forms of consumption; dress, for example, reflected and served to articulate gender identities among both women and men in England and France, though in different ways, during the eighteenth century (Solomon-Godeau, 1996; Kuchta, 1996). Beyond the specific identities that were reflected and articulated through the consumption of particular things in given contexts, the material well-being generated in middle- and upper-class quarters in northwestern Europe provided the background that articulated a European identity based on notions of progress and, of course, European superiority over the rest of the world (Woolf, 1992, p. 89).

In short, therefore, the development of European identity and European identities in response to global economic forces is not a new phenomenon. Some observers, such as the historically minded sociologist Immanuel Wallerstein, have argued that Europe has been part of a world economy since the sixteenth century (Wallerstein, 1983). This does not, however, mean that there is necessarily nothing new about the changes that are reshaping identities in Europe at the beginning of the twenty-first century. Rather, what it does is to alert us to the importance of historical context when examining these changes. It is vital, as the other chapters in this book suggest, to set recent pressures that are remaking identities in the context of a longer process of historical change.

This takes us back, then, to the question with which I began this section: what is new about what has been widely termed 'globalization'? What implications do global forces have for identities within Europe at the turn of this century? Obviously, these are enormous questions and the sketch I shall give below is far from a comprehensive answer. What I want to do, however, is outline some of the ways in which global processes have influenced culture and thus provided the background for the reshaping of identities. My outline is nevertheless partial and consequently I would encourage you to read it rather as a series of suggestions to help you think about the issues. You may, while reading what I write, think of other factors that I have not included.

If by the end of the eighteenth century the interplay between global processes and European societies had laid the foundation of a European identity that rested on notions of progress, by the beginning of the twenty-first century the situation was very different. As Cristina Chimisso shows in Chapter 2 of the first book in this series (Chimisso, 2003), the equation of trade and industrialization with notions of Europe as progressive enjoyed hegemony for the whole of the nineteenth century. These notions were disturbed by the crisis of confidence that resulted from the upheaval of the First World War and the uncertainty in Europe of the interwar years. The history of Europe during the twentieth century was dominated by the impact of the two world wars on the continent's polities and societies. This turbulent history was accompanied by changes in economic alignments; whereas during the nineteenth century Europe had been at the heart of the world economy, the twentieth century saw an increasing concentration of economic power in the hands of the United States. The consequence of this was the displacement of European states, particularly the United Kingdom, from their previous positions of dominance (Arrighi, 1994).

This rise of the United States as an economic power and the export of aspects of its economic model to Europe, a process defined by some as 'Americanization', have had profound consequences for Europe and European identities. Faced with the apparent modernity of American capitalism, European businesses at the beginning of the twentieth century were worried at the prospect, economically at least, of 'American invasion' (Arrighi, 1994, p. 241). During the first half of the twentieth century many European intellectuals were obsessed with a vision of 'America' as a new civilization capable of displacing the bourgeois Europe of the nineteenth century. Austrian author Robert Musil has commented, more than a little sarcastically, that

> an obsessive daydream has been a kind of super-American city where everyone rushes about or stands still, with a stopwatch in hand. Air and earth form an ant hill traversed, level upon level, by roads live with traffic. Air trains, ground trains, underground trains, people mailed through tubes special-delivery, and chains of cars race along horizontally, while express elevators pump masses of people vertically from one traffic level to another; at the junctions, people leap from one vehicle to the next, instantly sucked in and snatched away by the rhythm of it, which makes a syncope, a pause, a little gap of twenty seconds during which a word might be hastily exchanged with someone else.

> (Musil, 1995, pp. 26–7)

The United States did not merely offer the vision of a super-modern society, it also offered practical models that could serve to remake economies and forms of consumption in Europe itself. Among the most important of these was 'Fordism', which enabled the production of cheap mass-produced consumer goods. Pioneered by the Ford Motor Company at the beginning of the twentieth century, it revolutionized the production of the motor car. Prior to Ford's shift of the production system cars had been craft-built, requiring a large number of specialized skills; this limited production and made the car inherently expensive. Ford reorganized the process, breaking it down into a series of mechanical, standardized tasks. The performance of these tasks was coordinated by organizing them along an 'assembly line' in the factory, thus allowing for huge increases in productivity, increasing the volume of production and radically cutting the cost of the finished product. The economic results were impressive, allowing Ford to corner around half the US market by 1916 (Rabinbach, 1992, p. 282). While the car was, as Colin Chant shows in Chapter 5 of this book, 'Cars, contexts and identities: the Volkswagen and the Trabant', central to the experience of twentieth-century Europe, Fordist techniques were also systematically applied to the production of other goods in the United States during the first half of the twentieth century. As Eric Hobsbawm notes, 'the Fordist principle was extended into new kinds of production, from house-building to junk food' (Hobsbawm, 1994, pp. 263–4). Despite the attractiveness of Fordist models of mass production to European employers, their spread within Europe during the interwar years was uneven. It was not until the postwar boom that such processes were to become widespread across at least the western half of the continent.

While the spread of Fordist production regimes helped lay some of the material basis for consumption, cultural forms imported from the United States more directly affected patterns of everyday life and culture in twentieth-century Europe. During the interwar years, with the rise of the new technology of cinema, American mass culture was to spread across the continent. As early as 1927 one London-based journalist commented with alarm that in the British capital

> the bulk of the picture goers are Americanised to an extent that makes them regard the British film as a foreign film. They talk America, think America, dream America; we have several million people, mostly women, who, to all intents and purposes, are temporary American citizens.
>
> (Quoted in De Grazia, 1989, p. 53)

American forms of popular music, such as jazz, enjoyed considerable popularity among the young across the continent by 1940, a fact which provoked considerable alarm among some European governments, most notably the national socialist regime in Germany. With the Second World War and the participation of US forces in the liberation of the western half of Europe from Nazi rule, substantial sections of the population of the western and central parts of the continent came into direct contact with US troops and thus American culture. This was the case even in remote parts of western Europe like Iceland, which spent the Second World War under British military occupation and continued to experience a substantial US presence into the postwar period; as Icelandic novelist Einar Kárason remarks, 'the Americans arrived like beings from another planet' (Kárason, 1983, p. 11).

With the advent of the cold war and the postwar boom during the 1950s, western Europe developed its own versions of the American consumer society. In states along the frontiers of the superpowers' spheres of influence this was not simply the product of economic forces, but a matter of explicit political choice. In Austria, occupied by the four major powers until the conclusion of a peace treaty in 1955 and bordered by, among others, sovietized Hungary and Czechoslovakia, US agencies consciously promoted American popular culture. According to one historian, this resulted by the end of the 1950s in the creation of a youth culture that fused Austrian and

American elements; young Austrians were 'the children of Schmaltz and Coca-Cola' (Wagnleitner, 1994). The postwar boom, furthermore, led to the transformation of working-class household budgets in particular, permitting the generalization of a culture of mass consumption throughout the western European core. In the West German city of Kiel household budgets were dominated in 1950 by expenditure on the very basic necessities, a legacy of the difficult postwar economic situation in the country. By 1960 expenditure on foodstuffs accounted for only 34 percent of a household's average monthly budget (Wildt, 1996, pp. 37–62). In neighbouring France a developing consumer culture offered the middle class at least images of 'fast cars [and] clean bodies' (Ross, 1995). By the early 1960s West Germans were faced with a consumer culture which offered them fitted kitchens and instant meals that promised to bring world cuisine into the German home. It invited them to try new places to shop and a range of new publications to inform their consumption (Wildt, 1996).

During the postwar period central and eastern Europe were separated from the western half of the continent politically, although not entirely insulated from trends of cultural 'Americanization'. Societies in the region developed their own versions of mass consumerism. In the Soviet Union the promise of consumption was, even at the height of Stalin's productivist first five-year plan (1928–32), used by the regime as a propaganda tool to demonstrate the abundance that would result from the construction of socialism in the future (Kelly, 1998, p. 233). As we saw earlier in the second reading, the extract from Caroline Humphrey, from the advent of Khrushchev onwards the Soviet state sought to generate a domestic, socialist version of the consumer economy, though this often foundered on the reality of shortages. Further west, however, in central and eastern Europe from the mid 1950s onwards socialist regimes sought to buy political legitimacy by generating their own versions of a consumer society (Reid and Crowley, 2000). As David Crowley demonstrates in Chapter 6 of this volume, 'Making the socialist home in postwar eastern Europe', consumer cultures in central and eastern Europe, particularly those centring on the home, were developed in part in response to ideas that permeated Soviet-type societies from the United States, showing an intriguing interplay between global processes and local circumstances. And as Colin Chant shows in the preceding chapter, the most archetypal of 'American' consumer goods, the mass-produced motor car, formed a central part of the consumer culture of socialist East Germany.

The end of the postwar boom in western Europe brought considerable change in its wake, as governments responded to economic difficulties over the following twenty years by embracing policies of financial and commercial deregulation and by privatizing state industries. Moreover, these changes coincided with economic crisis in the states of the Soviet Union and east-central Europe, which combined with popular discontent to produce the revolutions of 1989. These processes set in train a new series of shifts, which were described in greater depth in the second section of this chapter ('Consumerism as a case study: global process and cultural identities'), when the socialist consumer cultures in the region were replaced with those associated with global capitalism.

Other global processes, not the least migration from the poor south of the globe to the rich countries of the north, Europe included, are shaping changes to which European identities have had to respond. The postcolonial migration into countries such as the UK, France and the Netherlands as well as the economic migration into countries like West Germany during the postwar period are discussed in the second book of this series (Pittaway, 2003). These tendencies have persisted as economic disparity has continued to drive migrants from the south into Europe (Hobsbawm, 1994, p. 364). This has been coupled with the movement of people from the poorer post-socialist states of central and eastern Europe to their western neighbours. Continual migration into the region has made immigration a visible political issue, shedding light on racist sentiment among sections of the population across the continent.

The last global process worthy of note that is reshaping identities at the start of the twenty-first century is the increasingly transnational nature of media and of communications. This has both been driven by and has driven processes of financial and economic deregulation that have gripped European states since the end of the postwar boom. Television and particularly national broadcasting accompanied the spread of mass consumption in much of Europe during the postwar period; with the advent of cable and satellite television providers their influence over national societies has been increasingly eroded. Transnational channels like the German-language SAT-1 are not only aimed at audiences within Germany, but carry programming tailored to German-speaking audiences in Austria and Switzerland as well. The development of transnational forms of communication has not, however, been restricted to television; as David Reynolds has remarked, 'mobile phones and satellite TV, PCs and the Internet, opened up a vast range of communications that transcended state boundaries' (Reynolds, 2000, p. 654).

Reconstructing European identities

EXERCISE

I'd like you to think very carefully about my sketch of global and globalizing processes, set in their historical context, given above. Try to answer the question I posed in the previous section as to whether there is anything very new about globalizing processes at the turn of this century and, if so, what. I'm also inviting you here to think critically about the argument I'm presenting.

DISCUSSION

By way of a discussion I want to summarize the argument that underpins the sketch presented above. I seek to argue that Europe, and identities within Europe, have been influenced by different global processes over the past 200 years. This interaction has allowed some identities to develop and others to fail to develop. The situation at the beginning of the twenty-first century is the culmination of a series of global processes which have produced a relatively homogeneous transnational consumer culture, the effective globalization of finance and some branches of production, and a greater mobility of people between different states and parts of the world (and I might have added, but did not, a greater mobility of people within state boundaries).

Whether one terms these phenomena 'globalization' is a matter of terminology, but they are nevertheless real. This brings me on to the related question of their impact on the development of European identities. Pressures for cultural homogeneity have produced some political responses; we have discussed the range of projects that aim to create an all-encompassing European identity, largely to support European institutions. In our discussion earlier in this chapter of the spread of global consumer cultures around Europe's fluid borders, we observed that reactions were by no means uniform. The Muscovites studied by Caroline Humphrey in the second reading remained suspicious and mistrustful of global consumer culture. Their suspicion rested on identities as consumers that were derived from the recent Soviet past. While Hungarian consumers more eagerly embraced the consumption patterns that were promoted in Budapest's shopping malls during the mid 1990s, their reactions also revealed the articulation of identity. The likening, for example, of shopping malls to Soviet tanks showed the traces of the articulation of national identities in a homogenized, multinational consumer culture. In short, therefore, when attempting to examine European identities in a globalized world it is important to look for particular responses to these processes. For example, while 'on the Internet, for instance, English was the dominant language ... minority languages like Welsh and Galician, found that the Net gave them a louder and cheaper voice than traditional media like radio' (Reynolds, 2000, p. 655). One could also add that both the creation of the euro and the nationally based resistance to it across the continent are in their own ways local responses to the process of globalization.

The existence of ever more homogeneous consumer cultures and ever greater mobility has, however, increased the importance of more particular identities and the greater emphasis on the rediscovery of roots. In order for you to gain an appreciation of this issue I should like you to turn to the fourth reading. This is an edited extract from a book entitled *Theatres of Memory*, vol. 1: *Past and Present in Contemporary Culture* (1994), written by the British historian Raphael Samuel. The work is an exploration of the way in which Britain's multiple histories were reflected in British culture by the 1990s.

Resurrectionism

The last thirty years have witnessed an extraordinary and, it seems, ever-growing enthusiasm for the recovery of the national past – both the real past of recorded history, and the timeless one of tradition. The preservation mania, which first appeared in reference to the railways in the early 1950s, has now penetrated every department of national life. In music it extends from Baroque instruments – a discovery of the early 1960s, when concerts of early music began to be performed for the *cognoscenti*[11] – to pop memorabilia, which bring in six-figure bids when they are auctioned at Christie's or Sotheby's. In numismatics it has given trade tokens the status of Roman coinage. Industrial archaeology, a term coined in 1955, has won the protective mantle of 'historic' for abandoned or salvaged plant. The number of designated ancient monuments (268 in 1882, 12,900 today) also increases by leaps and bounds: among them is that brand-new eighteenth-century industrial village – product of inspired scavengings as well as of Telford New Town's search for a historical identity – Ironbridge. Country houses, on their last legs in the 1940s, and a Gothic horror in British films of the period, attract hundreds of thousands of summer visitors and have helped to

---

[11] For some of the difficulties and excitements of this, Harry Haskell, *The early Music Revival*, London 1988; Tess Knighton and David Fallows, eds., *Companion to Medieval and Renaissance Music*, London 1992; Christopher Page, *Discarding Images: Reflections on Music and Culture in Medieval France*, Oxford 1993.

make the National Trust (no more than a pressure group for the first seventy years of its existence) into the largest mass-membership organization in Britain. New museums open, it is said, at a rate of one a fortnight and miraculously contrive to flourish in face of repeated cuts in government funding: there are now some seventy-eight of them devoted to railways alone.[12]

One feature of the historicist turn in national life – as of the collecting mania – has been the progressive updating of the notion of period, and a reconstruction of history's grand narrative by reference to the recent rather then the ancient past. Thus in TV documentary, the British Empire is liable to be seen through the lens of 'The Last Days of the Raj', as it is in Paul Scott's [*Jewel in the Crown*] trilogy, or the films of Merchant–Ivory. The year 1940 – replacing 1688, 1649 or 1066 as the central drama in the national past – becomes, according to taste, 'Britain's finest hour' or a privileged vantage point for studying the national decadence. Twentieth anniversaries, these days, seem to excite as much ceremony and rejoicing as for centenaries or diamond jubilees. Very pertinent here is what Fredric Jameson calls 'nostalgia for the present'[13] – the desperate desire to hold on to disappearing worlds. Hence it may be the growth of rock pilgrimages and the creation of pop shrines. Hence too, it may be – memorials to the fragility of the present rather than the past – the multiplication of commemorative occasions, such as 40th and 50th birthdays, and the explosive growth in the production of commemorative wares. The past under threat in many retrieval projects, as in the mass of 'do-it-yourself' museums, and self-made or family shrines, is often the recent past – the day before yesterday rather than as, say, in nineteenth-century revivalism, that of the Elizabethan sea-dogs, medieval chivalry or Gothic architecture.

[12] For the way these museums have become national monuments in their own right, see Ronald Maddox's 'Industrial Archaeology' postage stamps of 1989 with pictures of Ironbridge; St Agnes tin mine, Cornwall; New Lanark mill, and a Clwyd viaduct. They are reproduced in *The Stanley Gibbons Book of Stamps and Stamp Collecting*, London 1990, p. 76.

[13] Frederic Jameson, *Postmodernism, or the Cultural Logic of Late Capitalism*, London 1992.

British postage stamps, which ever since the Benn–Gentleman revolution of 1965–6,[14] have set out to represent this country pictorially rather than, as previously, regally and symbolically, seem finally to have caught up with the car-boot sales, the flea markets and the private collection of bygones and memorabilia. A recent set of greeting stamps falls firmly within the category of what is known in the auction rooms as juvenilia. Designed by Newell and Sorrell, they feature characters from children's literature, with Dan Dare, the comic superhero of the 1950s, enjoying parity of esteem with Biggles, the famous fighter pilot invented by Captain W.E. Johns. The Three Bears, who first appeared in Robert Southey's *The Doctor* (1837) are matched by Rupert Bear, from the *Daily Express* comic-strip, and Paddington Bear, who first appeared in 1958. Among the female role models, a rather vexed Alice, still bearing the traces of Tenniel's Gothic, offsets the sweetness of Little Red Riding Hood and Orlando the Marmalade Cat.

At the other end of the chronological spectrum, the New Agers and the organic farmers, proclaiming a spiritual and material kinship with the earliest inhabitants of these islands; the environmentalists, calling themselves 'Friends of the Earth'; and the ecologists, pondering the question of whether the Iron Age or the Dark Ages were the last time when Man and Nature were still in balance, have each in their own way helped to make prehistory

[14] The philatelic revolution, to follow the numerous diary entries Benn devotes to it, was undertaken in a modernizing spirit. He wanted to get the Queen's head off the postage stamps (an object in which he was defeated by the guile of the Palace, and the outrage of the Establishment); to democratize, or broaden, the iconography of national life; and to reflect best practice contemporary design. David Gentlemen, his fellow worker, or conspirator – 'about my age and ... undoubtedly one of the best ... stamp designers in this country' – shared Benn's radicalism, but artistically he was a late offspring of English neoromanticism, having trained under Edward Bawden. In his postage designs, as in his 'Eleanor Cross' mural, which give Charing Cross tube station a striking medieval motif, or his illustrations to the Suffolk oral histories of George Ewart Evans, he seems closer in spirit to the book illustrations of Walter Crane or Thomas Bewick than to either Festival of Britain modernism or 1960s pop art. In any event, from Benn's time onwards postage stamps have been resolutely historical, pouncing on commemorative occasions, and giving a public platform for such historicist enthusiasms as industrial archaeology. For the struggle with Buckingham Palace, see Tony Benn, *Out of the Wilderness: Diaries 1963–7*, London 1987, pp.218–20, 229–32, 234, 237, 279–82, 284–5, 287–8, 296–300, 313, 316–17, 364–5, 391–3, 408–9, 411,15, 420, 428–31. For David Gentleman's historicism, see his *Britain* (1982); his *London* (1988) and the *pièce justificatif* for his design on the Northern Line platform at Charing Cross, *A Cross for Queen Eleanor: the Story of the Building of the Medieval Charing Cross*, London Transport 1979. *Design in Miniature*, London 1972, is an autobiography; and *A Special Relationship*, London 1987, an unexpectedly fierce little portfolio of sketches directed against Mrs Thatcher and President Reagan.

much more vividly present. Taking legend seriously, and arguing that it represents oral tradition and oral history, at many generations remove, they set out to discover its lost and hidden landscapes. Summer solstice celebrations, such as the mass open-air festival at Glastonbury, or the 'New Age' travellers' rave-ups, resuscitate the memory of ancient shrines, and create a whole network of new ones. Through the medium of ley-lines, or what one of New Age's more critical writers calls 'Astro-Archaeology', every old footpath is liable to be the vestige of some ancient British trackway.[15] By the same token ecologists, anyway the self-styled 'Merlin' ecologists, argue that Celtic and druidical place names are clues to aboriginal settlement.[16] Old landmarks, under an optic like this, become the survivals of an ancient civilization, on a par with Pompeii and Herculaneum. The standing stones at Land's End, if we interpret them rightly, are the cabbala of what one writer calls 'megalithic science',[17] while Cheesewring on Bodmin Moor is 'one of the wonders of prehistoric engineering.'[18]

New Ageism has a huge cult following among the young. It finds echoes in rock music, and outer circles of influence in fringe medicine, holistic therapies and radical feminist activism. More recently it has emerged as a potent new force in environmentalist campaigning, bringing its own sacred geography into the arena; calling up a pharaoh's curse on those – like the motorway builders – who disturb the bones and the spirit of the dead; and using the occult, in the form of chants and charms, to give demonstration and protest a runic edge. Thus the Dongas tribe (white witches) and the Elfs,[19] (the eco-saboteurs or the Earth Liberation Front) backed by such New Age outriders as 'cyclists from Mother Urf'[20] made the running in the Battle for Twyford Down, a Greenham Common-like action directed against the extension of the M3, with

---

[15] *Early British Trackways* (1922) was the first book of Alfred Watkins, the original creator of the idea of ley-lines. Jennifer Westwood, Albion, A Guide to Legendary Britain, London 1985 is a place by place inventory of such legends.

[16] John Michel, *A Little History of Astro-Archaeology – Stages in the Transformation of Heresy*, London 1979.

[17] John Michel, *The Old Stones of Land's End: an Enquiry into the Mysteries of Megalithic Science*, London 1974, quoted, with suitably critical commentary, in Tom Williamson and Liz Bellamy, *Ley Lines in Question*, Tadworth 1983.

[18] Williamson and Bellamy, *Leylines*, p.149 quoting Michel, *A Little History*.

[19] For the role of Elfs in the battle of Twyford Down, see 'Explode a Condom, Save the World', *Guardian*, 10 July 1993.

[20] *Catalyst*, May-June 1993.

hundreds of protesters invading the construction site. In the brilliantly successful battle for Oxleas Wood in southeast London, 'the biggest victory for environmentalists for several years', it was the People of Dragon, 'a pagan group that brings together witches, odinists, druids, magicians and the many other elements of the neo-pagan revival now taking place in Britain' who led the way in the resistance ...

Environmentalists, after their own fashion, can be quite as ecstatic about Neolithic times as New Agers. Thus Richard Mabey, in his interesting credo, *The Common Ground*, conjures up that Arcadian time, 'about 7,000 years ago, when the wetlands were still undrained', the climate was 'agreeably warm', and about two-thirds of the land surface was thickly wooded.[21] Like the New Agers, too, though for different reasons, environmentalists, oppressed by the knowledge of disappearing or endangered species, are apt to make a fetish of relics and survivals – 'old' grasses, 'vintage' herb-rich meadows, 'semi-natural' or 'ancient' woods. Nature Conservancy officers follow suit, keeping inventories of species at risk, making a shrine of wildlife reserves – 'Nature's Heritage' is the generic title given to them in Scotland – and waymarking them with interpretive panels where their history is set out.

Under the influence of the new arboriculture ancient woodland, which in the 1960s seemed on the point of extinction, is now treated as if it was a historic monument and promoted as one of Nature's antiquities: 'prehistoric wildwood', 'relics of the original forest'.[22] By 1989, as a result of careful management and a revival of the ancient forestry arts of coppicing, as well as the formation of local and national woodland trusts, there was actually more surviving 'ancient' woodland than there had been in 1975 ...[23]

The idea of re-enacting, or establishing a living connection with, prehistoric Britain seems also to have been one of the inspirations behind the long-distance walkers' routes developed by the

[21] Richard Mabey, *The Common Ground: A Place for Nature in Britain's Future*, London 1980, pp.69, 142. This book, written for the Nature Conservancy Council, uses photography quite brilliantly. The writer is also keenly aware of the historicity of the landscape.

[22] The Arboricultural Association was formed in 1964 at the same time as a group of three surgeons formed the Association of British Tree Surgeons and Arborists. Ten years later the two societies merged to form the Arboricultural Association. *Environment World*, March 1992.

[23] Oliver Rackham, *Trees and Woodlands in the British Landscape*, London 1990, p.198.

Countryside Commission.[24] Thus the South Downs Way, in the long stretch from Eastbourne to Petersfield, 'follows the ancient path used 5,000 years ago by early travellers'; while on the Cotswold Way, 'many hill forts are passed'[25]. The Ridgeway, 'one of the best used of all the prehistoric long-distance trade routes' was one of the models. In Wiltshire it ran round the Marlborough Downs to the Iron Age hill fort of Barbury Castle. In Oxfordshire it became the Icknield Way. In Norfolk it ended up at Grimes Graves – 'the Neolithic flint mines which seem to have produced the principal trade commodity for the route'[26].

More generally there is a strong historical element in the nature trails – or 'nature heritage' trails – developed, since the 1960s, as an educational device, and latterly as a tourist or visitor attraction. 'As you walk along the sandy rides, sharp eyes may see worked flints discarded by Neolithic hunters' runs the brochure for Thetford Forest Park, 'a cradle of British history'[27]. The interpretation panel at Reydon Wood, a little stretch of ancient woodland near Southwold currently being coppiced by a local trust, is equally insistent in drawing attention to the medieval earthworks. The Derwent County Park, Gateshead, includes the remnants of old ironworks, mill dams and waterways on its Nature Detective Trails.[28]

Conservation, a minority cause in the early 1960s when the term entered common currency, and restricted at the outset to the protection – or attempted protection – of well-known historic landmarks, is today the most favoured outlet for the reformist impulse in national life, mobilizing a vast amount of voluntary effort and enjoying the nominal support of politicians of all stripes. In schemes of environmental improvement, it occupies the ideological space accorded in the 1940s to modernization and planning; under the influence of ecology it has extended its activity from the built environment to bird sanctuaries and wildlife reserves. In the countryside, the Woodland Trust, which began its

[24] Hugo D. Westacott, *The Walker's Handbook*, London 1979; *Long Distance Footpaths and Bridleways*, Countryside Commission 1975. I am grateful to Alun Howkins for this reference.

[25] Senlac Travel, 'Long Distance Walk', 1992.

[26] Martin Robertson, *Exploring England's Heritage: Dorset to Gloucestershire*, London 1992. Old packhorse bridges and drovers' tracks also seem to be favoured for these long-distance walkers' routes.

[27] Thetford Forest Park brochure 1991.

[28] Derwent Walk Country Park brochures, 1993

life in 1972, now has some three hundred woods in its care. The Council for Small Industries in Rural Areas designates priority areas for the revival of traditional crafts. 'Enterprise Neptune' fights to protect the 'heritage' coast from pollution; while the National Trust, to judge by the tastefully lettered signposts which confront the modern rambler, has contrived to take every beauty spot in the country into its care.

No less symptomatic than the protection of the countryside is the 'historicization' of the towns, which has nowadays replaced streamlining and modernization as the great object of municipal idealism and civic pride. Glasgow's 'Merchant City' is an apparently successful example, the restoration and refurbishment of a run-down district of sweatshops and warehouses into one that is simultaneously pre-industrial and post-modern, exorcizing memories of the shipyards by resurrecting the commercial glories of the age of Adam Smith, while at the same time providing a showcase for modern fashion and a new business headquarters for information technology. A more macabre example would be the Rhondda Heritage Park, built on the corpse of the recently closed pits, occupying a site where less than ten years ago miners were staging a sit-down strike. 'Operation Groundwork', a partnership between government, local councils and private enterprise first established in south west Lancashire in 1981, is now generalizing such refurbishments. Landscaping and recycling old industrial plant serves to attract new investment and development, providing new office blocks with a 'heritage' core, and associating them, through museums and concert halls, with both history and the fine arts.

The historicist turn in national life may be dated to the 1960s, when it appeared as a pole of opposition to the modernizations of the time, though it also bore their impress. It was then that the museums movement got under way, and that projects for 'folk' museums, or 'industrial parks', were widely adopted by county and municipal authorities, though the newly appointed curators, painstakingly relocating and reconstructing old buildings and plant, were so thoroughly engaged in the work of site assembly that it was not until the 1970s that they began to reveal their potential. Beamish Hall, the open-air industrial museum which today attracts some three hundred thousand visitors a year to its 'Northern Experience' theme park, was adopted by Durham County Council in 1965, and Frank Atkinson, the curator whose inspired scavengings brought it about, was outlining the idea of it as early as 1961, in the first issue of *Industrial Archaeology*, but it was not until 1971 that it opened its gates to the public. As the admissions figures show, once opened, the new museums attracted a large following ...

Environmental education, or 'field studies', promoted by the Schools Council and progressive education officers as a species of 'discovery learning' and an ideal framework for 'project' work, took on a historical hue, and indeed in the primary schools of the 1960s and 1970s was perhaps the main agency through which a 'new-wave' social history made itself felt. In either case, there was a well-developed faith in the local and the immediate. 'Hedges and Local History' was a favourite topic – a subject which (as in synaesthesia) could be simultaneously seen and touched and yet which opened up on to the largest questions of land use and settlement ...

Family history was one of the most striking discoveries of the 1960s. Towards the end of the decade, when the family history societies began their growth, it was giving rise to quite the most remarkable 'do-it-yourself' archive-based scholarship of our time – a movement which started literally on the doorstep and owed nothing to outside influence. In the early 1960s family history was, it seems, an unknown subject so far as university historians were concerned (Keith Thomas, addressing a *Past and Present* conference in 1962, casually remarked on its absence);[29] and it was still sailing under the aristocratic and heraldic flag of 'genealogy' when it was practised by amateurs and part-timers. Yet already Peter Laslett, a historian who had cut his teeth on the popular when working during the war in the Army Bureau for Current Affairs, and later on the BBC Third Programme, was launching the Cambridge group for the study of population, an extra-mural enterprise which made 'family reconstitution' the heart of its work, and enlisted the labour of hundreds of volunteers in transcribing parish registers.[30]

So far from wanting to construct an ideal pedigree, these new-wave genealogists can take a perverse pleasure in the transgressive. Thus Orpington, Bromley and North-west Kent family historians, maddened perhaps by the respectability which surrounds them on all sides, seem to be fastening on murder and mystery as a means

[29] 'The Study of the Family in England has simply not begun', Keith Thomas, conference address on 'History and Anthropology', reproduced in *Past and Present*, April 1963, p.15.

[30] Institute of Historical Research, interviews with historians, Peter Laslett interviewed by Keith Wrightson. Also *The World We Have Gained Essays presented to Peter Laslett*, ed. Lloyd Bonfield, Oxford 1986.

of keeping their ancestry up to the mark. Recent issues of the society *Bulletin* are positively ghoulish. 'Murder or Suicide' is the title of an article in which the author, not content with a coroner's inquest on one of his great-aunts, follows the death by TB of his grandfather's first wife. Another article, melodramatically titled 'Crushed to Death: Kiln Collapse at Swanscombe' chronicles the untimely death of a researcher's great-grandfather.[31] 'Killed in the Blitz' is a third which gives an inventory of an aunt's personal clothing ('white blouse, blue skirt, pink corset') and even of her dentures.[32]

In another area, reflecting 1960s pedagogic enthusiasm for project-work and 'learning by doing', the idea of family history was being taken up by progressive teachers in the schools. David Sylvester, later an HMI [inspector of schools], devoted a long chapter to it in *History for the Average Child* (1968)[33] and another HMI, R. Wake, defending the worth of history as a separate discipline, recommended it in an early issue of *Teaching History*:[34] 'Two unfailingly rewarding topics are: The day I was born; My great-grandfather/mother'. Primary and secondary school teachers in Berkshire and Hampshire collaborated in the scheme outlined by Don Steel and Lawrence Taylor in *Family History in Schools: An Interdisciplinary Experiment* (1968). By 1971 the new pedagogic enthusiasm was sufficiently well established for it to get BBC 2 airtime.

The 1960s take-off of 'living history' and the new appetite for 'living' nature were in Marxist (or Freudian) terms, overdetermined. In the case of the museums movement, a concurrence of different causes might be hypothesized: in one aspect it can be seen as a by-product or analogue of the antiques boom of the 1960s, and the collecting mania which sent scavengers and detectorists on the trail of the humblest artefacts. In another sense, it was the beneficiary of the local government reforms of 1962, under which the county councils were empowered to appoint their own archaeologists and take charge of the museum services. In yet another – the turn to 'hands-on', interactive display, and living, working exhibits – it could be seen as a museological or historical parallel to that very 1960s excitement, the 'happening'.

---

[31]   *North-West Kent Family History*, vol. 6, no. 9, April 1984.

[32]   *North-West Kent Family History*, vol. 6, no. 4, December 1992.

[33]   P. J. H. Gosden and D. W. Sylvester, *History for the Average Child*, Oxford 1968.

[34]   Roy Wake, 'History as a Separate Discipline', in *Teaching History*, vol. 1, no. 3, 1970.

Urban conservation was sparked into being, in the first place, as an alarmed response to the automobile revolution of the 1950s (car ownership tripled in the course of the decade) and the grandiose road-building programmes which followed in its wake. It was given a further fillip by the great rebuilding of the 1960s, and the destruction of old neighbourhoods which prepared the way for it. In quite another direction – the politics of the environment and the way it relates to changes in occupancy – reference might be made to the spread of home-ownership to 'period' properties, and the middle-class colonization of previously run-down streets. Here the rise of the amenity societies would be related to the influx of newcomers to the older Victorian suburbs, just as the spread of wildlife trusts in the same period – notoriously with 'townies' in the lead – might be explained in part by the growth of weekend commuting and the multiplication of 'second' (i.e. country cottage) homes. The enthusiasm for voluntary associations – reflected in the membership figures, and the readiness to undertake part-time volunteer work, as well as the protective nature of the causes themselves – has evident affinities with the 'new-wave' charities of the 1960s, such as Shelter and Oxfam, while the campaigning spirit in face of threat seems of a piece with the middle-class radicalism which, in Britain as in the United States, did so much to shape the politics of the decade.

As for the parallel rise, especially towards the end of the decade, of do-it-yourself history, a rather different set of causes might be hypothesized; one in which past–present relations were reworked as a way of taking refuge from the here-and-now. It cannot be an accident that labour history makes its appearance in the very decade which saw the start of a secular withdrawal of the working class from politics; that local history, so far as writing and often even readership was concerned, was so often in the hands of newly settled residents (the local amenity societies derived much of their energy from the same source); and that family history seems to have had a particular appeal to the geographically and socially mobile – i.e. those who, without the aid of history, were genealogical orphans. 'Feelings of rootlessness', as the family history societies themselves acknowledge, animated the new enthusiasm.[35] It gave to the territorially mobile the dignity of ancient settlement, to the limited nuclear family a far-flung kinship network, and to the urban and suburban a claim to 'country' origins.

---

[35] Royston Gambier, president of the Federation of Family History Societies, quoted in 'Digging Your Family Roots', *Morning Star,* 7 July 1979.

> One impetus for the historicist turn in national life, as also for the multiplication of retrieval projects and the growth of environmental campaigns and fears, was a vertiginous sense of disappearing worlds – or what was called in the early 1960s, when a V & A exhibition on the subject toured the country, 'Vanishing History'[36]. It was amplified in the 1970s by a whole series of separation anxieties which affected now one sector of national life, now another; by the destruction or run-down of regional economies; by threats to the living environment which put the taken-for-granted at risk; and not least by the rise of a cultural nationalism which spoke to a lost sense of the indigenous.
>
> (Samuel, 1994, pp. 139–50)

EXERCISE

Read this extract carefully and prepare responses to the following questions.

1   How did interest in the past manifest itself in Britain during the mid 1990s?

2   Do you think that Samuel is right to term this an 'enthusiasm for the recovery of the national past'? I'd like you to try to give some reasons for your answer.

3   What, according to Samuel, lies behind this new interest in the past?

DISCUSSION

1   There are countless examples of interest in the past in Samuel's text, ranging from interest in memorabilia to the attempts of new towns to construct histories for themselves; from political movements such as environmentalism to a rise in interest in family history; from attempts to conserve historical town centres to moves to create walks that connect 'historic' sites.

2   I included this question because when I read the original I started a little at Samuel's description of this enthusiasm as an attempt to recover a 'national' past. What I found particularly

---

[36]   The 'Vanishing History' exhibition, which later went on tour, was designed to 'draw public attention to the need for the recording of old buildings due for demolition', *Amateur Historian*, vol. 5, no. 6, Winter 1963, p.197. It is interesting that the summit of conservation ambition, in 1963, was to record; there was as yet no idea that the threatened buildings might be saved – i.e. listed and statutorily protected against clearance and vandalism.

interesting in his wealth of examples of how the past manifests itself in British culture is how little of that past speaks to any notion of a common, collective 'national' experience. It could be argued, for example, that family history is a clearly privatized form of history about the discovery of the 'heritage' of an individual and family unit. And some of these manifestations of the past that Samuel cites are about bolstering local identities – the preservation of heritage of place, for instance. Environmental concerns are about preservation of the landscape, which may carry certain ideas about national identity, but cannot be said to really connect to a 'national history'.

3   Though I detected something of a sneer in Samuel's exploration of people's motives for rediscovering elements of the past, I found his explanation compelling. He argues, fundamentally, that the appropriation of the past in its various manifestations is about an attempt by individuals to construct identities in the face of changes, which have eroded previously existing collective identities. As such, the fragmented attempts to use the past in culture that Samuels describes could instead be seen as a response to the crisis of either national, class or other identities.

Two of the other chapters in this volume make points which parallel those made by Samuels in this extract. In Chapter 3, 'From Keltoi to cybercelts: continuity and change in Celtic identities', Marion Bowman presents the shifting content of pan-Celtic identities in contemporary Europe, showing how notions of Europeanness, ethnicity and memory have been redeployed and reshaped by changing contexts. Furthermore, in Chapter 4, 'Architecture and identities: from the Open-Air Museum Movement to Mickey Mouse', Tim Benton focuses on a particular form, the open-air museum, which relies on notions of the past that are often bound to identities, particularly national identities. He shows how these have been reflected in particular national, regional and temporal contexts. He links these to notions of how ideas of European pasts and assumed national identities have been represented in theme parks created by giant multinational media conglomerates, such as Disneyland Paris. The ways, therefore, in which identities in Europe are being remade in response to global processes are many and varied.

Conclusion

In this chapter I have introduced you to some of the most important issues in considering the interaction between global processes, culture and identities in contemporary Europe. I have shown, I hope, that the apparent globalization of economic processes and their reflection in culture has not necessarily produced sameness. Indeed it would have been surprising if they had, for European identities have interacted with global processes for much of the last 250 years at least. The present situation is merely the result of the most recent of these global processes. This chapter is, however, only an introduction – the issues that are explored and introduced here are picked up and developed in the five chapters that follow.

References

Arrighi, G. (1994) *The Long Twentieth Century: Money, Power and the Origins of Our Times*, London/New York, Verso.

Árva, L. and Diczházi, B. (1998) *Globalizáció és Külföldi Tőkeberuházások Magyarországon*, Budapest, Kairosz Kiadó/Növekedéskutató.

Bartolovich, C. (2000) 'Global capital and transnationalism', in H. Schwarz and S. Ray (eds), *A Companion to Postcolonial Studies*, Malden/Oxford, Blackwell.

Bodnár, J. (2001) *Fin de Millénaire Budapest: Metamorphoses of Urban Life*, Minneapolis, MN/London, University of Minnesota Press.

Brewer, J. and Porter R. (eds) (1993) *Consumption and the World of Goods*, London/New York, Routledge.

Castells, M. (1997) *The Information Age: Economy, Society and Culture*, vol. II: *The Power of Identity*, Oxford, Blackwell.

Chimisso, C. (ed.) (2003) *Exploring European Identities*, Milton Keynes, Open University.

De Grazia, V. (1989) 'Mass culture and sovereignty: the American challenge to European cinemas, 1920–1960', *Journal of Modern History*, vol. 61, no. 1, pp. 53–87.

Ékes, I. and Ernst, G. (1995) *Rendszerváltó háztartások (1990–1994)*, Budapest, Szakszervezetek Gazdaság- és Társadalomkutató Intézete.

Emsley, C. (ed.) (2003) *War, Culture and Memory*, Milton Keynes, Open University.

Friedman, J. (1994) 'Global system, globalization and the parameters of modernity', in J. Friedman, *Cultural Identity and Social Process*, London, Sage.

Hobsbawm, E. (1994) *Age of Extremes: the Short Twentieth Century*, London, Michael Joseph.

Humphrey, C. (2002) *The Unmaking of Soviet Life: Everyday Economies after Socialism*, Ithaca, NY/London, Cornell University Press.

Johnson, L. R. (1996) *Central Europe: Enemies, Neighbors, Friends*, New York/Oxford, Oxford University Press.

Kárason, E. (1983) *Devils' Island*, transl. D. MacDuff and M. Magnusson, Edinburgh, Canongate.

Kelly, C. (1998) 'Creating a consumer: advertising and commercialization', in C. Kelly and D. Shepherd (eds), *Russian Cultural Studies: an Introduction*, New York/Oxford, Oxford University Press.

Klein, N. (2000) *No Logo*, London, Flamingo.

Kuchta, D. (1996) 'The making of the self-made man: class, clothing, and English masculinity, 1688–1832', in V. De Grazia and E. Furlough (eds), *The Sex of Things: Gender and Consumption in Historical Perspective*, Berkeley, Los Angeles, CA/London, University of California Press.

Kürti, L. (2002) *Youth and the State in Hungary: Capitalism, Communism and Class*, London, Pluto.

McKendrick, N., Brewer, J. and Plumb, J. H. (1982) *The Birth of a Consumer Society: the Commercialisation of Eighteenth-Century England*, London, Hutchinson.

Miller, D. (1998) *A Theory of Shopping*, Cambridge, Polity.

Mintz, S. W. (1986) *Sweetness and Power: the Place of Sugar in Modern History*, Harmondsworth, Penguin.

Musil, R. (1995) *The Man without Qualities*, transl. S. Wilkins and B. Pike, London, Picador.

Pittaway, M. (ed.) (2003) *The Fluid Borders of Europe*, Milton Keynes, Open University.

Rabinbach, A. (1992) *The Human Motor: Energy, Fatigue and the Origins of Modernity*, Berkeley, Los Angeles, CA/London, University of California Press.

Reid, S. E. and Crowley, D. (2000) (eds) *Style and Socialism: Modernity and Material Culture in Postwar Eastern Europe*, Oxford/New York, Berg.

Reynolds, D. (2000) *One World Divisible: a Global History since 1945*, Harmondsworth, Penguin.

Robertson, R. (1992) *Globalization: Social Theory and Global Culture*, London, Sage.

Ross, K. (1995) *Fast Cars, Clean Bodies: Decolonization and the Reordering of French culture*, Cambridge, MA/London, MIT Press.

Samuel, R. (1994) *Theatres of Memory*, vol. 1: *Past and Present in Contemporary Culture*, London, Verso.

Schama, S. (1987) *The Embarrassment of Riches: an Interpretation of Dutch Culture in the Golden Age*, London, Collins.

Solomon-Godeau, A. (1996) 'The other side of Venus: the visual economy of feminine display' in V. De Grazia and E. Furlough (eds), *The Sex of Things: Gender and Consumption in Historical Perspective*, Berkeley, Los Angeles, CA/London, University of California Press.

Tripathi, S. (2001) 'Put out less flags', *Index on Censorship*, vol. 30, no. 2, pp. 78–80.

Wagnleitner, R. (1994) *Coca-Colonization and the Cold War: the Cultural Mission of the United States in Austria after the Second World War*, transl. D. M. Woolf, Chapel Hill, NC/London, University of North Carolina Press.

Wallerstein, I. (1983) *Historical Capitalism*, London/New York, Verso.

Wildt, M. (1996) *Vom kleinen Wohlstandt: eine konsumgeschichte der fünfziger Jahre*, Frankfurt-am-Main, Fischer Taschenbuch Verlag.

Woolf, S. (1992) 'The construction of a European world-view in the revolutionary-Napoleonic years', *Past & Present*, no. 137, pp. 72–101.

Zukhin, S. (1995) *The Culture of Cities*, Oxford, Blackwell Publishers.

The Council of Europe: defining and defending a European identity

HUGH STARKEY

Introduction

This chapter examines the ideals and principles underlying the creation and operation of the European intergovernmental organization with the widest membership. In 2001 the Council of Europe had forty-three member states. Its aim is to further European unity in order to achieve a peaceful continent in a peaceful world. Its strategy for achieving this is to insist that its member states are fully democratic and that all individuals living in Europe should have their human rights protected. These founding principles are claimed to be the 'common heritage of [European] peoples' and therefore an essential feature of European identity. In this chapter we trace the origin and development of this conception of what it means to be European.

Imagining a peaceful Europe

At the height of the Second World War (1939–45), far-sighted leaders and political activists from a number of countries made intense efforts to ensure that the outcome of the conflict would be the establishment of strong international institutions capable of promoting and preserving peace. At a global level, Britain and the USA signed the Atlantic Charter in August 1941 and twenty-six states signed the Declaration by United Nations in Washington in January 1942. Representatives of fifty states met in San Francisco in May and June 1945 to draw up the Charter of the United Nations which came into force on 24 October 1945.

In Europe, the failure of the well-intentioned League of Nations to prevent a second war between European states gave impetus to the creation of continental as well as world institutions. By the early 1940s movements of resistance to fascism and Nazism, elaborating their postwar strategies, were actively promoting the idea of European unification (Urwin, 1989, p. 90). One of the most influential documents in circulation was the Ventotene manifesto, drafted in 1941/2 by the anti-fascist resister Altiero Spinelli in his prison camp on the island of Ventotene under the title 'Towards a Free and United Europe'. This text, published with a preface by Eugenio Colorni in January 1944, became the founding document of the Italian Movement for European Federation. Similar movements existed in a number of European countries at this time. The first reading consists of extracts from the manifesto.

The Ventotene manifesto

I – The crisis of modern civilization

Modern civilization has taken the principle of freedom as its basis, a principle which holds that man must not be a mere instrument to be used by others but an autonomous centre of life ...

The absolute sovereignty of national States has led to the desire of each of them to dominate, since each feels threatened by the strength of the others, and considers that its 'living space' should include increasingly vast territories that give it the right to free movement and provide self-sustenance without needing to rely on others. This desire to dominate cannot be placated except by the hegemony of the strongest State over all the others.

As a consequence of this, from being the guardian of citizens' freedom, the State has been turned into a master of vassals bound into servitude, and has all the powers it needs to achieve the maximum war-efficiency. Even during peacetime, considered to be pauses during which to prepare for subsequent, inevitable wars, the will of the military class now holds sway over the will of the civilian class in many countries, making it increasingly difficult to operate free political systems. Schools, science, production, administrative bodies are mainly directed towards increasing military strength. Women are considered merely as producers of soldiers and are rewarded with the same criteria as prolific cattle. From the very earliest age, children are taught to handle weapons and hate foreigners. Individual freedom is reduced to nothing since everyone is part of the military establishment and constantly called on to serve in the armed forces. Repeated wars force men to abandon families, jobs, property, and even lay down their lives for goals, the value of which no one really understands. It takes just a few days to destroy the results of decades of common effort to increase the general well-being ...

II – Post-war tasks. European unity

Germany's defeat would not automatically lead to the reorganization of Europe in accordance with our ideal of civilization. In the brief, intense period of general crisis (when the States will lie broken, when the masses will be anxiously waiting for a new message, like molten matter, burning, and easily shaped into new moulds capable of accommodating the guidance of serious internationalist minded men), the most privileged classes in the old national systems will attempt, by underhand or violent methods, to dampen the wave of internationalist feelings and passions and will ostentatiously begin to reconstruct the old State institutions ...

The uselessness, even harmfulness, of organizations like the League of Nations has been demonstrated: they claimed to guarantee international law without a military force capable of imposing its decisions and respecting the absolute sovereignty of the member States. The principle of non intervention turned out to be absurd: every population was supposed to be left free to choose the despotic government it thought best, in other words virtually assuming that the constitution of each individual State was not a question of vital interest for all the other European nations.

(Federal Union website)

EXERCISE _____

In the manifesto, Europe is defined by reference to 'modern civilization'. From the analysis of the defects of pre-war and wartime Europe contained in the reading, what do you conclude are likely to be the necessary fundamental features of a Europe defined as a modern civilization?

DISCUSSION _____

Modern civilization is defined in the manifesto as based on 'the principle of freedom'. This is further qualified as the principle that any human being 'must not be a mere instrument to be used by others but an autonomous centre of life'. Slavery, for instance, is thus ruled out. It is not compatible with modern civilization because it involves the loss of the capacity to be 'an autonomous centre of life' and further reduces the human being to the status of 'mere instrument to be used by others'. In this respect Nazi Germany, to which the fascist Italian state was allied, while being in many respects modern, particularly in its technology, is implicitly defined by the manifesto as falling outside the category of a 'civilization', as slavery and forced labour were instruments of the Nazi state.

The Nazi ideology, as described in the second paragraph of this extract, was based on an extreme form of competition between nation-states and the acquisition of sufficient 'living space' for Germany to be self-sufficient. In other words it denied the value of international cooperation, focusing only on competition and, indeed, conquest. The obverse of this state of affairs is a vision of cooperating nations, resolving their differences and disputes within the framework of an overarching European identity with its own institutions.

The third paragraph is a criticism of the militarization of the state. A militarized state cannot be truly democratic because the interests of the military always take precedence over civil society. Thus the institutions of the state, even education, become instruments of military objectives and ideology, rather than protectors of individual freedoms. Young people in schools may be taught to 'hate foreigners' and even to handle weapons. Moreover, the state's attitude to its women citizens is determined by a perceived need to produce enough children to provide the armed forces of the future. (This view was widespread among militarized regimes in the 1930s and 1940s, as witness Marshal Pétain's famous capitulation speech on 17 June 1940 when he called for the French to support an armistice with the Germans and blamed the defeat on 'too few children' (Rémond, 1988, p. 299) – in other words insufficient numbers of French soldiers.) Enforced military service in peace or wartime disrupts civil life and the manifesto notes that 'It takes just a few days to destroy the results of decades of common effort to increase the general well-being.'

The discussion of postwar reconstruction in the next paragraph of the reading envisages the possibility of 'the reorganization of Europe in accordance with our ideal of civilization'. This is seen to depend on 'the guidance of serious internationalist minded men' (*sic*). This 'civilized' Europe is one where individual freedom is protected, in other words it will be based on human rights.

The criticism of the League of Nations in the final paragraph of the extract relates to its incapacity to intervene in the internal affairs of member states. If every people is 'left free to choose the despotic government it thought best' this is bound to have repercussions on surrounding states. This was clearly the case with respect to Nazi

Germany. Interestingly it was also later the case with Serbia and the rump Yugoslavia. The decision by Nato, with the support of the European Union and the United Nations, to intervene militarily in Kosovo in 1999 was taken precisely on the grounds that the racist policies of the Milošević regime were causing refugee flows that threatened the stability of surrounding democratic states.

In conclusion, a Europe based on the notion of 'modern civilization' is characterized by the existence of institutions that protect human rights and fundamental freedoms on an international basis. This conception of Europe is one that underpins all subsequent developments of European institutions.

Churchill and the Congress of Europe at The Hague

Within Britain there was much sympathy for the idea of an international body of peaceful and democratic European states. Indeed, much of the intellectual and practical underpinning of the Ventotene manifesto has been attributed to the British diplomat Philip Kerr, Lord Lothian (1882–1940) (Guderzo, 1986, p. 9).

In a wartime broadcast in 1943, the British prime minister, Winston Churchill, proposed a regional Council of Europe to complement the United Nations. Even when out of power in 1946 Churchill, then leader of the opposition in the UK parliament, continued to argue for the creation of a United States of Europe. On 9 May 1946 he delivered a major speech in The Hague entitled 'The United States of Europe', following this on 19 September 1946 in Zurich with 'The Tragedy of Europe'. In this speech he concluded:

> I must now sum up the propositions which are before you. Our constant aim must be to build and fortify the strength of U.N.O. [the United Nations Organization] Under and within that world concept we must re-create the European family in a regional structure called, it may be, the United States of Europe. The first step is to form a Council of Europe.

(Churchill, 1948)

In December 1947 Churchill convened an International Committee of the Movements for European Unity, which organized the Congress of Europe in The Hague from 7 to 10 May 1948, with Churchill as honorary president. A total of 663 delegates from 16 European states attended, along with observers from other European states and from the USA and the British Commonwealth. Churchill made an opening speech in the Netherlands parliament buildings. The main work of the Congress was conducted in three committees: political; economic and social; cultural. Each committee produced a resolution and all were adopted unanimously in plenary session on 10 May, along with a 'Message for Europeans', which summarized the main policies agreed at the Congress.

The fact that these final resolutions were adopted unanimously does not imply an unproblematic consensus. While united in a desire for new European institutions, activists argued fiercely as to their scope, their powers and their ultimate purpose.

All three resolutions of the Congress make reference to human rights, though the Economic and Social Resolution does not actually use this expression. The next three readings are extracts from these resolutions.

Economic and Social Resolution of the Congress of Europe, The Hague, May 1948

The exigencies of modern economic development must be reconciled with the integrity of human personality ...

Conclusion

Such is the economic basis on which the peoples of Europe will find the opportunity – and the duty – not only to put a stop to the present decline in their standard of living, but also to ensure that all shall enjoy better conditions of life, both material and cultural, which is the ultimate and sole aim of every economic activity. Under these improved conditions, when the petty rivalries of national states have been laid aside, we may look forward to the development of a harmonious society in Europe. In such a society the rights of the family would be respected, the free association of individuals and groups and the protection of the weak and infirm guaranteed, and scope given to all to develop in freedom and concord a full and balanced personality. We look forward to a social and economic existence, in which Europe may play her proper role in the world as a constructive element and a force for peace.

(Grand-Place Europe website)

EXERCISE

Read the above extract and explain the vision of Europe expressed in it. In particular, what relationship is implied between the economic and the social and cultural dimensions of European construction?

DISCUSSION

The clear intention is the creation of a humane economy, one that is 'reconciled with the integrity of human personality'. In other words the economy should support 'better conditions of life, both material and cultural', rather than be an end in itself. Freedom is an objective of the economy, but this is not the freedom of unfettered economic development. Rather it is freedom as applied to individuals and groups, aimed at producing 'a harmonious society in Europe'. Such a Europe will be a model, seen 'as a constructive element and a force for peace'. To achieve this harmonious society requires 'the free association of individuals and groups', including cultural groups, political parties and trade unions. Individuals should be given the scope 'to develop in freedom and concord a full and balanced personality'. This implies that individuals are not just workers, but that they should have opportunities for rest, leisure and cultural activities. Certain categories will require special consideration, as expressed by the phrase 'the protection of the weak and infirm guaranteed'.

The Marshall Plan, announced the previous year (5 June 1947), provided substantial American aid for European economic reconstruction. This is acknowledged in the preamble to this resolution: 'Thanks to the generous assistance of the United States of America there is a unique opportunity to build a new and better Europe.' However, the expressly anti-communist terms of the aid package, expounded by President Truman, were seen as divisive for Europe by many of the delegates. There is consequently no mention or acknowledgement of a trans-Atlantic dimension in this or the other resolutions. In avoiding reference to the Americans, the delegates were consciously defining a specifically European programme.

This European identity is expressed as being founded on individual self-expression, freedom of association for political, social and cultural purposes, and the rights of disadvantaged persons to social and economic security.

Political Resolution of the Congress of Europe, The Hague, May 1948

THE CONGRESS:

1. RECOGNIZES that it is the urgent duty of the nations of Europe to create an economic and political union in order to assure security and social progress.

2. NOTES with approval the recent steps which have been taken by some European Governments in the direction of economic and political co-operation, but believes that in the present emergency the organizations created are by themselves insufficient to provide any lasting remedy.

Sovereign Rights

3. DECLARES that the time has come when the European nations must transfer and merge some portion of their sovereign rights so as to secure common political and economic action for the integration and proper development of their common resources.

4. CONSIDERS that any Union or Federation of Europe should be designed to protect the security of its constituent peoples, should be free from outside control, and should not be directed against any other nation.

5. ASSIGNS to a United Europe the immediate task of establishing progressively a democratic social system, the aim of which shall be to free men from all types of slavery and economic insecurity, just as political democracy aims at protecting them against the exercise of arbitrary power ...

European Assembly

8. DEMANDS the convening, as a matter of real urgency, of a European Assembly chosen by the Parliaments of the participating nations, from among their members and others, designed

    (a) to stimulate and give expression to European public opinion;

    (b) to advise upon immediate practical measures designed progressively to bring about the necessary economic and political union of Europe;

(c) to examine the juridical and constitutional implications arising out of the creation of such a Union or Federation and their economic and social consequences;

(d) to prepare the necessary plans for the above purposes.

Charter of Human Rights

9. CONSIDERS that the resultant Union or Federation should be open to all European nations democratically governed and which undertake to respect a Charter of Human Rights.

10. RESOLVES that a Commission should be set up to undertake immediately the double task of drafting such a Charter and of laying down standards to which a State must conform if it is to deserve the name of a democracy.

11. DECLARES that in no circumstances shall a State be entitled to be called a democracy unless it does, in fact as well as in law, guarantee to its citizens liberty of thought, assembly and expression, as well as the right to form a political opposition.

12. REQUESTS that this Commission should report within three months on its labours.

Supreme Court

13. IS CONVINCED that in the interests of human values and human liberty the Assembly should make proposals for the establishment of a Court of Justice with adequate sanctions for the implementation of this Charter, and to this end any citizen of the associated countries shall have redress before the court, at any time and with the least possible delay, of any violation of his rights as formulated in the Charter.

(Grand-Place Europe website)

EXERCISE

Read the extract from the political resolution above. Then

1 Identify the expectations of the common basis on which states can apply to become members of the proposed European Union.

2 Note the features of the key political structure proposed, namely the European Assembly.

3 Consider why a political resolution gives so much emphasis to a Charter of Human Rights and a Supreme Court.

DISCUSSION _____

1   Under Article 3, there is an expectation that nations wishing to be members of the European Union will 'merge some portion of their sovereign rights'. A further clear expectation is adherence to the principles of democracy. This is most obviously expressed in Article 9, which would restrict membership of 'the resultant Union or Federation' to 'European nations democratically governed'. What is meant by 'democratically governed' is defined in the final section of Article 9 and in Articles 10 and 11. The first condition is that a State will 'undertake to respect a Charter of Human Rights' (Article 9). The European Union to be created will lay down 'standards to which a State must conform if it is to deserve the name of democracy'. The second condition is that these standards, to be codified in a charter, should really be upheld and the rights in the charter guaranteed 'in fact as well as in law'. Article 11 also gives an indication of the political rights to be contained in the charter, namely 'liberty of thought, assembly and expression, as well as the right to form a political opposition'. In addition, Article 5 sets out the intention to establish a 'democratic social system'. The purpose is stated as being 'to free men [*sic*] from all types of slavery and economic insecurity'.

2   The European Assembly, as defined in Article 8, is to be drawn from members of the parliaments of member states. In other words, it is not to be directly elected. However, since it is to be composed of members with an elected mandate, it can claim to 'give expression to European public opinion' as well as to 'stimulate' it. The assembly is intended to take forward 'the necessary economic and political union of Europe'. It will 'advise upon ... practical measures' and 'prepare the necessary plans'. Thus it is not expected to have an executive function. Rather, it is to 'examine the juridical and constitutional implications' of a European Union and consider their 'economic and social consequences'. Not surprisingly, given the speed at which the European dimension of postwar reconstruction was developing, there is relatively little detail of the political structures and little attention given to how precisely the new structures can be put in place.

3   The members of the Political Committee of the Congress are concerned primarily to keep the momentum going, hence the convening of the assembly is 'a matter of real urgency'. They see their other function as the laying down of basic principles as to what constitutes a European democratic state, hence the emphasis on the Charter of Human Rights and the Supreme Court to uphold these rights. A European union or federation,

the committee suggests, should be 'free from outside control' and 'not be directed against any other nation'. We may detect here a desire to distinguish a European identity from an American one. The term 'outside control' may suggest a refusal to accept Marshall Plan aid with strings attached, and particularly the desire to retain an independent position vis à vis the Soviet Union (the 'other nation'?) at a time when the Berlin blockade was increasing tensions and foreshadowing the cold war.

The first of the postwar European institutions, the Committee for European Economic Cooperation (CEEC), had been created in Paris in July 1947. Following the ratification by the US Congress of the Marshall Plan in April 1948, just a month before the Hague Congress, the CEEC became the Organization for European Economic Cooperation (OEEC, precursor of the current Organization for Economic Cooperation and Development, or OECD). The mission of the OEEC was to coordinate the application of Marshall aid and it was therefore strongly influenced, if not dominated, by the Americans. The resolutions of the Hague Congress can be seen as an attempt to offer Europe an alternative vision to that proposed by the Americans, namely an insistence on political, economic and cultural rights as the basis for the reconstruction and development of Europe.

Cultural Resolution of the Congress of Europe, The Hague, May 1948

THE CONGRESS:

1. **Believing** that European Union is no longer a Utopian idea but has become a necessity, and that it can only be established on a lasting basis if it is founded upon a genuine and living unity;

Believing that this true unity even in the midst of our national, ideological and religious differences, is to be found in the common heritage of Christian and other spiritual and cultural values and our common loyalty to the fundamental rights of man, especially freedom of thought and expression;

Believing that efforts to unite must be sustained and inspired by an awakening of the conscience of Europe, and that this must be informed, stimulated and provided with the means of expression;

Believing that for this definite purpose, world-wide cultural institutions such as UNESCO cover too vast a field while national

..

institutions are too limited in scope, so that there do not exist in practice European institutions capable of carrying out the above tasks;

Taking note of Article III of the Treaty of Brussels which urges the governments concerned to promote cultural exchanges by conventions between themselves or by other means;

[Recommends the setting up of a European Cultural Centre and a European Youth Institute and]

Human Rights

4. AFFIRMS that human rights are the essential bases of our efforts for a United Europe and that a Charter of Human Rights is insufficient unless rendered legally binding by agreement to be reached between the member-states of the European Union.

5. CONSIDERS it essential for the safeguarding of these rights that there should be established a Supreme Court with supra-state jurisdiction to which citizens and groups can appeal, and which is capable of assuring the implementation of the Charter.

(Grand-Place Europe website)

EXERCISE

Note the beliefs expressed in the preamble to the resolution, particularly as they refer to the 'genuine and living unity' of European people. Consider the reasons why the Cultural Committee, as well as the Political and Economic and Social Committees, is so emphatic about the necessity for human rights to be enshrined in a charter and protected by a Supreme Court.

DISCUSSION

The Cultural Committee expresses the conviction that there is a European culture that overrides the all too apparent 'national, ideological and religious differences' between states. This culture is based on two dimensions, namely:

● 'the common heritage of Christian and other spiritual and cultural values';

● 'our common loyalty to the fundamental rights of man, especially freedom of thought and expression'.

We can note that although Christianity is singled out, it is not the sole defining 'common heritage', for 'other spiritual and cultural values' are equally recognized as essentially European. Thus humanists, Jews, Hindus and Muslims, while not mentioned specifically, are not excluded from the definition of European culture.

The second dimension is believed to be a 'common loyalty'. This is a loyalty to concepts codified in the late eighteenth century as 'the rights of man' (*sic*). In this resolution the emphasis is on those rights that are essential for cultural expression, namely 'freedom of thought and expression'. These are set out in Articles 10 and 11 of the French Declaration of the Rights of Man and Citizen (1789) as follows:

> 10. No one is to be disquieted because of his opinions, even religious, provided their manifestation does not disturb the public order established by law.

> 11. Free communication of ideas and opinions is one of the most precious of the rights of man. Consequently every citizen may speak, write and print freely, subject to responsibility for the abuse of such liberty in cases determined by law.

> (Laqueur and Rubin, 1979, p. 119)

This formulation, going much further than the English Bill of Rights of 1689 which merely guaranteed freedom of speech in parliament, was included in successive constitutions of French republics. (Periods of imperial and monarchist rule in France brought with them restrictions to these rights, as did the short-lived Vichy regime of 1940–2.) However, this encoding of rights was a feature of national laws and constitutions. There were no international human rights instruments or even declarations until 10 December 1948, when the Universal Declaration of Human Rights was proclaimed.

The Cultural Committee makes a confident statement about common European values without necessarily being able to justify it at the time. That said, it tends to be governments that wish to restrict freedom of expression, whereas individual citizens are likely to welcome intellectual, religious and cultural freedoms. Such an aspiration to freedoms to be guaranteed by governments quickly found mass public support in Europe. It was entirely in the spirit of the Enlightenment, to which so many European philosophers, lawyers and thinkers had contributed.

For European culture to flourish, the basic minimum is the protection of fundamental freedoms. This had been absent from parts of Europe during the 1920s and 1930s and from virtually all of Europe during the war. Hence the emphasis at The Hague on a charter to codify human rights and a Supreme Court to uphold them.

The Treaty of Brussels (17 March 1948), referred to at the end of the preamble to this resolution, was signed just two months before the Hague Congress. Its full title was the Treaty of Economic, Social and Cultural Collaboration and Collective Self-Defence. The signatory states were Belgium, France, Luxembourg, the Netherlands and the UK. In the treaty, the heads of state resolved:

● to reaffirm their faith in fundamental human rights, in the dignity and worth of the human person and in the other ideals proclaimed in the Charter of the United Nations;

● to fortify and preserve the principles of democracy, personal freedom and political liberty, the constitutional traditions and the rule of law, which are their common heritage.

The reference to 'common heritage' is another example of a group of European states defining a collective identity, built on human rights, democracy and the rule of law.

Article 3 of the Brussels treaty, cited in the Cultural Resolution of the Hague Congress, reads as follows:

> The High Contracting Parties will make every effort in common to lead their peoples towards a better understanding of the principles which form the basis of their common civilization and to promote cultural exchanges by conventions between themselves or by other means.

This appears to admit that the leadership in Europe is possibly running ahead of public opinion. For such treaties and developments to be successful, the public requires 'a better understanding of the principles which form the basis of their common civilization'. That said, the treaty commits the member states to 'make every effort to lead their peoples towards a better understanding', which implies, at the least, some public education about human rights, democracy and the rule of law.

The conclusions of the Congress of Europe at The Hague were summarized in a final 'Message to Europeans' which pulls together the main recommendations of the three committees. It contains five pledges, the first calling for a 'United Europe' and the last promising support for this aim. The other three pledges concern the institutional structures on which European unity can be built.

Message to Europeans, The Hague, May 1948

Europe is threatened, Europe is divided, and the greatest danger comes from her divisions.

Impoverished, overladen with barriers that prevent the circulation of her goods but are no longer able to afford her protection, our disunited Europe marches towards her end. Alone, no one of our countries can hope seriously to defend its independence. Alone, no one of our countries can solve the economic problems of today. Without a freely agreed union our present anarchy will expose us tomorrow to forcible unification whether by the intervention of a foreign empire or usurpation by a political party.

The hour has come to take action commensurate with the danger.

Together with the overseas peoples associated with our destinies, we can tomorrow build the greatest political formation and the greatest economic unit our age has seen. Never will the history of the world have known so powerful a gathering of free men. Never will war, fear and misery have been checked by a more formidable foe.

Between this great peril and this great hope, Europe's mission is clear. It is to unite her peoples in accordance with their genius of diversity and with the conditions of modern community life, and so open the way towards organized freedom for which the world is seeking. It is to revive her inventive powers for the greater protection and respect of the rights and duties of the individual of which, in spite of all her mistakes, Europe is still the greatest exponent.

Human dignity is Europe's finest achievement, freedom her true strength. Both are at stake in our struggle. The union of our continent is now needed not only for the salvation of the liberties we have won, but also for the extension of their benefits to all mankind.

Upon this union depend Europe's destiny and the world's peace.

Let all therefore take note that we Europeans, assembled to express the will of all the peoples of Europe, solemnly declare our common aims in the following five articles, which summarize the resolutions adopted by the Congress:

PLEDGE

1. We desire a **United Europe**, throughout whose area the free movement of persons, ideas and goods is restored;

2. We desire a **Charter of Human Rights** guaranteeing liberty of thought, assembly and expression as well as the right to form a political opposition;

3. We desire a **Court of Justice with adequate sanctions** for the implementation of this Charter;

4. We desire a **European Assembly** where the live forces of all our nations shall be represented;

5. And pledge ourselves in our homes and in public, in our political and religious life, in our professional and trade union circles, **to give our fullest support to all persons and governments working for this lofty cause**, which offers the last chance of peace and the one promise of a great future for this generation and those that will succeed it.

(Grand-Place Europe website)

EXERCISE

The Message to Europeans contains a pessimistic analysis of the probable consequences of inaction and an optimistic vision of a future Europe. What are the dangers catalogued and the claims made, both for the basis of a European union and for the expected contribution of such a union to the wider world?

DISCUSSION

The dangers are said to be a result of a divided Europe: 'the greatest danger comes from her divisions'. Between nations there are 'barriers that prevent the circulation of her goods', but these borders are said to do little to afford protection. The situation in 1948 is described as 'present anarchy' which leaves Europe exposed to 'forcible unification whether by the intervention of a foreign empire or usurpation by a political party'. By implication, the consequences of inaction are 'war, fear and misery'.

The vision is of the creation of 'the greatest political formation and the greatest economic unit our age has seen'. It is characterized as the most powerful ever 'gathering of free men' (*sic*).

European unity is to be based on diversity, for which European peoples have a 'genius'. They wish to create 'modern community life' and 'organized freedom'. These steps will 'revive [Europe]'s inventive powers', particularly in defence of 'the rights and duties of the individual'. Again Europe is characterized as 'the greatest exponent' of the protection of human rights. This stems from 'Europe's finest achievement', which is 'human dignity'. This is seen as a gift to the world, a benefit that can be extended 'to all mankind' and hence create 'the world's peace'.

The founding of the Council of Europe (5 May 1949)

The resolutions of the Congress of Europe at The Hague were developed by the European Movement, an unofficial body set up to maintain the momentum of the Congress. The European Movement formally presented its proposals to the five member states of the Brussels Treaty Organization: Belgium, France, Luxembourg, the Netherlands and the UK. In March 1949 a further five nations (Denmark, Ireland, Italy, Norway and Sweden) were invited to join the organization with a view to preparing a formal constitution for a body to give institutional weight to European unity.

These ten founding member states met at St James's Palace, London, on 5 May 1949 to formally establish the Council of Europe. The Statute of the Council of Europe is thus also known as the Treaty of London (1949). The founder members were joined by Greece and Turkey in August and by Iceland and the Federal Republic of Germany the following year (1950).

The founding member states agreed that the headquarters of the Council of Europe would be the frontier city of Strasbourg, on the Rhine, symbolizing reconciliation. The first meeting of the assembly was held in the Great Hall of the University of Strasbourg on 10 August 1949. By 4 November 1950 the European Convention on Human Rights and Fundamental Freedoms was ready for signature by the fourteen member states meeting in Rome. The assembly (which became the Parliamentary Assembly) and the European Convention on Human Rights are still two pillars of the Council of Europe.

The Statute of the Council of Europe: preamble

The Governments of the Kingdom of Belgium, the Kingdom of Denmark, the French Republic, the Irish Republic, the Italian Republic, the Grand Duchy of Luxembourg, the Kingdom of the Netherlands, the Kingdom of Norway, the Kingdom of Sweden and the United Kingdom of Great Britain and Northern Ireland,

Convinced that the pursuit of peace based upon justice and international co-operation is vital for the preservation of human society and civilization;

Reaffirming their devotion to the spiritual and moral values which are the common heritage of their peoples and the true source of individual freedom, political liberty and the rule of law, principles which form the basis of all genuine democracy;

Believing that, for the maintenance and further realization of these ideals and in the interests of economic and social progress, there is a need of a closer unity between all like-minded countries of Europe;

Considering that, to respond to this need and to the expressed aspirations of their peoples in this regard, it is necessary forthwith to create an organization which will bring European States into closer association,

Have in consequence decided to set up a Council of Europe consisting of a committee of representatives of governments and of a consultative assembly, and have for this purpose adopted the following Statute.

(Statute of the Council of Europe, p. 3)

EXERCISE

The rationale for creating the Council of Europe is said to be 'the maintenance and further realization of these ideals'. Which specific concepts are claimed to be ideals and how do they relate to each other?

DISCUSSION

The second paragraph suggests that 'human society and civilization' is itself an ideal. It is certainly something under threat, needing to be preserved. The antithesis that the signatories had in mind was clearly Nazi Germany. The Nazi regime was linked with barbarity in the minds of the democrats constructing new international institutions. For instance, the second paragraph of the Universal Declaration of Human Rights, proclaimed by the General Assembly of the United Nations on 10 December 1948 (six months before the Treaty of London), states: 'Whereas disregard and contempt for human rights have resulted in barbarous acts which have outraged the conscience of mankind ...'

Perhaps the overarching ideal is 'peace'. This is clearly recognized as not a state, but a process, something that has to be pursued. Hence the formula is 'the pursuit of peace'. Peace is then broadly defined as not just a passive state of subject peoples, but rather 'based upon justice and international co-operation'.

The third paragraph defines a European understanding of 'civilization'. It is based on 'genuine democracy'. European democracy is based on key principles, namely 'individual freedom, political liberty and the rule of law'. These principles are said to be derived from long-standing 'spiritual and moral values'. These values are given the weight and the authority of tradition passed down through the generations by being termed 'the common heritage of [European] peoples'.

Thus the statute defines peace with justice as the ideal and democracy based on shared values and principles as the means to this end. The vision is largely that of the Enlightenment and what Klug (2000, p. 71) calls 'First-Wave Rights', whose defining feature is 'liberty from state tyranny and religious persecution'. There is little in the preamble to prioritize 'Second-Wave Rights', which promote human dignity (Klug, 2000, p. 94). All that supports a broader view of rights is the assumption, included without definition or qualification, that 'economic and social progress' is a goal also to be pursued through the 'closer association' of European states.

The Statute of the Council of Europe: aims

Chapter I – Aim of the Council of Europe

Article 1

a   The aim of the Council of Europe is to achieve a greater unity between its members for the purpose of safeguarding and realizing the ideals and principles which are their common heritage and facilitating their economic and social progress.

b   This aim shall be pursued through the organs of the Council by discussion of questions of common concern and by agreements and common action in economic, social, cultural, scientific, legal and administrative matters and in the maintenance and further realization of human rights and fundamental freedoms.

c   Participation in the Council of Europe shall not affect the collaboration of its members in the work of the United Nations and of other international organizations or unions to which they are parties.

> d   Matters relating to national defence do not fall within the
>   scope of the Council of Europe.
>
> (Statute of the Council of Europe, p. 3)

EXERCISE

Article 1 of the statute has two paragraphs framed in positive terms
and two in negative terms. How do the aim and two purposes in 1a
relate to the more general statements in the preamble? How is the
scope of the work of the Council defined in Articles 1b and 1d, also
with reference back to the preamble? Why do you think those
drafting the treaty felt it necessary to include the negative Articles 1c
and 1d?

DISCUSSION

The overall aim of the Council of Europe is 'to achieve a greater
unity between its members', which relates to the fourth and fifth
paragraphs of the preamble. The first purpose is 'safeguarding and
realising the ideals and principles which are their [members']
common heritage', as defined in the third paragraph of the
preamble. The second purpose is 'facilitating their [members']
economic and social progress'. This is given much greater emphasis
than in the preamble's fourth paragraph.

The scope of the council is broad but does not include defence, the
subject of the Treaty of Washington, signed a month previously
(4 April 1949), which created the North Atlantic Treaty Organization
(Nato).

The remit of the Council of Europe is on the one hand 'economic,
social, cultural, scientific, legal and administrative matters', and on
the other hand 'the maintenance and further realization of human
rights and fundamental freedoms'.

The first part of the remit is the responsibility of two 'organs'
mentioned in the sixth paragraph of the preamble, namely 'a
committee of representatives of governments', subsequently known as
the Committee of Ministers, and 'a consultative assembly',
subsequently known as the Parliamentary Assembly. The functions of
these bodies are further defined in the statute in Chapters III, IV
and V.

The reference to the United Nations in Article 1c is designed to
emphasize the key role of the European organization within the UN
and in support of the UN's charter and aims. This is entirely in

accord with the view expressed in Churchill's 1946 Zurich speech (see the earlier section, 'Churchill and the Congress of Europe at The Hague').

The Statute of the Council of Europe: conditions of membership

Chapter II – Membership

Article 2

The members of the Council of Europe are the Parties to this Statute.

Article 3

Every member of the Council of Europe must accept the principles of the rule of law and of the enjoyment by all persons within its jurisdiction of human rights and fundamental freedoms, and collaborate sincerely and effectively in the realization of the aim of the Council as specified in Chapter I.

Article 4

Any European State which is deemed to be able and willing to fulfil the provisions of Article 3 may be invited to become a member of the Council of Europe by the Committee of Ministers ...

Article 8

Any member of the Council of Europe which has seriously violated Article 3 may be suspended from its rights of representation and requested by the Committee of Ministers to withdraw under Article 7. If such member does not comply with this request, the Committee may decide that it has ceased to be a member of the Council as from such date as the Committee may determine.

(Statute of the Council of Europe, p. 4)

EXERCISE

The Council of Europe reserves membership for states that respect certain common principles and commitments. Make notes on these, as they are stated in Article 3 and the sanctions available under Article 8. Drawing on your knowledge of European history since

1945, consider possible points of tension in the organization and reasons for expansion as the Council of Europe grew to forty-three member states by May 2001.

DISCUSSION

The ten founder members had grown to eighteen by 1970. In order of accession, Greece (August 1949), Iceland (March 1950), Turkey (April 1950) and West Germany (July 1950) joined as the institutions were still being created. There was then a gap and Austria (April 1956), Cyprus (May 1961), Switzerland (May 1963) and Malta (April 1965) formed the next wave of signatories.

In 1967 a putsch in Greece brought to power an undemocratic military regime and the other member states decided to act under Article 8 and expel Greece. In fact the colonels' regime anticipated this decision and withdrew. Greece rejoined in November 1974 after the restoration of democracy. However, in the summer of 1974 the intervention of Turkish forces in Cyprus led to the partitioning of that island, at a time when Greece was suspended, and the Council of Europe was unable to have an impact on the situation.

Around this time, first Portugal and then Spain emerged from long periods of dictatorship and joined the Council of Europe in September 1976 and November 1977, respectively. This illustrates the specificity of the Council of Europe as a democratic and cultural organization. Portugal was able to be a founder member of Nato, for example, in spite of being a dictatorship.

The only other occasion on which Article 8 has been invoked was in 1981, when the Turkish delegation to the Parliamentary Assembly was refused the right to take its seats. Turkey was readmitted following free elections in 1984.

The fall of the Berlin Wall in 1989 and the dismantling of the Soviet Union led the way to a doubling in size of the Council of Europe in the 1990s, following the accession of Finland in 1989. Initially, from 1989, the Parliamentary Assembly granted special guest status to parliaments accepting the Helsinki Final Act and the UN Covenants on Human Rights (see below). This led the way to formal admission to the Council of Europe on the signing of the European Convention on Human Rights to the following countries: Hungary (1990); Poland (1991); Bulgaria (1992); Czech Republic, Estonia, Lithuania, Romania, Slovakia, Slovenia (1993); Albania, Latvia, FYR Macedonia, Moldova, Ukraine (1995); Croatia, Russia (1996); Georgia (1999); Armenia, Azerbaijan (2001).

Helsinki Final Act

The Conference on Security and Cooperation in Europe (CSCE), opened at Helsinki on 3 July 1973, continued at Geneva from 18 September 1973 to 21 July 1975, and was concluded at Helsinki on 1 August 1975 by the High Representatives of Austria, Belgium, Bulgaria, Canada, Cyprus, Czechoslovakia, Denmark, the Federal Republic of Germany, Finland, France, the German Democratic Republic, Greece, the Holy See, Hungary, Iceland, Ireland, Italy, Liechtenstein, Luxembourg, Malta, Monaco, the Netherlands, Norway, Poland, Portugal, Romania, San Marino, Spain, Sweden, Switzerland, Turkey, the Union of Soviet Socialist Republics, the United Kingdom, the United States of America and Yugoslavia. In the words of the preamble to the Helsinki Final Act, the signatories were

> motivated by the political will, in the interest of peoples, to improve and intensify their relations and to contribute in Europe to peace, security, justice and cooperation as well as to rapprochement among themselves and with the other States of the world.

> (Seerecon website)

They aimed, at the height of the cold war, 'to broaden, deepen and make continuing and lasting the process of détente'.

The Helsinki Final Act lays down specific principles for the conduct of relations between states, notably:

- respect for sovereignty and non-intervention in internal affairs;
- renunciation of the use of force in settling disputes;
- respect for human rights;
- territorial integrity of states.

In 1995, the CSCE became the Organization for Security and Cooperation in Europe (OSCE). In 2001 it had fifty-five member states.

UN covenants on human rights

There are two UN covenants on human rights, one covering economic, social and cultural rights and the other covering civil and political rights. Together with the Universal Declaration of Human Rights these form the International Bill of Human Rights. The two covenants were an initiative of the General Assembly of the UN and opened for signature in 1966. They aim to give legal force to the human rights covered by the Universal Declaration. Both came into force in 1976, having been ratified by the required minimum of thirty-five member states of the UN.

The principles underlying the European Convention on Human Rights and Fundamental Freedoms (4 November 1950)

The European Convention on Human Rights and Fundamental Freedoms, unlike the United Nations Universal Declaration of Human Rights, is a treaty, binding on its signatories. It sets out to provide strong protection for all the inhabitants of member states, whether or not they have formal citizenship.

The previous texts we have examined in this chapter, apart from the Treaty of London, are resolutions, manifestos and statements of intent. Even the Universal Declaration of Human Rights is, as its name implies, a declaration of the General Assembly of the UN, with great moral but no legal force.

The fact that European states have been prepared collectively to accept obligations to ensure 'a high standard of human rights protection' (Gomian, 1991, p. 7) is a source of pride to the Council of Europe. It claims to have established 'the most sophisticated and effective human rights treaty in the world' and is also said to be 'the guardian of the European human rights heritage' (Gomian, 1991, p. 8). The principles which it upholds are defined in the preamble to the European Convention on Human Rights and Fundamental Freedoms. The next reading is an extract from this preamble (note that other extracts from the European Convention may be found in the appendix to this chapter).

The European Convention on Human Rights and Fundamental Freedoms: preamble

The Governments signatory hereto, being Members of the Council of Europe,

Considering the Universal Declaration of Human Rights proclaimed by the General Assembly of the United Nations on 10 December 1948;

Considering that this Declaration aims at securing the universal and effective recognition and observance of the Rights therein declared;

Considering that the aim of the Council of Europe is the achievement of greater unity between its Members and that one of the methods by which the aim is to be pursued is the maintenance and further realization of Human Rights And Fundamental Freedoms;

Reaffirming their profound belief in those Fundamental Freedoms which are the foundation of justice and peace in the world and are best maintained on the one hand by an effective political democracy and on the other by a common understanding and observance of the Human Rights upon which they depend;

Being resolved, as the Governments of European countries which are like-minded and have a common heritage of political traditions, ideals, freedom and the rule of law to take the first steps for the collective enforcement of certain of the rights stated in the Universal Declaration ...

(HR-Net website)

EXERCISE

Compare the preamble of the European Convention on Human Rights and Fundamental Freedoms with the preamble to the Statute of the Council of Europe (quoted above as the sixth reading). Each preamble has five substantive paragraphs. Consider the ways in which the preamble to the European Convention develops the view of European unity and identity compared with the earlier text.

DISCUSSION

The two documents are slightly different in nature. The preamble to the statute may be compared to that of the Charter of the United Nations. In other words it is about setting up a new intergovernmental organization. The preamble to the European Convention can then logically be said to be more similar to that of the Universal Declaration of Human Rights. That said, it is nonetheless interesting to compare the preambles to the statute and the convention.

The preamble to the statute makes no specific reference to human rights. Rather it refers to 'principles which form the basis of all genuine democracy'. These principles are 'individual freedom, political liberty and the rule of law'. They are said to derive from 'spiritual and moral values which are the common heritage of [European] peoples'. In other words the statute bestows the authority of tradition ('heritage') on values that support 'genuine democracy'. European identity is defined in terms of attachment to democracy. It is assumed that these values are widely held in 'like-minded countries of Europe'.

According to the statute democracy is but a means to an end. The goal is 'human society and civilization'. This is assumed to have been achieved by some countries, because it is to be preserved. It is clearly perceived to be fragile, however, as witnessed by the recent (1933–45) political history of a very well-educated German nation. Hence the need for 'the preservation of human society', which is seen to depend on 'the pursuit of peace based upon justice and international co-operation'. This is the definition of the European project, namely peace, to be achieved by a common commitment to 'genuine democracy' and leading to 'economic and social progress'. Such a project is perceived to have the mandate of the peoples of the signatory states, for it is presented as a response to their 'expressed aspirations'.

The preamble of the European Convention on Human Rights and Fundamental Freedoms reaffirms the claim that there is an essentially European identity based on 'a common heritage of political traditions, ideals, freedom and the rule of law'. European countries, including the early signatory Turkey, are said to be 'like-minded', a term also used in the statute.

However, the view of European identity has changed, or developed, since the time of the statute. This is clear in the convention's placing of this identity firmly in the context of a commitment to human rights. Human rights are universal (as in the Universal Declaration), so Europe, in the Enlightenment tradition, embodies a commitment to universal values. Although the Universal Declaration of Human Rights (10 December 1948) pre-dates the Statute of the Council of Europe, it is not mentioned in the statute's preamble. However, the preamble to the European Convention does begin with a reference to the Universal Declaration. Whereas European unity in the statute is to be achieved by creating an organization (the Council of Europe), in the preamble to the convention unity is to be achieved *inter alia* through 'the maintenance and further realization of Human Rights and Fundamental Freedoms'.

What the statute refers to as 'individual freedom, political liberty and the rule of law' has become encapsulated in the convention as 'Fundamental Freedoms which are the foundation of justice and peace in the world'.

Thus both documents stress world peace based on justice as their aim. References to 'civilization' have disappeared from the convention. The phrase 'genuine democracy' is replaced by 'effective political democracy'. Peace and justice in the convention will be protected, on the one hand, by this 'effective political democracy' and, on the other, by a 'common understanding and observance of the human rights upon which they depend'. Hence the need for an explicit statement of European human rights, so that there can be a common understanding. European human rights are universal human rights, but not all the rights in the Universal Declaration could be guaranteed in 1950, so the convention refers to enforcing 'certain of the Rights stated in the Universal Declaration'.

The other implication of 'common understanding' is that there should be public education, in and out of school, about the rights and the commitments that states enter into on signing the convention.

The Council of Europe, the European Economic Community and successors

The promotion and protection of human rights in Europe are but one, albeit major, function of the Council of Europe. The European Court of Human Rights, based in Strasbourg, received submissions from over 45,000 individuals in the first fifty years after the European Convention was signed. Until 1998 most of these were filtered by the European Commission of Human Rights and actual judgements during this period numbered about 900. Only cases that the commission judged to be well founded were submitted to the court. Since 1998 cases go directly to the court, where they are usually dealt with by a bench of three of the forty-plus judges (there is one for each member state).

Historically a disproportionate number of cases originated in the UK, because until the Human Rights Act of 1998 UK citizens had no opportunity to challenge violations of the convention in their own country, but had to make their case direct to Strasbourg.

Other aspects of the Council of Europe's work include education, cultural heritage, sport, youth, the media and local government (Huber, 1997; Coleman, 1999). Since 1983 there has been a particular emphasis on human rights education and education for democratic citizenship (Starkey, 1991; Osler and Starkey, 1996). Another major strand of the council's education programme has been the development of the teaching and learning of languages (Sheils, 1996). These educational programmes and initiatives aim to promote a culture of human rights as basic European values in order to safeguard fundamental freedoms.

Since 1989 the Council of Europe has been engaged with supporting the democratizing countries of central and eastern Europe. Its activities have included helping prospective member states to develop effective liberal political and judicial systems, and observing elections. The Council of Europe is also a major partner in the Stability Pact for South East Europe. In particular it supports a programme to develop education for human rights and democratic citizenship.

The institutions aimed at promoting the economic development of Europe developed simultaneously. In 1951 Belgium, France, Italy, Luxembourg, the Netherlands and Federal Republic of Germany signed the Treaty of Paris which established the European Coal and Steel Community (ECSC). This led directly to the European Economic Community (EEC), founded by the Treaty of Rome in 1957.

Although all member states of the ECSC and the EEC were also signatories of the European Convention on Human Rights, it was not until 1986 that the European Community explicitly acknowledged that its unity and identity are also based on human rights. The Single European Act (1986), signed by twelve member states, makes specific reference to the European Convention on Human Rights in its preamble. The subsequent Treaty of European Union, signed at Maastricht in 1992, states in the preamble that member states confirm an 'attachment to the principles of liberty, democracy and respect for human rights and fundamental freedoms and of the rule of law'.

The Treaties of the European Communities (TEC) contain several references to the Council of Europe, notably Article 149 on cooperation in education, Article 151 on cooperation in cultural matters and Article 303 on general overall cooperation (European Communities, 1999).

The fact remains, however, that the European Union has no human rights instrument of its own, and since it is not itself a sovereign state it cannot be a state party to the European Convention on Human Rights. Another difficulty is that the Treaties of the European Communities have no provision for the EU as a body to sign international treaties or conventions. The EU is nonetheless profoundly concerned to promote human rights; a number of its policy initiatives and regulations strengthen in particular the struggle against discrimination on grounds of sex, race and disability. The European Parliament (not to be confused with the Parliamentary Assembly of the Council of Europe) adopted its own Declaration of Fundamental Rights and Freedoms on 12 April 1989. This consists of twenty-eight articles laying down the basic principles of 'a common legal tradition based on respect for human dignity and fundamental rights' (Duparc, 1992, pp. 38–42).

A convention of representatives of the European communities, including members of the European Parliament, has also drafted a Charter of Fundamental Rights of the European Union, which is intended to reaffirm those rights already contained in EU provisions. At the time of writing its official status is still uncertain. Nonetheless, it is another instrument intended to reinforce the perception, and self-perception, of a European culture defined as founded on a commitment to human rights. The preamble to the draft charter states:

> The peoples of Europe, in creating an ever closer union among them, are resolved to share a peaceful future based on common values.
>
> Conscious of its spiritual and moral heritage, the Union is founded on the indivisible, universal values of human dignity, freedom, equality and solidarity; it is based on the principles of democracy and the rule of law. It places the individual at the heart of its activities, by establishing the citizenship of the Union and by creating an area of freedom, security and justice.
>
> (Draft Charter of Fundamental Rights of the European Union website)

European signs and symbols

The European flag is a circle of twelve gold stars on a blue background, representing the unity of European nations. It was adopted by the Committee of Ministers of the Council of Europe in 1955 following a resolution of the assembly. The number of stars is an ideal and has no relation to the number of member states. The flag was also adopted in 1986 as the symbol of the European Union.

The European anthem is an arrangement of the prelude to the 'Ode for Joy' from Beethoven's Ninth Symphony. It was adopted by the Council of Europe in 1972.

Conclusion

By adopting a cultural rather than an economic approach to European unity, the Council of Europe is a less politically contentious international organization than is the European Union. Nonetheless the moral authority of the Council of Europe is strong and since 1949 it has promoted the development of a European culture of human rights which it has defined as forming part of European heritage. The widening of the definition of Europe to include all forty-three member states makes sense essentially because the claim to cultural unity is sustainable. For this reason the Council of Europe's programmes of education, youth work and cultural heritage can be seen as contributing to the democratization of the continent and to peace and stability.

There are still powerful forces within European countries, and linked internationally, that deny human rights and therefore challenge democracy and seek to undermine it. Perhaps the most pernicious of these forces is racism or sectarianism. When politically exploited in the name of nationalism or ethnic superiority this has led to destabilization, armed conflict and attempts at 'ethnic cleansing'.

The institutions of Europe were set up precisely to counter such threats to peace. By celebrating and taking forward Europe's contribution to a peaceful international and world order, namely the development of institutions based on human rights, the Council of Europe helps to provide peace and stability. It can be argued that the cultural task of developing a European identity based on a commitment to human rights has been greatly instrumental in the economic development and security of the continent.

Appendix: The European Convention on Human Rights and Fundamental Freedoms

The rights protected under the convention are closely defined in fourteen articles and several additional, voluntary articles known as protocols. In many cases the rights are qualified. States may limit them in certain circumstances. For instance, the right to peaceful assembly (Article 11) may be limited where the restrictions are

> prescribed by law and are necessary in a democratic society in the interests of national security or public safety, for the prevention of disorder or crime, for the protection of health or morals or for the protection of the rights and freedoms of others.

> (HR-Net website)

The following extracts show the main rights guaranteed and indicate some of the restrictions to these rights.

ARTICLE 1 [Obligation to respect human rights]

> The High Contracting Parties shall secure to everyone within their jurisdiction the rights and freedoms defined in Section I of this Convention.

SECTION I [Rights and freedoms]

ARTICLE 2 [Right to life]

1.   Everyone's right to life shall be protected by law. No one shall be deprived of his life intentionally save in the execution of a sentence of a court following his conviction of a crime for which this penalty is provided by law.

2.   Deprivation of life shall not be regarded as inflicted in contravention of this article when it results from the use of force which is no more than absolutely necessary:

(a)   in defence of any person from unlawful violence;

(b)   in order to effect a lawful arrest or to prevent the escape of a person lawfully detained;

(c)   in action lawfully taken for the purpose of quelling a riot or insurrection.

ARTICLE 3 [Prohibition of torture]

No one shall be subjected to torture or to inhuman or degrading treatment or punishment.

ARTICLE 4 [Prohibition of slavery and forced labour]

1.   No one shall be held in slavery or servitude.

2.   No one shall be required to perform forced or compulsory labour ...

ARTICLE 5 [Right to liberty and security]

1.   Everyone has the right to liberty and security of person. No one shall be deprived of his liberty save in the following cases and in accordance with a procedure prescribed by law:

(a)   the lawful detention of a person after conviction by a competent court ...

(f)   the lawful arrest or detention of a person to prevent his effecting an unauthorized entry into the country or of a person against whom action is being taken with a view to deportation or extradition.

2.   Everyone who is arrested shall be informed promptly, in a language which he understands, of the reasons for his arrest and the charge against him.

3.   Everyone arrested or detained ... shall be brought promptly before a judge ... and shall be entitled to trial within a reasonable time or to release pending trial ...

ARTICLE 6 [Right to a fair trial]

1.   In the determination of his civil rights and obligations or of any criminal charge against him, everyone is entitled to a fair and public hearing within a reasonable time by an independent and impartial tribunal established by law.

ARTICLE 7 [No punishment without law]

1.   No one shall be held guilty of any criminal offence on account of any act or omission which did not constitute a criminal offence under national or international law at the time when it was committed ...

ARTICLE 8 [Right to respect for private and family life]

1.   Everyone has the right to respect for his private and family life, his home and his correspondence ...

ARTICLE 9 [Freedom of thought, conscience and religion]

1.   Everyone has the right to freedom of thought, conscience and religion; this right includes freedom to change his religion or belief, and freedom, either alone or in community with others and in public or private, to manifest his religion or belief, in worship, teaching, practice and observance.

2.   Freedom to manifest one's religion or beliefs shall be subject only to such limitations as are prescribed by law and are necessary in a democratic society in the interests of public safety, for the protection of public order, health or morals, or the protection of the rights and freedoms of others.

ARTICLE 10 [Freedom of expression]

1.   Everyone has the right to freedom of expression. This right shall include freedom to hold opinions and to receive and impart information and ideas without interference by public authority and regardless of frontiers. This article shall not prevent States from requiring the licensing of broadcasting, television or cinema enterprises.

2.   The exercise of these freedoms, since it carries with it duties and responsibilities, may be subject to such formalities, conditions, restrictions or penalties as are prescribed by law and are necessary in a democratic society, in the interests of national security, territorial integrity or public safety, for the prevention of disorder or crime, for the protection of health or morals, for the protection of the reputation or the rights of others, for preventing the disclosure of information

received in confidence, or for maintaining the authority and impartiality of the judiciary.

ARTICLE 11 [Freedom of assembly and association]

1. Everyone has the right to freedom of peaceful assembly and to freedom of association with others, including the right to form and to join trade unions for the protection of his interests.

ARTICLE 12 [Right to marry]

Men and women of marriageable age have the right to marry and to found a family, according to the national laws governing the exercise of this right.

ARTICLE 13 [Right to an effective remedy]

Everyone whose rights and freedoms as set forth in this Convention are violated shall have an effective remedy before a national authority notwithstanding that the violation has been committed by persons acting in an official capacity.

ARTICLE 14 [Prohibition of discrimination]

The enjoyment of the rights and freedoms set forth in this Convention shall be secured without discrimination on any ground such as sex, race, colour, language, religion, political or other opinion, national or social origin, association with a national minority, property, birth or other status.

(HR-Net website)

References

Churchill, W. (1948) *The Sinews of Peace*, London, Cassell.

Coleman, J. (1999) *The Council of Europe*, Strasbourg, Council of Europe.

Draft Charter of Fundamental Rights of the European Union website: http://ue.eu.int/dfdocs/EM/04422en.pdf

Duparc, C. (1992) *The European Community and Human Rights*, Luxembourg, Commission of the European Communities.

European Communities (1999) *European Union: Selected Instruments Taken from the Treaties*, Luxembourg, Office for Official Publications of the European Communities.

Federal Union website: http://www.federalunion.uklinux.net/archives/ventotene.htm

Gomian, D. (1991) *Short Guide to the European Convention on Human Rights*, Strasbourg, Council of Europe.

Grand-Place Europe website: http://www.eurplace.org/thehague.congress/history/

Guderzo, G. (ed.) (1986) *Lord Lothian: una Vita per la Pace*, Pavia, La Nuova Italia Editrice.

HR-Net website: http://www.hri.org/docs/ECHR5O.html

Huber, D. (1997) *Decade that Made History*, Strasbourg, Council of Europe.

Klug, F. (2000) *Values for a Godless Age: the Story of the United Kingdom's New Bill of Rights*, Harmondsworth, Penguin.

Laqueur, W. and Rubin, B. (1979) *The Human Rights Reader*, New York, Meridian.

Osler, A. and Starkey, H. (1996) *Teacher Education and Human Rights*, London, Fulton.

Rémond, R. (1988) *Notre siècle*, Paris, Fayard.

Seerecon website: http://www.seerecon.org/RegionalInitiatives/SabilityPact/helsinki.htm

Sheils, J. (1996) 'The Council of Europe and language learning for European citizenship', *Evaluation and Research in Education*, vol. 10, nos 2, 3, pp. 88–103.

Starkey, H. (ed.) (1991) *The Challenge of Human Rights Education*, London, Cassell.

Statute of the Council of Europe, 5 May 1949, with amendments, European Treaty series nos 1/6/7/8/11.

Urwin, D. (1989) *Western Europe since 1945: a Political History*, 4th edn., Harlow, Longman.

3

From Keltoi to cybercelts: continuity and change in Celtic identities

MARION BOWMAN

Introduction

What makes someone European? Is 'Europeanness' to do with where you live? Who decides whether or not that place counts as Europe? Is it enough for your parents, or grandparents, or even great-grandparents to have come from Europe for you to be a European? Or is residence in Europe enough to make you European, regardless of your family roots? Is it to do with history? If where you live now was once part of Europe – or at least under European influence in some way – does that make you European? Is it to do with language? Do you have to speak a European language to be European? Who decides what counts as a European language? Does learning a language give one culture or nationality? Is Europeanness imposed, assumed or actively embraced? Is it a cultural affair, affected by the clothes you wear, the customs you keep, the religion you observe? Is it a national, local, group, family or individual matter? What do you have to do to establish, express or enhance your Europeanness? Or is it enough simply to 'feel' European? And how relevant is it to try to define or even talk about Europeanness in an era of increasing globalization?

An official European Commission report has declared the need

> to make the European citizen aware of the different elements that go to make up his [*sic*] European identity, of our cultural unity with all its diversity of expression, and of the historical ties which link the nations of Europe.
>
> (CEC 1988, p. 9, quoted in Shore, 2001, p. 31)

One way of establishing – or at least implying – 'historical ties which link the nations of Europe' has been to invoke a shared Celtic past. An international exhibition of Celtic art and artefacts held in Venice in 1991 was entitled 'I Celti: la prima Europa'. In Wales, at Celtica (a 'visitor centre presenting the history and culture of the Celts') the Celts are presented as 'people whose culture has influenced European history over 3000 years' (Celtica website). There is even potentially a Celtic Euro-religion: École Druidique des Gaules (EDG) believes that 'on the deep roots of Druidry, Europe could be rebuilt, and that the spirituality of the Celts is the only one which represents the collective Indo-European heritage common to all Europe' (Shallcrass and Restall Orr, 2001, p. 80).

It seems, then, that the Celts are increasingly being used in the promotion and expression of European unity. But who are these Celts and where do they come from? Does an appeal to a common 'Celticity' simplify or complicate issues of European identity? Just as there are many European identities, and very varied understandings of what it means or what it takes to be European, Celtic identities are similarly complex. All the questions I posed in the first paragraph in relation to Europeanness are issues that have been and continue to be contested in relation to Celtic identity.

In this chapter we are going to explore different types of Celtic identities and various ways in which, over the centuries, Celticity has been and continues to be constructed, construed and commodified. I should make it clear at the outset that I am not making a case either for or against the notion of the Celts as the first Europeans. I am, rather, interested in the different ways in which people have sought to evaluate, establish and express Celticness, both in the past and now, and by extension what we can learn from this in relation to issues of European identity. Thus, throughout the chapter, while I am writing about Celtic identities you should be making connections with and reflecting on what you have learned so far about European identities. However, we shall also be looking at Celticity *beyond* Europe, in the context of contemporary globalization, Americanization and the virtual identities offered by cyberspace. How fixed or meaningful can *any* identity be in an increasingly and self-consciously global milieu?

Celticism

What we shall be dealing with in relation to Celtic identities is largely 'Celticism', defined by Celtic scholar Joep Leerssen as not the study of the Celts and their history, but rather the study of their reputation and of the meanings and connotations ascribed to the term 'Celtic'. To the extent that 'Celtic' is an idea with a wide and variable application, Celticism becomes a complex and significant issue in the European history of ideas: the history of what people wanted that term to mean.

(Leerssen, 1996, p. 3)

Here we shall be concentrating primarily upon the ways in which images of the Celts and Celticity have developed in the anglophone world. Archaeologist Simon James uses the term 'Atlantic Celts' for the people who are considered or consider themselves to be modern Celts geographically, living on the 'Atlantic façade' of Europe (James, 1999). The term Atlantic Celts is also apposite because, in the English-speaking world, the majority of people of conventionally defined 'Celtic' ancestry now live on the other side of the Atlantic in the Americas (such as the descendants of Irish and Scots people in North America, and of Welsh people in Patagonia). We should also remember that there are millions of people in the Celtic diaspora (including Australia and New Zealand), which makes Celticity a global rather than a purely British or European issue. As Leerssen points out, 'Celticism is a multi-genre, multinational phenomenon' (Leerssen, 1996, p. 20)

EXERCISE

Before we go any further, stop for a moment to reflect on your own images of Celts and what it means or what it takes to be Celtic. Please now list what you consider to be three Celtic places, three Celtic characters, three Celtic languages, and whatever you think of as three typically Celtic things – these might be characteristics, artefacts, examples of music or art – whatever you envisage when you hear the term Celtic. (You might find it interesting and instructive to get someone else to draw up a 'Celtic list' to compare with yours.)

DISCUSSION

There are, of course, no right or wrong answers here as I have asked you about your *perceptions* of Celticity. Asking people what they envisage when they hear the term Celtic invariably produces a range of responses – bagpipes, Irish pubs, rain, Stonehenge, tartan, Asterix, Iona, Runrig, Druids, intricately carved crosses, *Riverdance*, windswept hills, harp music, highland games, *Braveheart*, the Book of Kells and Carnac, to give but a few examples. If you have access to the internet, entering 'Celtic' on a search engine and then observing the results will give you some idea of the diversity of usage and connotations the term has.

Where you are or where you are from may well have influenced your list. In the European Community, it might make a difference whether you are in/from Ireland, Portugal, France, Germany or Italy, for example; in Britain, whether you are in/from Belfast, Skye, Edinburgh, Cardiff, Anglesey, the Isle of Man or Cornwall could have some bearing on your responses. In the Americas, lists in New York, California, Cape Breton (the self-consciously Scottish part of Nova Scotia, Canada), or Patagonia (where there is a significant Welsh cultural enclave) could be expected to show considerable variety. There is a plethora of images of the Celts (when they were/are; who they were/are; what they were/are; where they were/are) and a variety of criteria for Celticity – language, ancestry, geography and (increasingly significant) religiosity. There is thus a convergence of complexities when Celticness or Celticity also gets pressed into service as a marker, measure or model of Europeanness.

'The authorized version'

In order to understand why Celts are currently being invoked as 'the first Europeans' or proto-Europeans, it will be useful to read the following account by archaeologist Simon James, which is a thumbnail sketch of the mainstream model of Celtic history.

Standard Histories: assumptions, limitations and objections

Just as there are innumerable conceptions of the insular Celts, so there are many versions of their history. By no means everyone would subscribe to the 'canonical' account presented here, but versions more or less like it are commonly to be found in popular books and on numerous web-sites. It is obviously a vast simplification, but represents the kind of thumbnail sketch most of us have as our model of the history of a particular region or people.

Such mainstream models of Celtic history see the insular Celtic peoples as being related to the Gauls and other continental Celts of the first millennium BC; indeed, they have long been thought of as invading and migrant populations, arriving during the Iron Age [Figure 1]. The apparent similarities and connections between continental and insular Celts have long been emphasized, in language, art, religion, warfare and social customs, and settlements. Hillforts, particular types of arms and jewellery, and patterns of decoration seem to bespeak a prehistoric Celtic commonwealth stretching from Scotland to Portugal and Turkey. This is an elaborately documented, well-established view of the past, widely regarded as the foundation for modern Celtic identities.

The first known Celts

By around 800–600 BC, in the lands just north of the Alps, peoples had appeared whom their literate Greek neighbours to the south came to call *Keltoi*, the first time we encounter their name. Around

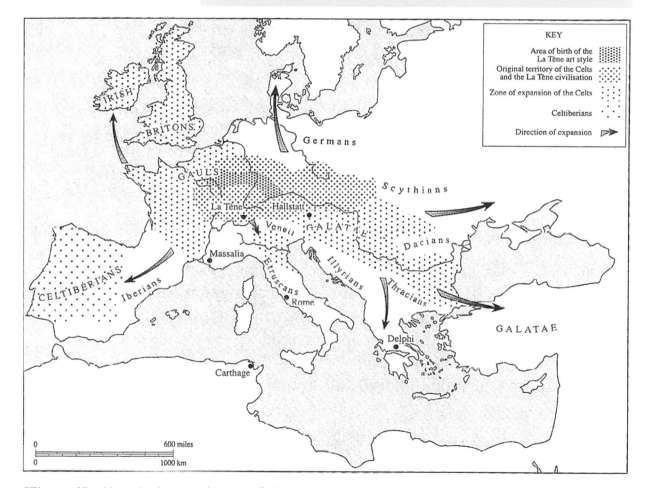

[**Figure 1**]   How the later prehistoric 'Celtic world' has often been envisaged during the twentieth century, with migration in almost all directions from a supposed original 'homeland' in central Europe. (Based on Megaw and Megaw 1989, fig. 2.)

the same time, Celts are attested in Spain too. Because they were non-literate, we have no accounts written by themselves; these were therefore still 'prehistoric' peoples, although their societies were evidently sophisticated and technologically skilled. Iron-working had recently been introduced, hence archaeologists call this last phase of European prehistory the 'Iron Age'. These earliest-known Celts formed principalities which traded with the Greeks and Etruscans. Around 500 BC the rich hillforts at the centres of these principalities were violently destroyed.

During the fifth century BC, in a band of territory stretching across Europe from eastern France through Germany, Austria and into Bohemia, new groups arose, characterized by, among other things, particular types of graves (including those of warriors) and a new kind of art. Archaeologists have given the name 'La Tène culture' to the physical remains of these groups who, around 400 BC, suddenly erupted into Italy and began to settle in the Po Valley.

The Celtic Gauls: fearsome barbarian invaders

These were the ancient continental Celts *par excellence*, otherwise known as Gauls (*Galli* in Latin). No longer a distant curiosity for Greek travellers and scholars, the Celts were suddenly a fearsome and immediate 'barbarian' danger. Around 390 BC, the Gallic *Senones* sacked Rome itself, but were driven back and largely contained beyond the Apennines, in the Po Valley which to the Romans became *Gallia Cisalpina*, 'Gaul this side of the Alps'.

The Galatians of Turkey

Migrating Celtic groups also invaded the Balkans and, in 279 BC, attacked Delphi, the greatest shrine in Greece. Beaten back with terrible losses, some nevertheless crossed into what is now Turkey and established a 'robber-kingdom' around modern Ankara. Known by the Greek equivalent of the Roman name 'Gauls', these *Galatae* gave their name to the land, Galatia, and so to the Galatians of the New Testament.

The Celts in the West

It has also long been assumed that there were waves of Celts moving westwards and north-westwards from the Central European homeland, to match the historically attested Mediterranean migrations – even though there were no literate observers in these areas to record such invasions. Nonetheless, the Romans found people calling themselves Celtiberians in Spain, and there are traces of Celtic dialects in various parts of the Iberian peninsula. These have been explained as a result of early, unrecorded Celtic invasions.

Inferring Celtic invasions of Britain and Ireland

Likewise, it has long been believed that there were Celtic invasions of the islands. Caesar recorded that Gauls, especially *Belgae*, had settled in Britain. Identical tribal names are found on the continent and in Britain (e.g. *Atrebates, Parisi*). Modern language studies have shown that the indigenous tongues of the British and the Irish are closely related to that of the ancient continental Gauls; they are all members of the Celtic family of languages. As archaeology developed, the artefacts characteristic of Iron Age Britain and Ireland began to be identified, and revealed important links with the world of the continental Celtic Gauls: all three groupings produced the same kind of characteristic La Tène-style 'Celtic' art with swirling lines, suggesting vegetation, and perhaps stylized faces of people and animals. There seemed to be a common emphasis on weapons, strongholds and warfare, and historical documents suggested institutions in common, too, not least in religion – Druids, for example, are attested amongst all three groups.

The Ancient British and Irish, then, came to be seen as Celts like the Gauls and related continental peoples from Spain to Turkey. Further, the available evidence was assumed to mean that they arrived as waves of invaders, mostly or entirely during the Iron Age.

Iron Age Celtic society

All these Iron Age societies, from Ireland to Galatia, tend to be seen as variations on a well-defined conception of a typical Celtic society. This is usually envisaged as possessing a characteristic social organization (with a social hierarchy including specialized classes of aristocratic warriors, Druids and other priests, and privileged people with specialist skills, such as bards and smiths) and exhibiting characteristic cultural traits, including, centrally, Celtic language, rich oral traditions (of oratory and literature), music and material arts. Such societies tended to bellicosity, but this is often seen as reflecting fierce independence and pride, which extended to women as well, in a way which shocked the Graeco-Roman world. They were also deeply religious, their beliefs and cults focusing especially on natural places such as woodland groves, pools and water-courses. 'Celtic spirit' is perhaps best exemplified in the Celtic love of both feasting and religious observances.

Roman conquest: destruction of continental 'Celtdom'

During the last three centuries BC, the expanding Roman empire gradually subjugated all of the continental Celtic world, except for areas north of the Rhine and Danube, which were soon overrun by another group of 'barbarian' peoples, the early Germans.

Many of the wholly or partly Celtic areas, such as the 'Three Gauls' (roughly modern France and the Rhineland) and Hispania (Spain and Portugal), became prosperous Roman provinces, but Celtic language and lifestyle did not survive the process of 'Romanization'. All these lands came to speak Latin dialects, ancestral to the 'Romance' languages of today (Spanish, French, Portuguese, Catalan, etc.). Rome all but extinguished 'Celticity' on the European mainland.

Britain, Ireland and Rome

In Britain, Roman occupation of, roughly, the lands which would one day be England and Wales led to a similar loss of Celtic language and culture in the east of the island, although it proved more tenacious in the west. And there was continuity of independence among the free 'barbarians' of Caledonia (northern Scotland), while Ireland was never invaded by Rome at all. (Drumanagh in County Dublin, a long known but little investigated site recently claimed to have been a Roman military base, was in fact almost certainly a trading centre.)

Picts and Scots

As the empire began to decay in the third and fourth centuries, the remnants of the free Celts moved onto the offensive. In Caledonia a new confederation, the Picts, appeared. These threatened the Roman frontier, while Irish sea-raiders, known as *Scotti*, raided the western coasts, even as Germanic Angles and Saxons were raiding the east.

Catastrophe for the Britons

In the fifth century AD Roman Britain collapsed, and the Anglo-Saxons invaded and settled the east, eventually to establish Germanic-speaking England. They pressed the native British groups, whom they called 'Welsh' ('strangers' or 'foreigners'), ever westwards, into the land which would become Wales and Cornwall.

The conquest of Brittany

From the west, some Britons crossed to Armorica, the western extremity of Gaul, even as that land was becoming France (after the name of its new Germanic overlords, the Franks). The British migrants were not so much refugees from Anglo-Saxon invasion as invaders themselves: many peoples were on the move at this time, and the Britons took this opportunity for some expansion of their own. Henceforth, the island of Britain was distinguished as 'great Britain' to avoid confusion with this new 'little Britain' (Brittany).

The Irish in Britain: the origin of Scotland

The Irish, too, joined in the military free-for-all, slave-raiding their fellow Celts in Britain (their most famous captive being, of course, the young St Patrick). They also settled in Britain, most importantly on the west coast of Scotland, which was to take its name from these settlers in Argyll; the land of these *Scotti* became *Scotia*. Eventually, wars with the Picts and other lesser kingdoms led to union as the historic kingdom of Scotland, in AD 843.

Ireland becomes the land of saints and scholars

Ireland itself became a Christian land as a result of the work of St Patrick in the fifth century, and became one of the greatest centres of piety and learning in Europe during the seventh and eighth centuries AD, its clerics and artists having a profound influence in Britain (not least among the English) and on the continent.

The Celts in medieval times and beyond

BRITTANY, an independent kingdom in the ninth century, became one of the various almost-independent duchies which made up medieval France. As central royal power grew in the fifteenth century, so Brittany's independence dwindled, and it was politically absorbed by France in 1532.

WALES remained a separate principality, but came under increasing English dominance from the tenth century. In 1485 the Welshman Henry Tudor became King of England, but his totally Anglicized son Henry VIII united Wales politically to England by Acts of Parliament between 1536 and 1543. Much of Welsh native culture disappeared in the sixteenth century with the abolition of Welsh law.

SCOTLAND was culturally divided, roughly, between the Gaelic (Irish Celtic, 'Erse') speakers of the Highlands and those who spoke

Scots (a Germanic dialect, close to English) in the Lowlands. The warlike clans and chieftains of the Highlands were often in conflict with their Lowland neighbours, who thought them cattle-thieving barbarians. This formed the background to their eventual brutal suppression after their support (albeit equivocal) for the Catholic Bonnie Prince Charlie's attempt in 1745–6 to seize back from the Protestant Hanoverians the British throne for the ancient Scottish Royal House of Stewart.

IRELAND Once the Vikings began to raid in 795, Ireland was increasingly dominated, partly or wholly, by foreigners. The Vikings were followed by the Anglo-Normans in the twelfth century. During the sixteenth century the English colonial grip tightened, and relations were further embittered by the Reformation. Protestant England kept Catholic Ireland under subjugation, sometimes incredibly brutal. From 1800 until after the First World War, Ireland was a largely reluctant part of the United Kingdom.

THE GREAT MIGRATIONS All these lands saw substantial or massive migrations, especially from the eighteenth century onwards. Migrants were partly lured away from often terrible conditions and starvation on the land (culminating in the catastrophe of the Irish potato famine of the 1840s) to equally squalid, but more reliably paid, employment in the industrial cities of Britain, or to the promise of land and liberty in the Americas and Australasia. Many of them, especially in Ireland and Scotland, were unwilling to leave, but were driven away by lairds and landlords who put profits above the welfare of their own people.

The rediscovery of a common Celtic heritage

The eighteenth century saw the beginnings of nationalism in Ireland and elsewhere, and the rediscovery of a common Celtic heritage. The study of language, and the beginnings of archaeology, laid the foundation for more detailed understanding of the histories of these peoples, and contributed to growing national self-consciousness, exhibited in politics and in cultural forms, not least art and literature. Perhaps this process reached maturity with the establishment of an independent Irish state in 1921.

The Celts today: homelands and 'diaspora'

Today, the Celtic countries are undergoing a period of political and cultural renewal, with a wealthy and confident Irish Republic, hopes of constitutional rapprochement in Northern Ireland, and devolution in Wales and Scotland. In the lands of the diaspora and indeed around the globe, Celtic culture, not least music, enjoys great prestige and popularity.

It may be thought that a people should be best placed to know its own story, which will preserve traditions passed from generation to generation, learned at the grandparent's knee: outsiders question it at their peril. But there are very good reasons to challenge such a judgement, for *any* established, popular outline of ethnic or national history, and specifically in the case of the Celts. The claims of *all* such histories should be questioned and tested as a matter of course ...

[T]he startling reality is that no one in Britain or Ireland called themselves 'Celtic' or 'a Celt' (and no one applied such names to them either) until after 1700. No early Irish or Welsh source, nor any Greek or Roman author before them, ever calls the peoples of the isles 'Celts'. So can the outline of 'Celtic' history set out above possibly be valid?

References

Megaw, M. R. and Megaw, J. V. S. (1989) *Celtic Art from its Beginnings to the Book of Kells*, London/New York, Thames & Hudson.

(James, 1999, pp. 26–32)

EXERCISE

That thumbnail sketch may have been familiar to you; it certainly underpins many current assumptions about Celts and Celticity. This is still the backdrop to most of what is said/written/believed about Celts, and against which some contemporary scholars are reacting, as we shall discuss later. You might want to consider how convincing you find this conventional account, and make a note of points that you consider either support or weaken the image of Celts as the first Europeans, and their suitability as role models in the present situation.

DISCUSSION

The map reproduced in Figure 1 obviously shows areas covered by many already in, or aspiring to become part of, the European Community. On the other hand, it is clear that quite distinct groups of people are involved (many of whom, as far as we know, never identified themselves as Celts) and according to the conventional account they had a tendency to spread their influence through invasion and warfare. The statues of 'Celtic' heroes displayed in many European nations (for example, Queen Boudicca in London; Vercingetorix in Clermont-Ferrand, France; Ambiorix in Tongeren, Belgium) are of people who *resisted* homogenizing European (in those cases Roman) rule (see Leerssen, 1996, p. 16).

Furthermore, as archaeologist Angela Piccini cautions,

> Archaeologists are now questioning the validity of a scholarly tradition which conflates Greek and Roman written sources with early historic Irish and Welsh tales in order to explain British Iron Age material culture in light of migrations of warrior peoples sweeping across the Hungarian steppes to take up residence on the misty shores of Ireland.
>
> (Piccini, 1996, p. 87)

Constructing the Celts

Classical Celts

In order to appreciate issues of Celtic identity in the contemporary milieu, we need to look at the various markers, measures and models of Celticity that emerged in previous periods and the uses to which they have been put. This is a context in which the religious studies' usage of 'myth' as 'significant story' (regardless of considerations of truth) is particularly useful.

As we have seen from James's account, three of the main sources traditionally used in relation to the identification of the Celtic past – and, by extension, Celticity in the present – have been classical, archaeological and linguistic material. I shall now highlight the main issues thrown up by these, in relation to both past and present constructions of the Celtic.

The first documented mention of the Celts is generally agreed to be by Hecateus of Miletus writing in the sixth century BCE about the Keltoi of Massilia (Marseilles). According to Plato, the Keltoi are 'one of the six barbarian warlike people who are given to drunkenness as opposed to Spartan restraint' (quoted in Tierney, 1960, p. 194). What follows is Angela Piccini's brief but helpful summary of the sort of information we get about Celts from the classical sources.

Celtic art: images and imagination

MARION BOWMAN

One of the most significant ways in which people become interested in or attracted to Celticity is through Celtic art and artefacts. These might be encountered through exhibitions and lavishly illustrated books, reproductions of Celtic jewellery, or cards, t-shirts and other items bearing Celtic motifs. But what is Celtic art? What makes an artefact or image Celtic? Is it where it was made or found? Is it the use of particular motifs? Is it the purpose for which it was made, or the spirit in which it was created? Does Celtic art consist of images from the past, or is Celtic art a recognizable, evolving, contemporary art form? Is Celtic art about copying or creativity, representation or appropriation, imagination or identity?

Can something consistently, recognizably 'Celtic' be found in images and artefacts produced in different places, in varied cultural and religious contexts, over a period of c. 2,500 years? The following illustrations have been chosen to demonstrate a broad range of art and artefacts that might be considered Celtic. The illustrations are, for the most part, arranged chronologically. We start with archaeological finds conventionally classified as Celtic, including a buckle, the Battersea Shield, a mirror, and the Gundestrup Cauldron, an intriguingly decorated metal vessel found in a Danish peat bog. You might like to think how or whether these artefacts relate to classical accounts of Celts. After these, you see examples of Irish Christian art from The Book of Kells, an intricately ornamented gospel book dated to c. 800 CE and two highly ornate specimens of metalwork with Christian connections, the Ardagh Chalice and the Shrine of St Patrick's Bell.

There then follows a set of illustrations relating to the Tara Brooch, which was found in the nineteenth century at Bettystown, County Meath, Ireland, but on account of its fine craftsmanship, associated with Tara, the official residence of the ancient High Kings of Ireland. In addition to the original Tara brooch, you will see a nineteenth century copy (of the type worn by those recreating noble Irish dress at the Pan-Celtic Congress) and twentieth- and twenty-first-century artefacts inspired by it.

'St Bride' is by the late nineteenth/early twentieth-century Celtic revivalist artist, John Duncan, who was inspired by a number of characters and scenes from Celtic myth. In 'St Bride', Duncan is depicting the legend that Bride, daughter of a Druid, was miraculously conveyed by angels to Bethlehem to become an assistant to Mary and foster-mother of Christ.

'Hiraeth' is a modern picture inspired by the image of Celts leaving their homelands; it is by American artist and musician Cindy Matyi, who finds Celtic art 'a wonderful instrument for depicting contemporary messages of peace, environmental concern and personal growth' (http://home.fuse.net/smatyi).

The next section consists of four pictures by Steve O'Loughlin, an American artist of Irish descent and 'self-confessed Celtophile' (O'Loughlin, 1999, p. 83). O'Loughlin's fascination with Celtic art started with The Book of Kells, and he considers one of the great attractions of Celtic art is its 'spiritual quality'.

The final picture deals with inward migration to a 'Celtic' country and what might be termed 'multi-cultural Celticity'. 'Mr Singh's India' was commissioned by Iqbal Singh, a self-made millionaire originally from the Punjab, now resident in Scotland and originator of the Singh tartan.

He wanted a painting that linked his Sikh heritage to his adopted Scottish culture, and for that chose British artists of Indian descent, Amrit and Rabindra Kaur Singh, twin sisters whose work is inspired by the Indian miniature art tradition. The picture includes a wealth of detail reflecting both historical and contemporary events and characters, and stereotypes of Scottish/Celtic culture.

How do these illustrations relate to what you learned in Chapter 3? What do you consider distinctly 'Celtic' about all – or any –of them? Spend some time looking at each image, deciding what it is that you see, and considering whether, had you seen it outside the context of this visual essay, you would have thought of it as 'Celtic'. Do you see any continuity between all of these images?

Look at the details of each image (date, provenance, artist's comments, etc.) and work out how, or indeed if, it fits into *your* understanding of Celtic art and by extension, *your* image of Celticity. What can these pictures tell us about the construction and location of Celticity in the twenty-first century?

1 Bronze buckle, La Tène, found Holzelsau, Germany, 5–4th century BCE. Photo: Archologische Staatssammlung, Museum für Vör-und Frühgeschichte

3 Decorated bronze mirror, Iron Age, found Desborough, Northamptonshire, England, 50 BCE–50 CE. Photo: British Museum P&EE 1924-1-9-1

2 Battersea Shield, Iron Age, found in River Thames near Battersea Bridge, London, England, 350–50 BCE. Photo: British Museum P&EE 1857.7-15.1

Think how these three examples of decorated metalwork relate to early accounts of the Celts. To what extent can you discern distinctly 'Celtic' decoration upon them? What Celtic character traits might be deduced from these artefacts?

4 and 5 Gundestrup Cauldron, metal vessel, silver, gilt, La Tène, found Gundestrup, Denmark, first century BCE. Photo: The National Museum of Denmark

The Gundestrup Cauldron is a large metal vessel, thought to date from the first century BCE. As the Cauldron did not come handily labelled with an explanation of either its purpose or the images upon it, it has been much speculated upon. What do you see on the panels?

4 Some contemporary pagans suggest that this panel depicts a shaman communicating with animal spirits while in a trance state, while more often in the past this image has been captioned as a representation of Cernunnos, a Celtic horned god.

5

6 Portrait of Christ in the Gospel of Matthew, The Book of Kells, f32 V, ninth century CE. Photo: Trinity College, Ireland

The Book of Kells is a highly ornamented gospel book, with minutely detailed illustrations and highly abstract designs. Many claim such Celtic Christian manuscripts show a perfect blending of pre-Christian and Christian motifs.

The Book's provenance is contested, but as the monks of Iona (a small island off the west of Scotland) sought refuge in Kells (north west of Dublin, Ireland) after a Viking attack in 806 CE, some believe it was created on Iona.

Since 1661 the Book of Kells has been in the possession of Trinity College Dublin Library, where it is now an important tourist attraction.

7 Detail of Canon Table, The Book of Kells, ninth century CE. Photo: Trinity College, Ireland

Ireland boasts numerous examples of beautifully crafted and decorated metalwork from the early medieval period, characterized by abstract knot work and interlacing figures which are not obviously Christian in symbolism and appearance.

Found in 1847 by a boy digging for potatoes, the Ardagh Chalice is a highly decorated example of a metal vessel. As its name implies, it has been assumed that it was crafted for liturgical use in the Christian ritual of eucharist.

8 Ardagh Chalice, c. 800–899 CE, silver, silver gilt and enamel. Photo: © National Museum of Ireland

9 Shrine of St Patrick's Bell, bronze with silver plating and filigree, c.1100 CE. Photo: © National Museum of Ireland

Numerous Celtic saints seem to have carried a bell, which after the saint's death became an important relic. The Shrine of St Patrick's Bell, with its exquisite interlaced decoration, is an outstanding example of the elaborate covers made for such relics. As St Patrick is traditionally credited with Christianizing Ireland, his bell would have been an especially valued relic.

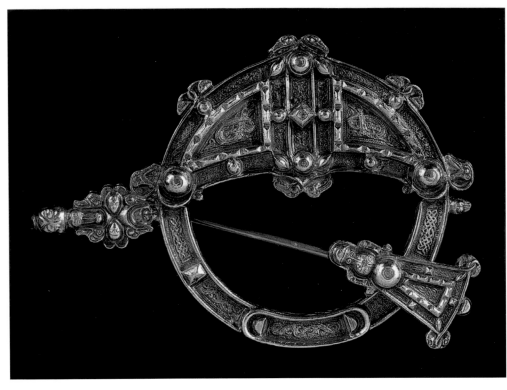

11 Copy of Tara Brooch, parcel gilt, 1850s, Waterhouse and Co., Dublin. Photo: © Ulster Museum, Belfast; photograph reproduced with the kind permission of the Trustees of the National Museums and Galleries of Northern Ireland

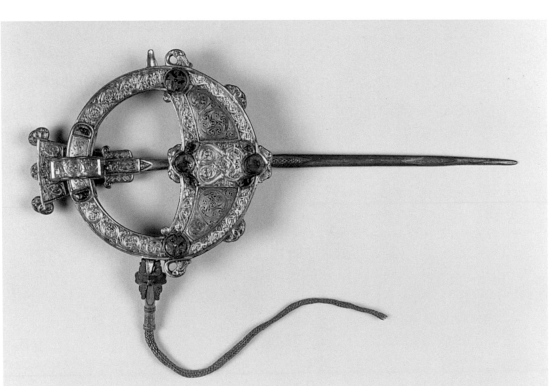

10 The Tara Brooch, silver gilt with added amber, gold, glass and copper; eighth century CE. Photo: © National Museum of Ireland

An internet search on Tara Brooch brought up these modern artefacts. What do these reveal about levels of interest in and understanding of Celtic art, and how it is marketed?

13 Tara Brooch by Tara Jewellery, Ireland. Photo: Anthony Nichols Group

'Tara Brooch ... the design of this piece of jewellery was inspired by the world famous Book of Kells ... The unique designs contained in the Book have inspired Irish artists for centuries. These designs are brought to life by the ancient art of enamelling. Tara Jewellery carries on this traditional art with skilled and dedicated crafts people to bring you a unique, original piece of Irish made jewellery. A true heirloom to be treasured now and handed down for future generations'
(http://shop.store.yahoo.com/irishop/tarabrooch.html)

12 Tara Brooch by Kilteel Copper Crafts, Co. Longford, Ireland. Photo: John Cassin/Copper Crafts

'The Tara Brooch is a classic example of Bronze Age craftsmanship and is probably the most celebrated of all Celtic jewellery ... This handcrafted Tara Brooch will enhance the surroundings in any home. It has a hook for secure hanging and is 20 inches long and 15 inches wide'
(http://www.celtlinks.com)

14 John Duncan, *St Bride*, 1913, tempera, 47 × 56 inches. Photo: © National Gallery, Scotland

Inspired by the Celtic revival and Celtic myth, Duncan depicts the miraculous journey of St Bride to Bethlehem. Note the detail on the angels' robes, the left dealing with the Nativity and the right with the Crucifixion. In what ways are Celtic motifs and images used in this picture?

15 Cindy Matyi, *Hiraeth*, 1997. Photo: © Cynthia Matyi

Artist Cindy Matyi writes of 'Hiraeth', 'This ancient Welsh word meaning "love of ... or longing for ... homeland" is used here to describe the scattering of Celtic peoples from Ireland, Scotland and Wales, often due to unwanted exile ... In the left border and across the bottom are seen the faces of many who were forced to start their lives over in a new land and some who died at sea. The strongest made the choice of carrying their culture abroad, dispersing like the wild geese in the right side border of the painting. The Celtic Tree of Life is symbolic of this continuum, the interconnectedness of humanity with nature, and the legacy of hope which our ancestors left to their children' (http://home.fuse.net/smatyi)

What influences and images of the Celts do you think this artist draws on?

16 Steve O'Loughlin, *Remote Control*, oil on canvas, 5' × 4'. Photo: Steve O'Loughlin

O'Loughlin describes 'Remote Control' as 'my tribute to the excesses of television. This is especially true here in Los Angeles. The Celtic deity Cernunnos, the horned god, is emerging from the television set with his antlers full of cables, televisions and speakers' (O'Loughlin, 1999, p. 85).

'Believing an artist should reflect the world around him, I try to incorporate the things I see around me. By juxtaposing contemporary scenes next to archetypal images I hope to show how close we are to the spiritual world even if it is cloaked in modern trappings', Steve O'Loughlin (http:// www. stevenoloughlin.com)

17 Steve O'Loughlin, *Freewayman*. Photo: Steve O'Loughlin

In 'Freewayman', O'Loughlin is using motifs from Celtic art to comment on American car culture. 'The running figure in Freewayman is entangled in an endless ribbon of traffic. I wanted to express the caught-in-traffic anxiety we live in' (O'Loughlin, 1999, p. 85).

18 Steve O'Loughlin, *Peace Mandala*. Photo: Steve O'Loughlin

Found in Buddhist and Hindu art, the mandala is usually a circular design, symbolizing the universe, frequently used for meditative purposes. O'Loughlin created 'Peace Mandala' after the 1992 Los Angeles riots as 'a healing gesture'; 'African, Asian, Hispanic and Western cultures are all represented separately, then blended together'(O'Loughlin, 1999, p. 85).

'It is the intention of my work to show the universal patterns symbolized in these ancient art forms at work in our modern world … The use of knotwork on the limbs of the figures comes directly from Celtic art. This knotwork for me symbolizes the bond and commonality between people' (http:// www. stevenoloughlin.com).

19 Steve O'Loughlin, *Four Celts*. Photo: Steve O'Loughlin

'Celtic art has been around for thousands of years and continues to evolve in our fast-paced world. I see my own work as a continuation of Celtic art, not just a glimpse into the past, but a vehicle for the future. I hope my insights will inspire other artists to push the boundaries of Celtic art' (O'Loughlin, 1999, p. 85).

O'Loughlin's image of Four Celts both confirms and challenges some of the stereotypes of Celts and Celtic art. Do you find the merging of old and new convincing or contrived, derivative or innovative? Do you regard this art as a successor to, or on a continuum from, the Gundestrup Cauldron, the Tara Brooch or the Book of Kells? Whatever your response, think about how you arrived at it.

20 Amrit and Rabindra Kaur Singh, *Mr Singh's India*, 1999/2000, 23.5" × 30". Photo: Copyright The Singh Twins – Collection of Glasgow Gallery of Modern Art

Inspired by the film *Braveheart*, the artists decided to highlight parallels between William Wallace and the heroic Punjabi historical figure Maharajah Ranjit Singh. The two heroes are pictured dining together, alongside the artists who are wearing traditional Punjabi dress in Singh tartan. Other connections between Scottish and Sikh / Punjabi culture include the heraldic lion rampant of Scotland and the Lion symbol of Sikhism (the name Singh means Lion).

Reference

O'Loughlin, Steve (1999) 'Steve O'Loughlin' in D. James and S. Booth (eds) *New Visions in Celtic Art: The Modern Tradition*, London, Blandford.

> They fight 'in rage and spirit like wild beasts without reason' at the battle of Themopylae, while at Telemon it is their 'vanity and bravado in fighting naked, their head-hunting, their use of trumpets, their reckless courage and self-sacrifice in battle and their mass suicide on defeat' that are described (Tierney 1960, 196, 197) ...
>
> In the commentaries of Athenaeus, Diodorus Siculus, Strabo, and Julius Caesar, the texts most often used to create a picture of those peoples now fixed as Celts, Gauls are described as 'exceedingly fond of wine ... sat[ing] themselves with the unmixed wine imported by merchants.' Diodorus Siculus (5.26.3) goes on to say that 'their desire makes them drink it greedily and when they become drunk they fall into a stupor or into a maniacal disposition' ...
>
> They are described as 'madly fond of war, high-spirited and quick to battle, but otherwise straightforward and not of evil character' (Strabo 4.4.2) ... [T]hese Gauls possess 'frankness and high-spiritedness,' 'childish boastfulness and love of decoration,' and a vanity which makes them 'unbearable in victory and so completely downcast in defeat' (Strabo 4.4.5).
>
> (Piccini, 1996, p. 88)

It is important to remember that we hear about a *variety* of peoples from classical sources. There are thus plenty of references to Keltoi, Celtae, Galatai and Galli, but these occur over a long a period of time, in different places, by a variety of authors writing with varying degrees of closeness to their subjects (see Tierney, 1976). It also needs to be remembered that 'The Celts were only one of many groups described as being quick to anger, illogical and intemperate – the direct opposite of how the Greek and Roman societies liked to view themselves' (Piccini, 1999, p. 19). Anthropologist Malcolm Chapman has likewise suggested that when the term 'Keltoi' was used, this often denoted not a careful ethnography of a particular people, but a conflation of 'foreigners' (Chapman, 1992, p. 33). It has therefore been argued that ancient Greek and Roman authors writing about the 'strange' people with whom they came in contact frequently tell us as much about themselves and their attitudes to 'others' as they do about those being described. (In *Inventing Ireland*, the Irish academic Declan Kiberd makes the similar point that 'Through many centuries, Ireland was pressed into service as a foil to set off English virtues' (Kiberd, 1995, p. 1).) Thus Piccini concludes, 'I cannot distil a Celtic essence from these writings, nor should that be my aim' (Piccini, 1996, p. 88). That, however, is what has traditionally been done – and I wonder how many of you were making comparisons between the classical comments quoted by Piccini and contemporary Celts!

Archaeological Celts

The James extract outlined how the physical remains of the material cultures of the many Iron Age peoples of Europe have conventionally been used to give a picture of Celtic life and culture, and there is a huge literature on such material. Indeed Celtic remains, artefacts and artwork are possibly among the best known and most attractive aspects of Celtic culture. (This is explored in more depth in the visual essay in this volume, 'Celtic art: images, imagination and identity'.)

However, the archaeologist Timothy Champion makes the point that 'Archaeological remains do not speak for themselves, they have to be interpreted' (Champion, 1996, p. 62). In Britain in the eighteenth century, for example, at the time of Romantic speculation about the ancient inhabitants of the British Isles, there was a tendency among antiquarians such as William Stukeley to declare *all* prehistoric structures 'Celtic' or 'Druidic'. In an article entitled 'The Celt in archaeology', Champion shows how European archaeologists of different nationalities at various times have focused on specific aspects of Celtic material culture in order to emphasize what best suited their purposes – Celts as warriors, Celts as artists, Celts as king-makers, Celts as resistance fighters. Thus archaeology

> served to provide Celts suitable to the needs of nineteenth-century Europe, whether that was for an artistic society in need of control, or for heroes and heroines to authenticate the aspirations of European nation states ... The society of the Iron Age Celts was reconstructed as the wished-for prototype of nineteenth-century patriarchy and militarism.
>
> (Champion, 1996, p. 75)

Furthermore, the contested nature of archaeological interpretation is such that Simon James has gone so far as to suggest that developments in archaeological technology, the discrediting of earlier theories of mass migration and waves of invasions, and a fresh appraisal of the diversity of archaeological evidence from Iron Age communities in the British Isles lead to the conclusion that 'our established belief that these islands, like much of continental Europe, were occupied by Celts in later prehistory, is simply wrong: the insular Ancient Celts never existed' (James, 1999, p. 16). Some have accused James of 'genocide', while others (such as archaeologists John Collis (1996) and Angela Piccini (1996) and anthropologist Malcolm Chapman (1992)) join him in questioning conventional wisdom on the origins, spread and existence of a Celtic culture.

Thus, at a time when in popular culture we are surrounded by 'proofs' of the Celts' ancient and continued existence – Celtic languages, Celtic music, Celtic artefacts, Celtic exhibitions, Celtic art, Celtic writings, Celtic ceremonies, a huge Celtic industry and myriad forms of Celtic spirituality – some scholars are actually questioning the whole concept of an ancient, identifiable Celtic culture. (It should be stressed that what is being contested here are the *conclusions* drawn from the archaeological remains, not the existence of the material itself.)

Champion notes that the Celts are again being 'rewritten' in the current context of political moves towards a unified Europe. This was evident in both an exhibition of the early Iron Age **Hallstatt** culture held in Austria in 1980, with the subtitle 'An early form of European unity', and the spectacular 1991 Venice exhibition entitled 'The Celts: the origins of Europe'. For the latter,

The earliest phase of the pre-Roman Iron Age in Central Europe is named the Hallstatt period after the finds discovered at a prehistoric site near Hallstatt, Austria, in 1846 (see Maier, 1998, pp. 142–3).

> Circumstances demanded that the artistic rather than the military side of the Celts was stressed, and it was without doubt the biggest and most stunning exhibition of Iron Age artistic and technical achievement ever gathered together ...
>
> Nevertheless, it required considerable distortion of the archaeological evidence to accommodate the vision of a pan-European Celtic culture zone as a precursor of the longed-for federal Europe, but this was simply the most recent example of the dynamic interaction between the interpretation of the archaeological evidence and the wider intellectual and political context of archaeological practice that has shaped our vision of the Celts for the last three hundred years.

(Champion, 1996, p. 76)

So, from classical sources and archaeological remains we have information and material, but much of it is open to a variety of interpretations and inferences. When thinking or reading about, or, as some are trying to do, capturing the spirit of the Celtic past, we need to be aware of the contested and contingent nature of history.

As James contends, we do not discover history as 'unambiguous truth', we *create* history.

> In the broadest sense – covering both document-based historical studies and material-based archaeology – history is the construction by modern minds of imagined (although not wholly imaginary!) pasts, from the fragmentary surviving debris of past societies. History is what *we* think, say and write about the evidence of the past.

(James, 1999, p. 33)

121

Linguistic Celts

One of the most tangible sources of information about the Celts is that of Celtic language and literature. The continental Celtic group of languages includes Gaulish, Celtiberian, Lepontic and Galatian, all of which had died out by the early Middle Ages, while the insular Celtic group comprises Breton, Cornish, Cumbrian, Irish, Manx, Scottish Gaelic and Welsh (Maier, 1998, p. 165). The academic discipline of Celtic Studies has thus come to be based on the study of 'all linguistic utterances of the Celtic peoples from ancient times to the present day' (Maier, 1998, p. 66).

The presence of language can be used in both the measurement and construction of Celticity. It is important to realize that the very term 'Celtic languages' had political overtones in the British context. It was the Welsh scholar and patriot Edward Lhuyd, Keeper of the Ashmolean Museum in Oxford, who in 1707 published *Archaeologia Brittanica*, 'a significant landmark in the history of the study of language' (James, 1999, p. 45). After years of research into the ancient and modern languages of Ireland, Scotland, Wales, Cornwall and Brittany, Lhuyd identified a family of languages related to the extinct language of the ancient Gauls of France, which he called 'Celtic'. We should bear in mind the political climate of the time, for 1707 was also the year that the Treaty of Union between England and Scotland officially created 'a new *political* identity called "British"' (James, 1999, p. 47). Thus

> the name of Briton – the best, and time-honoured, potential collective label for those peoples of the island who saw themselves as other than English – was appropriated for all subjects of the new, inevitably English-dominated superstate.
>
> (James, 1999, p. 48)

Edward Said describes orientalism as 'the corporate institution for dealing with the Orient – dealing with it by making statements about it, authorizing views of it, describing it, by teaching it, settling it, ruling over it: in short, Orientalism as a Western style for dominating, restructuring, and having authority over the Orient' (Said, 1995, p. 3).

Lhuyd's work was not only of scholarly interest, then, but it provided 'the basis for a wholly new conception of the identities and histories of the non-English peoples of the isles, which at that moment were under strong political and cultural threat' (James, 1999, p. 47). Just as philology, the study of languages, was extremely influential in the early academic study of religion and the creation of '**orientalism**', philology in the eighteenth and nineteenth centuries played a considerable part in the creation of Celticism.

In order to understand the role of language not only in defining both the Celts and Celticity, but also in relation to broader European ideas of language, race and culture, it will be helpful at this point to turn to the second reading, an extract from Malcolm Chapman's book *The Celts: the Construction of a Myth*.

'A Branch of Indo-European'

The adjective 'Celtic' has its most respectable and formal use within linguistics. The idea of the Indo-European languages is a result of the increasingly scholarly and scientific study of language in the eighteenth and nineteenth centuries. Similarities between otherwise very different languages in Europe had long been noticed, with erudite Romans speculating on the relationship of their own language to Greek. Gerald of Wales made some thoughtful suggestions about the relationships between disparate languages in the late twelfth century, which have been seen as an early attempt at comparative Indo-European linguistics. Only in the late eighteenth century, however, did thoughts on this subject begin to assume their modern form. Before then, attempts to understand the relationships between different languages had usually aimed at derivation from Greek or Latin (as privileged languages of ancient scholarship), or from Old Testament Hebrew. In 1786, however, William Jones, in a now famous address to the Royal Asiatic Society of Bengal, noted that Sanskrit, the language of Indian religious learning, had remarkable affinities with Latin and Greek. He further suggested that these three languages, and indeed other European languages, and Persian, had a common origin. As Lockwood says, 'the modern science of comparative philology had begun' (Lockwood, 1969:22).

The progressive scholarly elaboration of these ideas represents, perhaps, the greatest modern intellectual achievement in the humanities. The group of related languages to which Jones had drawn attention came to be called 'Indo-European' (although, in studies written in German, as many were, 'Indo-Germanic' was also commonly used). The theory of the Indo-European languages supposed that there was, behind all the modern Indo-European languages, a single common ancestor language (a 'Common Indo-European'), from which all the different modern languages had, over the years, diverged. This 'Common Indo-European' was not attested, in that no record of it survived, but increasingly sophisticated study of the earliest recorded forms, and of the laws of sound change, enabled the construction of hypothetical common forms. From this reconstructed 'Common Indo-European', the rest of the languages of the group were then derived, according to systematic developments of various kinds. So, from the 'Common Indo-European' of very early date developed the ancestor languages of the major different modern groups of languages – 'Common Germanic', 'Common Slavonic', 'Common Celtic', 'Common Italic', 'Common Hellenic', 'Common Indo-Iranian', and so on (as well as the ancestor languages of historically attested languages or language groups which have now disappeared – Tocharian, Anatolian, and others). These then gave rise, over time, to the languages we know today: for example, 'Common Germanic' produced German, Dutch, Danish, Norwegian and English; 'Common Italic' Latin, and thence French, Spanish, Italian, Portuguese, Catalan and Provencal; 'Common Slavonic' Russian, Polish, Czech, Serbo-Croat and Bulgarian; 'Common Celtic' Welsh, Breton, Irish and Scottish Gaelic; and so on.

This is to put the matter crudely, but a crude understanding is also a common one, and as such is useful in dealing with popular handling of these ideas. The development over time of the Indo-European languages is often expressed figuratively in a dendritic model (Figure [1]). This figure represents only a selection of western Indo-European languages, and the full picture is very much more complicated. A more detailed picture, for the Celtic languages, might look like Figure [2].

The model of the development of the Indo-European languages was elaborated in Europe during a period of strenuous and strident nationalism and nation-building. The nineteenth century in Europe is justly called an 'age of nationalism', and efforts in linguistic scholarship were closely tied to the political and ideological sphere. Before this period, the relationship of language and political institutions was far from close. The phenomenon of the 'nation', so normal now as to seem virtually part of the natural order, is of relatively recent date, deriving from the gradual transformation and decline of the power of the Catholic Church in Europe, much accelerated after the Reformation. The nations (if we may call them such) of pre-nationalist Europe were united as much by the common interests of an aristocratic or mercantile class, as they were by the common language and culture of all the inhabitants. The language spoken by the lower orders was often a matter of indifference to the upper orders, and some of the major political entities of Europe were linguistically exceedingly diverse (the Hapsburg Empire, for example).

Gradually, however, the idea developed that a nation should be characterised by a common language, spoken by all that belonged to it; and the same idea developed its reciprocal form – that every language *was*, or ought to be, a nation. Much has been written about these developments in recent years, in the general reappraisal of nationality that has followed the two devastating European wars of the twentieth century, wars for which nationalism might be blamed.

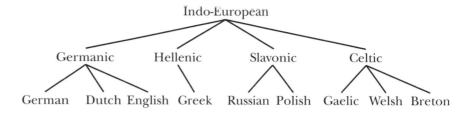

Figure [1]

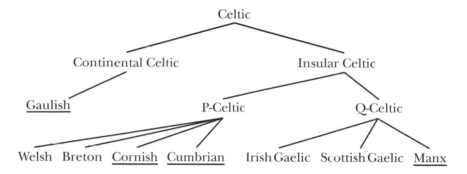

Figure [2] (extinct languages underlined)

Within the notion that a language was a nation, the dendritic model of language development provided by the Indo-European theory was not only a genealogy of languages – it was also a genealogy of peoples, races, nations and cultures. A near-mystical theory of the identification of race, nation and language was developed. The origins of this theory were rather diverse, but it is often credited to [Johann Gottfried] Herder, writing in German in the late eighteenth century.

The model of the development of the Indo-European languages was, within this framework, a kinship genealogy of the grandest kind. The figurative branching model was taken, quite literally, to represent demographic and geographical expansion. The political consolidation of nations which had names from within the model, seemed only like a realisation of the natural order. Language, culture, people, race and nation were, in important senses, the *same thing*. So, the fortunes of a language, of an ethnic or national label, or of an archaeologically definable culture-type, were all taken as evidence of one another, or rather of the same thing – the fortunes, so to speak, of the race. If a culture or a language seemed to expand, then this was taken to be evidence of the growth and vigour of a biologically definable human population; if an ethnic label moved across the map, this was taken to be a movement of flesh-and-blood people, carrying their language and culture with them.

Closely tied to the linguistic and nationalistic models of development were theories of human development of the most general kind. The notion that man had developed from more or less animal origins, through barbarism, and thence to civilisation, was an old one. In eighteenth-century Europe speculation upon this subject became particularly fashionable, and much was written about the relationship between modern European society, as it then was, and both the 'savage' societies discovered overseas, and the ancient barbarian societies attested by classical and mediaeval Latin and Greek sources. The idea that modern society was a refinement and a sophistication of an earlier and natural crudity came very readily to mind, and received various and diverse expressions. 'Civilisation' was generally regarded as a desirable development away from 'barbarity'; a development, however, that was neither inevitable nor irreversible (with the image of the decline and fall of Rome always in the imagination). There was also, however, a recognition, which Tacitus had developed in detail, and which was frequently echoed subsequently, that civilisation was not all gain: that while earlier society might have been less refined, it was also the better for it – more honest, natural, straightforward, and so on. Material concerning the Celts, increasingly available as it was both from modern and ancient sources, figured prominently in these discussions.

After 1859, such discussion was further fuelled, and given an apparently new and scientific legitimacy, by the publication of Darwin's *On the Origin of Species* (1859), which provoked a furious debate about the evolution of man and society, and the relationship of man to the natural world. This drew speculation about the history of society into the framework of biological evolutionary theory, with societies viewed as increasingly sophisticated adaptive mechanisms, which progressed from 'early primitive' forms to 'modern developed' forms. 'Modern' and 'developed' were usually taken to mean, unarguably, 'better' (although moral judgement is irrelevant to evolutionary theory as properly understood). Observers and theorists from modern Europe were strongly inclined to regard their own society and social practices as the most modern and developed, the 'best', and so set themselves to cultivating evolutionary trees which put themselves at the tops of the branches, and all other societies somewhere lower down. The best-known writer of this tendency was Herbert Spencer, a formidable Victorian polymath.

Congruent with this discussion of social evolution, was a discussion of the development of the 'races' of man. Mankind, it was argued, was divided into biologically different races. It had already been established, not without controversy, that all mankind was of one stock, of one biological origin. Nevertheless, the different races within this one species were involved in a 'struggle for survival', with the best and brightest coming to the top and forming great civilisations, and the dunces lagging behind in the backwater of Stone-Age savagery. It is easy, from our own vantage point, to see that these theories were by and for Europeans, and their self-congratulation and complacency has subsequently attracted a good deal of ridicule. It is worth remembering, however, that the industrialised European world in the late nineteenth century had undergone a period of remarkable change; evenness of judgement about such things could not have been easy. The stark clarity of the difference between 'savagery' and 'civilisation' required explanation, and gave an excitement and interest to all speculations on the subject. The place of the Celts in nineteenth-century European thought must be understood in the light of this.

Cultures and races were fitted, then, into an evolutionary scheme. The Indo-European language model, with its forward dendritic growth, seemed entirely congruent with models of the evolution of society and race. The units of these disparate models were, indeed, commonly understood to be essentially the same thing – races, that is, with societies and languages proper to them. So the adjective 'Celtic' denoted a language, a society and a race, forging its unique path through time ...

The Celts, therefore, have a long history of being tied up in a discourse of race, language and culture – a discourse which has indeed, in important senses, created them. Since the end of the Second World War, the more unattractive aspects of racial discourse are less conspicuous than once they were. The rethinking has, however, to date been very local in its effects. The revision or denial of the concept of 'race', for instance, is one which has so far an interestingly limited social distribution, and in world terms those who are prepared to dissociate biological and cultural inheritance completely are probably only a small minority. In the European intellectual context, the rethinking of the concept of 'race' is typically carried out against an intellectual obbligato of discussions of Nazi Germany and apartheid South Africa. On the political margins of Europe, however, in nations and areas that can feel that their role in the last war was one of virtuous innocence, and that they had no part (or no recent part) in colonialism and its works, a surprisingly innocent invocation of the desirability of purity of race can sometimes be found, along with an assertion of the necessary link between race, character, culture and language ... The discourse is not, in such cases, supremacist in the old ugly way, but it is happy to invoke what one might call 'desirable difference'. I make this point, because it might be felt that the discourse of 'race', in its old style, was completely discredited. This is true, but only in limited ways, and only in limited areas of thought.

Scholars today, however, often make at least some attempt to distinguish between different aspects of the once apparently unitary concept of race – language, culture, nation and people – and indeed to disavow the concept of 'race' altogether. Nevertheless, after all the disavowals have been made, the equation of language, culture and people is still regularly made, explicitly or otherwise. How else, after all, are we to take assertions of the kind ...

> It is a historical fact that the Celts in their heyday did traverse and occupy huge tracts of Europe in the second half of the first millennium BC, ranging from Galatia in the east (beyond Europe) in Asia Minor to Ireland in the west, from the Balkans and southern Italy and the Hispanic peninsula to lands bordering the North Sea and Scotland.
>
> (Evans 1980–2:234)

If there is no transfer from a linguistic definition of Celtic to a demographic definition, then how could a 'Celt' exist at all?

References

Evans, D. Ellis (1980–2) 'Celts and Germans', *Bulletin of the Board of Celtic Studies*, no. 29, pp. 230–55.

Lockwood, W. (1969) *Indo–European Philology*, London, Hutchinson.

(Chapman, 1992, pp. 14–18; 20–2)

EXERCISE

Having read the Chapman passage, think carefully about your own attitudes to and assumptions about language in relation to culture and identity.

To what extent do you think there is still a tendency to equate language and culture, language and nationality and, more controversially, language and race?

DISCUSSION

This exercise is about your attitudes and assumptions; there are no right or wrong answers. However, consider the prevalence of national stereotypes in Europe, and the extent to which they are related to different language groups ('Latin' passion and excitability, 'Germanic' efficiency and so on).

Undoubtedly, the conclusion that the Celtic languages formed an independent branch of the Indo-European linguistic family (which also includes Sanskrit), and the idea that there was one language group (albeit, as James (1999, p. 138) points out, 'a group of *mutually unintelligible* languages'), gave the popular impression of a common language, which was interpreted by some as evidence of a common culture, cultural identity and 'character'. In this perception of commonality lay the roots of pan-Celticism, which assumes that all Celtic cultures/peoples were/are the same, thought/think the same, and had/have similar tastes in cultural artefacts such as art and music. It also paved the way for the idea of a 'Celtic spirit'. However, reacting to assumptions that conflate Celtic language and a Celtic race, the spread of language and the movement of people, Chapman cautions,

> It takes only a moment ... to remember that adults can change their language during their lifetime, and that children very readily learn as their first language a language that is not mother tongue to their parents. People can change their 'ethnic' allegiance during their lifetimes; can change the label by which they are known and know themselves, according to biographical convenience. It is, therefore, simply unwarranted to continue treating the spread and survival of languages as being entirely congruent with the spread and survival of named biological populations.
>
> (Chapman, 1992, p. 22)

As you read through the rest of this chapter, look out for some of the eighteenth- and nineteenth-century assumptions about language and culture outlined by Chapman in relation to historical and contemporary attitudes to and images of Celts.

Mapping the Celts

We have already seen in the first reading, the extract from Simon James, the map of Europe produced by the 'Authorized Version' of the origins and spread of Celtic culture (Figure 1, p. 111). Now consider the importance and implications of a new mapping project.

As you read about it, bear in mind Chapman's comments on language, and also whether you think people find such data either significant or convincing in terms of Celtic/European identity.

In October 2000 the University of Aberystwyth announced its involvement in the *Atlas of European Celtic Languages*.

By studying the Geography of Ptolemy who recorded over 8,000 names throughout the known world around the middle of the second century AD, the travel records of Roman soldiers, and various local documents across Europe, Professor Patrick Sims-Williams and a small team of researchers from the University of Wales, Aberystwyth will draw a series of linguistic maps which will reveal the extent to which the Celtic languages were used in the British Isles and across the continent of Europe and Asia Minor.

According to Professor Sims-Williams, the earliest examples of Celtic inscriptions originate in the Mediterranean region, the home of literacy, and date from the sixth and fifth centuries BC, whilst the Celtic languages of the Middle Ages and the modern period are restricted to Britain, Ireland and Brittany.

'The evidence which we have at present suggests that Celtic languages were spoken over an extensive part of Europe, a region which extends from Scotland in the north to Tuscany in the south, from Portugal in the west to Galatia (Turkey) in the east, and not only in those countries which are today known as the Celtic countries.

'By comparing the number of Celtic names with the number which are not of Celtic origin in a specific area we will be able to measure the strength of the Celtic tradition there. Initial analysis on Ptolemy's work suggests that some areas in Spain were more Celtic than areas in Ireland during that period.

'As well as place-names we will also be concentrating on names of rivers and mountains. Frequently armies would rename towns and cities when they possessed new territories, but would adopt the native names of rivers and mountains. The fact that the names of many of the main rivers in England today have a Welsh origin is an example of this,' he added.

There is already evidence that three Celtic languages were in use during this period: Lepontic in northern Italy and southern Switzerland (approx. 600 BC), Celtiberian in Spain, and Gaulish in France (approx. 200 BC), and there are recent archaeological findings which confirm the connection between the Celts and Spain.

> Professor Sims-Williams hopes that this five-year project will lead to the earliest possible linguistic map of Europe, and thus provide a linguistic dimension to the work of archaeologists which has so far concentrated on physical evidence.
>
> (University of Aberystwyth website, 10 October 2000)

EXERCISE

It could be argued that this project appears to serve the agenda of Celts as first Europeans very well. However, how significant or convincing do you find such data in terms of Celtic or European identity? For example, would the knowledge that their river is called Avon because the Welsh word for river is *afon* make the residents of Stratford feel more Celtic and/or European?

To what extent do you think Celtic (or European) identity nowadays is based on, or influenced by, linguistic, archaeological or classical evidence? Which is more important – evidence, image, or personal perceptions?

Celtic revivals

From this very brief account of the sources traditionally drawn on for information on and conventional images of Celts, I have started to demonstrate the potentially problematic or contested nature of these. What we have by the beginning of the twenty first century are various images of the Celt and a variety of agendas utilizing Celticity. In order to understand contemporary commercial, political and spiritual agendas, we must look briefly at developments from the eighteenth century to the present.

Although we tend to talk of Celtic revivals, it may be more accurate to think of continuous interest in/manipulation of matters Celtic from the eighteenth century onwards, marked simply by peaks and troughs. However we perceive it, we can see that at the *fins des siècles* of the eighteenth, nineteenth and twentieth centuries there were periods of special interest in the Celts, for a variety of reasons, each revival marked by particular features and influences. Cultural historian Stuart Piggott, in relation to the history of ideas, writes of

> a recurrent series of speculations which seem to arise in civilized communities as the result of a subconscious guilty recognition of the inadequacy of the contemporary social order, and involve the concept of simpler and more satisfactory systems, remote either in time (Golden Ages in

the past), or in place (Noble Savages at or beyond the edges of contemporary geographical knowledge).

(Piggott [1968] 1993, p. 20)

A recurring feature of the Celtic revivals has been the extent to which the Celts have come to represent that which is lost but longed for in contemporary society.

Eighteenth-century Celts

The eighteenth century was a particularly important period for the study of Celticism, which flourished alongside Romanticism. While the seeds of the eighteenth-century revival had been sown earlier, a number of different factors converged then to bring Celts into the limelight. We have already seen how language became a major measure and marker of Celticity at that time, and the extent to which the idea of a family of Celtic languages was deemed to support the notion of a Celtic race, with pronounced ethnic and cultural features, leading ultimately to pan-Celticism.

There was also a growing interest in ancient monuments, and in Britain this in turn was leading to increased speculation about the early inhabitants of these lands, a trend further fuelled by comparisons being made between ancient Britons and the so-called primitive peoples encountered in North America and elsewhere. By the sixteenth and seventeenth centuries, views of ancient Britons and Celts were being gained not so much from speakers of Celtic languages, but from accounts and illustrations of native Americans and other encounters with indigenous peoples, and pictures of newly encountered native peoples influenced artists' impressions of ancient Britons (see Piggott, 1989, pp. 13–33). John Aubrey, writing in the seventeenth century, described the ancient Britons of Wiltshire as 'two or three degrees I suppose less savage than the Americans' (quoted in Piggott, 1989, p. 130); by the late eighteenth century, however, the Celts had become in some eyes more noble than savage.

Literature was also to make an important contribution to the image of the Celt in the eighteenth century. In the 1760s the Scot James Macpherson (1736–96) published two highly controversial but influential 'translations' of epic poems (*Fingal*, 1761, and *Temera*, 1763) that he claimed to have discovered in the highlands, allegedly the work of a blind Gaelic bard called Ossian, son of the Scottish King Fingal, who had reputedly lived in the western highlands in the third century CE. There was controversy as to the authenticity of the material at the time, and Macpherson still has his supporters and detractors. (Celtic studies scholars tend to think that Macpherson did use some genuine Gaelic material as the basis of his translations, but that to a large extent he composed the works of Ossian himself; see

Porter, 2001.) However, what matters is that Ossian presented to a European audience noble and heroic highland warriors in a misty and mystical setting, and it became 'arguably the most influential piece of literature ever to have been concerned with the Highlands and Islands of Scotland' (Meek, 2000, p. 40). Composed after the defeat of the highlanders at the battle of Culloden, Ossian did much to transform their image from dangerous barbarians to romantic heroes:

> How people saw the Highland landscape, interpreted the mountains, the people, their actions, their literature – all of this was seen through the window of Macpherson's Ossian.
>
> (Meek, 2000, p. 40)

Napoleon is said to have carried the poems with him on campaign, and they influenced any number of paintings, including one by Girodet-Trioson commissioned by Napoleon which shows 'The ghosts of French warriors being brought before Ossian by Victory'. Ossian was also the inspiration for musical works such as Felix Mendelssohn's *Fingal's Cave* (Maier, 1997, p. 219). Folklorist James Porter has gone so far as to claim:

> [I]t is no exaggeration to say that the poems of Ossian are not just the key to European Romanticism – with its emphasis on individual sensibility and the sense of loss associated with a glorious past – but the key also to the beginnings of interest in a collective cultural history and tradition ... It is with Ossian, in fact, that we glimpse the stirrings of a fascination with orality, the evidence for oral composition and performance, along with the more controversial issue of authenticity, identity, and the creative uses of folklore.
>
> (Porter, 2001, p. 397)

We have seen elsewhere how important all this was for a variety of European identities.

The return of the Druids

Some contemporary Druids simply deny that there was ever any human sacrifice, claiming stories of it were 'smear tactics' employed by classical authors to discredit their enemies. Others claim that the sacrifices would have been of willing victims, for whom this was a great honour.

One striking feature of the eighteenth-century Celtic revival was the huge growth of interest in Druids. In classical sources Druids are described as the priestly caste of the Celts and associated with mistletoe, oak, golden sickles, sacred groves, esoteric learning and (rather more controversially, and variously interpreted) **human sacrifice**. Bards (concerned with poetry, genealogy and music) and ovates (concerned with healing) were also part of this hierarchy.

Though traditionally seen as the pagan enemies of Christianity, the image of Druids underwent considerable rehabilitation in the eighteenth century. In the 1780s and 1790s the Welsh patriot, freemason and Unitarian Edward Williams – better known as Iolo Morganwg – presented and promoted what he claimed was an authentic, ancient Druidic tradition of the British Isles which had survived in Wales through the bardic system, the distinctive Welsh-language poetic tradition. The first Welsh Gorsedd (assembly of bards or poets) was held in 1791 on Primrose Hill in London. In 1819 the Gorsedd became affiliated to the Welsh Eisteddfod (itself an eighteenth-century revival of a medieval literary and musical competition), which promotes Welsh language and culture and is still held annually in Wales. Morganwg claimed that ceremonies were to be held outside, 'in the eye of the sun', and were to start by honouring the four points of the compass; he also taught the Gorsedd prayer, which he attributed to the primeval bard Talhairn:

> Grant, O God! thy refuge,
> And in refuge, strength,
> And in strength, understanding,
> In understanding, knowledge,
> In knowledge, knowledge of right,
> In knowledge of right, to love it;
> In loving it, the love of all essences,
> In love of all essences, love of God,
> God and all Goodness.

(Quoted in Morgan, 1975, p. 51)

Morganwg's claims and writings were accepted as genuine at the time, and it was not until the late nineteenth century that they were revealed as forgeries. By that time, however, their influence had been established and it continues to this day – as we shall see.

Nineteenth-century Celts

In the course of the nineteenth century, as we have already seen, the Celts of archaeological, linguistic and to a lesser extent classical sources were being used for a variety of national agendas. Tartan, which had been banned after the 1745 Jacobite rebellion, was completely rehabilitated with the 1822 visit of George IV to Edinburgh (an event stage-managed by Sir Walter Scott) and was further popularized and made fashionable by Queen Victoria. Literature of various sorts continued to both reflect and mould ideas and images of the Celts. Heavily influenced by Macpherson's Ossian and Romanticism, for example, the Breton scholar Ernest Renan (1823–92) characterized the Celts as 'spiritual beings and visionary dreamers' (Meek, 2000, p. 46), with an enlightened approach to the integration of paganism and Christianity.

In fiction, the romantic novels of authors such as lowlander Sir Walter Scott continued the trend of Ossianism and further encouraged the romantic tourism to Scotland that had started in the previous century, now being made easier by improvements in transport. However, in terms of its influence on contemporary Celtic spirituality it was Alexander Carmichael's 'collection of a remarkable range of orally transmitted Gaelic lore' (Meek, 2000, p. 60), known as *Carmina Gadelica*, which was to become perhaps the most significant Celtic literary artefact of this period. Collected in Gaelic in the Hebrides in the late nineteenth century, the *Carmina Gadelica* includes a huge variety of prayers and invocations, blessings for everyday tasks (such as milking, weaving, grinding), addresses to saints, charms (for example, for toothache, the evil eye, indigestion), journey prayers and songs. *Carmina Gadelica* was first published in six volumes from 1900 onwards; Carmichael produced translations for the first two volumes, and over a period of years other English translations were completed.

Whereas earlier editions had Gaelic texts with English translations by Carmichael and others alongside, in the most recent edition (published by Floris in 1992 with subsequent reprintings) *Carmina Gadelica* appears only in English.

Carmichael was motivated by a number of factors in collecting the *Carmina*. It was a time when folklore collecting was being actively pursued for fear that such lore would be lost — and also when a certain amount of polishing, reworking or restoring of collected texts was common. There was a political aspect too, for Carmichael hoped

> that by making the book up in as good a form as I could in matter and material, it might perhaps be the means of conciliating some future politician in favour of our dear Highland people.
>
> (Quoted in Meek, 2000, p. 61)

Very much a product of his time and echoing some of Renan's claims, Carmichael believed in the special spirituality of the highland Celt and in the antiquity of the material he had collected. In his introduction to the first volume of *Carmina Gadelica* he stated:

> It is the product of faraway thinking, come down on the long stream of time ... Some of the hymns may have been composed within the cloistered cells of Derry and Iona, and some of the incantations among the cromlechs of Stonehenge and the standing-stones of Callarnis.
>
> (Quoted in Meek, 2000, pp. 63–4)

This nineteenth-century collection thus became and remains regarded by many as *early* Celtic material, with extravagant claims made for both its antiquity and its spiritual qualities. As Piccini (1999, p. 20) puts it, in the course of the eighteenth and nineteenth centuries, 'Past and present in the western and northern reaches of Britain eventually came to be transformed into a Celtic always.'

Following on from the eighteenth-century Druidic 'revival', a number of Druid orders flourished, particularly the Ancient Order of Druids which in the nineteenth century spread widely in America, Canada, Australia and Europe (see Raoult, 1996). There were, broadly speaking, three main strands of Druidry: cultural Druidry on the Welsh bardic model; 'mutualistic' Druidry, primarily concerned with its members' welfare; and esoteric or religious Druidry. Of these, the bards as preservers and promoters of Celtic culture were to be most influential in terms of Celtic identity.

All in all, the nineteenth-century fascination with classification, 'progress' and 'survivals', together with the literary, scholarly and national developments outlined above, seemed to confirm relationships between the Iron Age peoples of Britain and Europe and the rural communities of the 'Atlantic façade'. This resulted in a firm belief in a pan-European Celtic people with identifiable cultural artefacts and specific personal qualities. The stage was set for pan-Celticism.

Pan-Celticism

Information on the Pan-Celtic Association is based on Marion Löffler's 'A Book of Mad Celts' (Löffler, 2000) and also from personal communication with her, for which I am most grateful.

The **Pan-Celtic Association** provides a fascinating insight into late nineteenth- and early twentieth-century notions of measures and markers of Celticity. In the course of the nineteenth century the Welsh Eisteddfodau had become the focus of pan-Celtic sentiment, and attempts had been made to foster pan-Celtic cooperation by various people, including in the 1860s Charles de Gaulle (great-uncle of the twentieth-century French general and president). By the 1890s organizations celebrating the Celtic culture of a number of regions had been formed, often with some form of annual festival. Examples are *An Comun Gaidhealach*, the Highland Association (founded in 1891) in Scotland, along with its festival, the *Mod*; the Gaelic League of Ireland (set up in 1893) with, from 1897, festivals called *Oireachtas* (or simply *Feiseanna*); *Kevredigez Vroadel Freiz*, the Breton National Union (established in 1898); and *Yn Cheshagh Ghailckagh*, the Manx Language Society (founded in 1899). These groups were at the heart of the Pan-Celtic Association, whose constitution had as its main objectives:

> The furtherance of Celtic studies, and the fostering of mutual sympathy and cooperation between the various branches of the Celtic race in all matters affecting their language and national characteristics.

The same constitution ruled that the Association should be non-political and non-sectarian. Members were urged to concentrate on matters of language, native sports, national music and costume, and to avoid overtly political expressions and actions ...

As part of the 'restoration of Celtic nationality' advocated by some members, it attached great importance to symbols such as monuments, banners, costumes and its Celtic anthem, the 'Heather Song'.

(Löffler, 2000, pp. 22–3)

The third reading is an account of the Celtic Congress of Caernarfon in 1904, taken from Marion Löffler's *'A Book of Mad Celts': John Wickens and the Celtic Congress of Caernarfon 1904* (2000). As you read, try to be aware of the assumptions underlying the Pan-Celtic Association's activities and keep a note of the various ways in which it was felt appropriate to mark and measure Celticity and express Pan-Celtic solidarity. Notice also the photographs by John Wickens for, as Löffler points out, they are a fund of information 'for those interested in the history of romantic nationalism and national dress, as well as for historians of Celticism and the Celtic revival of the nineteenth and early twentieth centuries' (Löffler, 2000, p. 20).

'A Book of Mad Celts'

The Celtic Congress of Caernarfon, 1904

One of the pinnacles of the Pan-Celtic Association's brief history was the flamboyantly romantic Celtic Congress held in Caernarfon in 1904. Under the leadership of T. Gwynn Jones and R. Gwyneddon Davies, the local secretaries of the Pan-Celtic Association, the town spent a year preparing for the influx of over 400 guests from all parts of Wales and the other Celtic countries. On the day before the festival the *North Wales Observer* reported that:

Monday saw the completion of the preparations on the part of the committee and hard-working secretaries. The townspeople responded loyally to the Mayor's request for bunting, and a festive character was secured to the streets through a liberal display of flags and banners. The hint as to the heather bloom was taken generally also, and he was a stranger indeed who forbore from sporting a sprig of the pretty 'blodau'r grug' in his buttonhole. The heather was the first suggestion of something novel in the occasion, something different from any other public display ever seen in the town. The second indication came in the appearance in the streets of men in quaint costume, speaking a tongue strange but familiar. They were the Breton delegates.[1]

This article set the tone for other newspapers. Although all of them dutifully outlined the Congress programme – the modern language section, the music section, the folklore and costume section and the international section – and gave summaries of the learned papers, their gaze was principally fixed on the novel ceremonies performed in costumes rarely seen before. Surprisingly, most papers, from the *Irish Times* to the *Western Mail* and the *Isle of Man Times* to the *Westminster Gazette*, commented favourably on the Congress and saw the gathering as a step towards greater understanding among the European nations. The *Western Mail*, for instance, rejoiced that:

> Between Wales and Ireland there was not only a feeling of coldness, but of actual hostility ... Possibly Welsh Protestantism was partly responsible for that feeling. Politics also helped to create it ... As to the Isle of Man and Gaelic Scotland, Welshmen troubled themselves very little about them ... Now, however, as Wales grows out of its religious prejudices and becomes more liberal, the sentiment of race and speech once more asserts itself. The same applies to the other Celtic kith and kin, and we see the result of it all in the movement which receives more or less support from the several branches.[2]

The newspaper coverage reflects how unusual such colourful ceremonies, processions, receptions and evening concerts were among the people of north Wales and also helps to explain why the outward symbols of the movement remained etched on their minds. The overwhelming impression they left is best conveyed in an inscription found in the album assembled for Gwyneth Vaughan: *A Book of Mad Celts by John Wickens*.

The Congress opened on Tuesday, 30 August, with the ceremony of assembling the Logan stone, a monument comprising five granite cubes, each representing a Celtic nation.[3] Led by Irish pipers and Highland pipers, a colourful procession, including the

---

[1] *North Wales Observer and Express*, 2 September 1904.

[2] *Western Mail*, 31 August 1904.

[3] By the end of the Congress, the Logan stone consisted of six granite cubes. Cornwall had been accepted as a Celtic nation, and a cube was added accordingly.

'presence in state of the Lord Mayor and Lady Mayoress of Dublin, and the mayors of Caernarfon, Bangor, Conway and Llandovery', wended its way from the station to the castle where the opening ceremony of building the monument was conducted.[4] The *North Wales Observer* enthused again:

> It is doubtful if a not only more picturesque but also more stately and impressive cavalcade ever passed through the streets of Caernarvon before ... a procession that was exceedingly attractive and yet presented no semblance of tinsel or make-belief – on the contrary, a well-sustained dignity and sincerity characterised it throughout, tending

[**Figure 1**]   Pan-Celts in the rain at the end of the Congress

4   *Irish Times*, 31 August 1904.

to impress upon the thousands who lined the pavements the reality of the Pan-Celtic ideas.[5]

Both the opening and closing ceremonies took place in the courtyard at the eastern end of Caernarfon Castle. After the leader of each delegation had set his nation's cube in place, the proceedings followed the model of the Welsh Gorsedd of the Bards, thereby underlining the power of Iolo Morganwg's invention.[6] This was partly due to the late Victorian *penchant* for the visualization of history, but it also owed much to the charisma of Hwfa Môn (1823–1905), who had been elected Archdruid in 1895 and who held office until his death in 1905. An immensely popular model, he was depicted by several painters and it was for him that the Bavarian artist Hubert Herkomer designed the archdruid's robe and regalia which have remained familiar to this day.[7] Hwfa Môn first wore this attire in 1896, the year the Celts assembled at Llandudno. In the same period the Welsh Gorsedd became the declared model for its sister institutions in Brittany (1901) and Cornwall (1928). It was invited to Brittany, Ireland, Scotland, and even America in order to lend a semblance of antiquity and dignity to newly-founded festivals. As every tribute in the memorial volume published a year after his death emphasized, Hwfa Môn seemed to personify everything that had been attributed to the Celtic Druids since the eighteenth century:

> In the Bardic Circle, he was like a King amidst the crowds, and everybody was prepared to let him rule in peace. One could have thought that he had been created for the purpose of being an Archdruid who was an adornment to this office and all its connections. The nations looked upon him with the greatest interest, and they believed that he was an incarnation on the secrets of the early bardic circle[8] ...

While Hwfa Môn and Baron Castletown preached Celtic unity and the symbols combined to reinforce their words, individual

---

[5] *North Wales Observer and Express,* 2 September 1904.

[6] Dillwyn Miles, *The Secret of the Bards of the Isle of Britain* (Llandybe, 1992), pp. 131–40.

[7] Hubert Herkomer, *Art Culture in Wales* (London, 1898), pp. 7–11; Peter Lord, *Y Chwaer Dduwies, Celf, Crefft a'r Eisteddfod* (Llandysul, 1992), pp. 64–5; Stephanie Jones, *Charles William Mansel Lewis: Painter, Patron and Promoter of Arts in Wales,* (Aberystwyth, 1998), p. 47.

[8] W. J. Parry, *Cofiant Hwfa Môn* (Manceinion, 1907), p. 10.

[Figure 2] Under the spell of Archdruid Hwfa Môn (Rowland Williams 1823–1905)

delegates did their best to demonstrate the visual manifestations of the national revival in their own countries. Influenced by the writings of influential nineteenth-century *savants* such as John Ruskin, it was argued that national costume was a morally edifying part of national identity and that therefore its revival or invention was imperative.[9] It is entirely understandable that the delegates were proud to pose as living examples of an essential part of a national tradition.

The first to reach Caernarfon were forty-eight Breton delegates, who immediately visited Caernarfon Police Court, where they were 'impressed by the matter-of fact way in which the proceedings were conducted by bench, council, police and witnesses in the Welsh language'.[10] They naturally wore regional variations of what they regarded as their national costume. The Bretons were the only

[9] E. Cooke and Alexander Wedderburn (eds.), *The Works of John Ruskin, Volume VII* (London, 1907), p. 428: Manx Museum and Library MS 140, Sophia Morrison, 'The Manx National Dress', *Manx Language Society Annual Meeting* (1901), pp. 8–11.

[10] *Western Mail*, 31 August 1904.

Celts who could boast a costume which continued an unbroken tradition and, in its regional variations, was still worn at Catholic Pardons Processions. Like many other European national costumes, it represented a stylized version of pre-industrial peasant dress. Marquis Régis de l'Estourbeillon de la Garnache (1858–1946), the leader of the delegation and of *Kevredigez Vroadel Freiz*, wore it and so did the photographer Émile Hamonic, the poet Theodore Botrel (1868–1925) and his wife Lena – all of whom were active in the separatist movement ...

The dress worn by the female Breton delegates is reminiscent of the national dress of the Sorbs, a Slavonic minority in the east of Germany. The use of layers of aprons is also to be found in the national dresses of nations in south-east Europe.[11] Madame Ange Mosher was an especially interesting delegate. She was born in America, to a Welsh mother, but spent most of her life in her adopted Celtic country Brittany, where she generously sponsored Breton drama and the separatist movement. Although Professor Ernest Rhŷs was moved by her rendition of a Breton 'grandmother's lullaby' during the Congress, the Welsh novelist Gwyneth Vaughan was less impressed.[12] In her photo-album the portrait was given the title 'An American impostor', which hints at the tensions which might have existed between 'true' and 'adopted' Celts.

Scotland's main representative Theodore Napier was a similar case. He had been born in Australia, but attended high school and university at Edinburgh before becoming secretary of the 'Legitimist Jacobite League of Great Britain and Ireland'. Between 1901 and 1912 he published the nationalist Jacobite journal, *The Fiery Cross*, and was extremely active in the Scottish national movement. The Scottish historian H. J. Hanham remarked of him: 'Though embarrassing for his nationalist allies, he was a remarkable man ... [he] gradually became a popular figure in Edinburgh, and when he left the country in 1912 there was a good deal of regret.'[13] ... For the benefit of the Celtic Congress he became Clanchief Napier, posing in the costume of a Highland chieftain of the Montrose period. This was a case of both invented identity and costume for, as Hugh Trevor-Roper has shown, the kilt had been devised by an English Quaker ironmaster at Glengarry near Inverness in the 1740s and had been popularized by Sir

---

[11]   Max Tilke, *Costume Patterns and Designs* (London, 1956).

[12]   Ernest Rhŷs, 'The Pan-Celtic Congress', *The Celtic Review*, I (1901), 191.

[13]   H. J. Hanham, *Scottish Nationalism* (London, 1969), pp. 84, 121.

Walter Scott in connection with the state visit of George IV to Edinburgh in 1822.[14] The seventy-year-old Napier cut a splendid figure in his kilt and drew the attention of crowds wherever he went. Equally impressive were the Highland pipers in their kilts. In the case of the female members of the thirty or so Scottish delegation, such as Ella Carmichael, editor of the *Celtic Review* and daughter of the famous folklorist Alexander Carmichael, fashionable Celtic adornments such as Celtic embroidery, brooch and shawl sufficed. No Celtic dress had been revived for them, and it would not be revived and displayed on a large scale until the Scottish National Pageant of Allegory, Myth and History in 1908[15] ...

After the Welsh, the Irish delegation of over ninety people was the strongest at the Congress. Most of the names associated with the Celtic renaissance in Ireland, from Lady Gregory and William Butler Yeats to Standish James O'Grady and Douglas Hyde, were present. Since many of them were Anglo-Irish, supporting the Irish language movement and resuscitating or inventing Irish traditions were means of asserting their own identity. John E. Geoghegan, for instance, scion of a well-known revivalist family, a cousin of the portrait painter Sarah Purser, and a patron of the arts in Ireland, posed proudly in a typical costume of eleventh-century cut, embroidered with late Bronze Age Celtic zigzag patterns, very similar to those shown in J. Romilly Allen's classic book, *Celtic Art in Pagan and Christian Times*, published in Dublin in 1904.[16] Another example of this style are Baron Castletown's Irish pipers, who led the processions, and who Taldir described as wearing ... 'the ancient Irish costume worn by the knights of King Lear (Leoghaire) at Tara castle when Saint Patrick came to preach Christianity to them'.[17] Among the women portrayed in revived Celtic dress was Alicia Needham, composer of Irish music. The Irish singer Agnes Treacy and harpist Esther Corless wore beautiful

---

[14]   Hugh Trevor-Roper, 'The Invention of Tradition: The Highland Tradition of Scotland' in Eric Hobsbawm and Terence Ranger (eds.) *The Invention of Tradition* (Cambridge, 1984), pp. 15–41.

[15]   Elizabeth Cumming, 'The Arts and Crafts Movement in Edinburgh' in Nicola Gordon Bowe and Elizabeth Cumming (eds.), *The Arts and Crafts Movements in Dublin and Edinburgh* (Dublin, 1998), pp. 35–6.

[16]   J. Romilly Allen, *Celtic Art in Pagan and Christian Times* (Dublin, 1904; reprint 1993), p. 27.

[17]   NLW, Department of Manuscripts and Records, François Jaffrennou (Taldir) Papers, Photo Album.

[Figure 3] The singer Agnes Treacy and the harpist Esther Corless in their tasteful dresses

robes also based on supposedly eleventh-century models, embroidered with bands of spirals and C-shaped curves found in Allen's writings.

The Irish costumes for men and women demonstrate a productive fusion which had occurred in Ireland, but not yet in Scotland or Wales. The Celtic theme for a national art revival had been set by Henry O'Neill's beautiful book, *The Fine Arts and Civilisation of Ancient Ireland*, in 1863. In the foreword he asserted:

> Irish Art has not received much attention till a comparatively recent period, yet this remarkable style was carried to an almost miraculous degree of excellence, and the best works in that style which still remain are, for inventive power, sound principles, and masterly execution,

the very finest examples of ornament that were ever executed ... The examples, we trust, will interest the mind by their novelty, and improve the taste by their excellence; they will gratify the national heart, because they are national and glorious.[18]

The items he chose to illustrate his claim to a national tradition, such as the famous Tara brooch and the cross at Drumcliff, were soon reproduced by the thousands and their patterns reworked in other materials. They were a welcome source of inspiration for the Irish domestic industries, which had been developed since the 1880s to assist poor women in the western areas especially in embroidery and lace-making, and for the numerous Irish art societies and schools of art[19] ...

In Wales the task of creating a tradition of national design and symbol had only just begun, although one of the most influential books in the field, *The Grammar of Ornament*, which had included Celtic patterns as early as 1856, was written by the Welshman Owen Jones.[20] Most of the efforts in this field concentrated on the National Eisteddfod and the Gorsedd, especially their robes and regalia. Members of the Gorsedd, such as Gwyneth Vaughan and Alfred Perceval Graves, chose to be photographed in their robes, while others, like T. Gwynn Jones, preferred civilian clothes. The Welsh national dress, which had been derived from regional Welsh peasant costume by Lady Llanofer in the 1840s, was unpopular among the upper and middle classes who provided the bulk of the Association's members. Because of its association with Lady Llanofer's court, where all the servants and court musicians were obliged to wear it, the national costume soon became associated with performers of traditional music ...

The Manx delegates had been criticized following the Dublin Congress of 1901 for wearing what was denounced as 'the garb of denationalisation', i.e. modern clothes. However, Sophia Morrison, secretary of *Yn Cheshagh Ghailckagh*, had sought the advice of E. E. Fournier d'Albe, the General Secretary, even before the first Congress and she was duly 'appointed a member of the Sub-

[18]   Henry O'Neill, *The Fine Arts and Civilisation of Ancient Ireland* (London, 1863), pp. v–vi.

[19]   Cyril Barrett and Jeanne Sheehy, 'Visual Arts and Society, 1850–1900' in W. E. Vaughan (ed.), *A New History of Ireland, VI: Ireland under the Union II, 1870–1921* (Oxford, 1996), pp. 436–74; idem, 'Visual Arts and Society, 1900–20', ibid., pp. 455–99.

[20]   Ivor Davies, 'Datblygiad Hanes Celf' in Ivor Davies and Ceridwen Lloyd-Morgan (eds.), *Darganfod Celf Cymru* (Caerdydd, 1999), pp. 15–16.

Committee of the Manx Language Society, for the purpose of designing a Manx National Costume'.[21] Together with Ada Corrin, she drew up a report on 'National Costume on the Isle of Man', which was presented several times between 1901 and 1907. It voiced their ideas of a dress 'modelled on the Irish costume of the 11th century ... in the hope that they may stimulate others to take up this important question, and evolve a costume for the Manx people, which, artistic and practical, shall at the same time be a symbol of their nationality and their patriotism'.[22] Sophia Morrison's efforts, however, never extended beyond initial contacts with the Scottish Home Industries Association and, as a result, the twenty-seven delegates from the Isle of Man appeared in modern clothes at Caernarfon. The most likely explanation is that the faithful few on the island lacked the resources to develop their ideas. They were obliged to give priority to collecting what remained of their language, conducting language classes and petitioning education authorities on the island and at Whitehall. The most famous Manx artist of the time, Archibald Knox (1846–1933), though designing decidedly Celtic-inspired patterns for Liberty & Co., London, did not choose Celtic themes for the few designs he executed for the national movement before the First World War[23] ...

An additional explanation for the lack of success in developing a national tradition of design may be that, of all the Celtic nations, the Isle of Man enjoyed the largest measure of political independence and thus it might not have felt the need to establish a connection with the past through costume[24] ...

From the outset the eight Cornish members of the Pan-Celtic Association encountered considerable problems. Their *Kowethas Kelto-Kernoweg* had been refused membership of the Association in 1901 on the grounds that Cornish was no longer a living language. The Celtic Congress of Caernarfon, however, decided to admit Cornwall as a Celtic nation. The leaders of the Cornish language revival, Henry Jenner, his wife, and the Reverend Percival Treasure chose to be photographed in their Gorsedd robes, although Jenner

---

[21] Manx Museum and Library, MS 9594, Sophia Morrison Papers, Box 8, E. E. Fournier to Sophia Morrison, 23 July 1901.

[22] Manx Museum and Library, MS 9594, Sophia Morrison Papers, MS 140.

[23] J. Tilbrook and G. House (eds.), *The Designs of Archibald Knox for Liberty and Co.* (London, 1976).

[24] R. H. Kinvig, *The Isle of Man: A Social, Cultural and Political History* (Liverpool, 1978), pp. 163–6.

had more than once presented himself at the National Eisteddfod in a revived Cornish costume, which was described as 'consisting of a blue tunic and kilt, relieved by the yellow Cornish national flower, the broom plant, with sandals and cap copied from old metal examples in the British Museum', where, incidentally, he worked[25] ...

Even though the ceremonies and costumes of the Pan-Celtic Association may appear fantastic and even ridiculous today, they were a Celtic reflection of the *Zeitgeist* of their times. The fact that most of the Pan-Celts chose to recommend eleventh-century costumes based on descriptions in the medieval Irish tales mirrors more general European tendencies of looking back to the craft-orientated middle ages for inspiration – from Wagner, the Pre-Raphaelites and Ruskin to the Arts and Crafts Movement and *fin-de-siècle* Vienna. In Britain this movement climaxed in a spate of historic pageants staged at the turn of the century, and into which the three Congresses held by the Pan-Celtic Association blended quite seamlessly. With the colourful National Welsh Pageant in Cardiff in 1909 and the celebrations performed on the occasion of the investiture of the Prince of Wales in Caernarfon in 1911, this trend came to an end. Like the Congresses of the Pan-Celtic Association, such ceremonies may have been designed 'to unite a beleaguered upper class searching for a new role in the nation' with the people, enabling the former to move from the periphery to the centre of their culture,[26] but, on a more general level, the delegates can be seen to have represented those stateless nations of Europe which were keen to close the gaps in their array of national customs. Celtic costumes, native sports, and traditional music and instruments were means of creating national traditions and supporting their claims to nationhood. With the end of the First World War, the political map of Europe changed radically and its cultural history took a different direction. The October Revolution in Russia opened a period of AgitProp and realism. Modernism was to rule supreme for the following fifty years and the hunt for a past appeared to be over.

(Löffler, 2000, pp. 28–32, 36–7, 40–4, 48–52, 58–64, 67–8)

---

[25] *North Wales Observer and Express*, 12 September 1902.

[26] Hywel Teifi Edwards, 'Pasiant Cenedlaethol Caerdydd 1909' in *Codi'r Hen Wlad yn ei Hôl, 1850–1914* (Llandysul, 1989), pp. 239–83; John S. Ellis, 'The Prince and the Dragon: Welsh National Identity and the 1911 Investiture of the Prince of Wales', *Welsh History Review*, 18, no. 2 (1996), 273.

EXERCISE

1   From your reading of the Löffler extract, what emerge as important markers and measures of Celticity in the Pan-Celtic Association, as demonstrated at the Caernarfon Congress?

2   How well would the concerns of the Pan-Celtic Association serve the current agenda of Celts as proto-Europeans?

3   How important do you think considerations such as language, costume, music and so on are to contemporary notions of Celticity?

DISCUSSION

1   From this account of the congress, you will have realized that language was considered the major criterion of Celticity for the Pan-Celtic Association. Indeed the Cornish Celtic cultural association, *Kowethas Kelto-Kernoweg*, was initially refused membership of the Pan-Celtic Association in 1901 on the grounds that Cornish was no longer a living language. However, in the course of the 1904 congress, Cornwall was admitted as a Celtic nation and a sixth stone, representing Cornwall, was added to the 'Logan stone' monument.

Traditional music, costume and 'native sports' were also considered important. Chapman and others have commented on the way in which archaic, previously general cultural features and artefacts, such as bagpipes (once common throughout Europe, but now associated with Scotland, Brittany, Ireland and Northumbria), have come to be seen as timelessly and typically 'Celtic' (Chapman, 1992, pp. 118–19).

You probably picked up on the extent to which 'traditional' costume was being invented or adapted. Dress was being used in a number of ways to establish distinct cultural identities; the jibe that the Manx delegates in modern dress were wearing 'the garb of denationalisation' is one demonstration of this. However, only the Bretons had a consistent tradition of dress, though it is interesting to note they had a variety of regional garbs to choose from. This indicates that the designation of one costume as national dress was a highly contrived activity to suit a nationalist agenda. The issue of class and the need for 'noble' attire are very obvious in relation to dress in Scotland, Wales and Ireland, indicating something of the social class of those involved in the Celtic revival and pan-Celticism. You might also have noticed the role of expatriate Celts such as Ange Mosher and Theodore Napier in this and other respects.

2   For the association, it would not have been good enough for
     people from parts of Europe where there had *once* been a Celtic
     language to present themselves as contemporary Celts. The *Atlas
     of European Celtic Languages* might be of historical interest, but the
     association was interested in Celtic as a living language. It is also
     worth noting that there was obviously a strong sense of Celtic
     regional identity amid the pan-Celticism, so that diversity as well as
     Celtic unity was expressed.

3   The extent to which such considerations are important vary. For
     example, Cornwall subsequently gained other markers of
     Celticity, including a Gorseth of bards on the Welsh model –
     established in 1928 and with distinctive pale blue robes (see Hale,
     2000) – and a Cornish tartan. These issues will be considered in
     more detail as we look at contemporary Celticity.

Contemporary Celtic identities: continuity and change

By the time of the most recent *fin de siècle* and its accompanying
Celtic revival, the parameters of Celticity had expanded considerably
for a variety of reasons, not least the influence of commodification
and globalization. (Reflect for a moment on the extent to which the
Irish pub has become a global phenomenon, and why.) A further
important aspect of the present revival is the increasing popularity
and diversity of Celtic spirituality (see Bowman, 2002).

While the Pan-Celtic Association had very clear criteria for Celticity,
in the course of the twentieth century 'Celtic' popularly became
increasingly broadly interpreted within the British Isles to embrace all
Scots, Irish, Welsh, Manx, Northumbrians and people from the west
country. Tim Sebastian, Chosen Chief of the Secular Order of Druids,
is of the opinion that ultimately everyone in Britain is of Celtic
descent; but anyway, he claims, as the term Celtic describes culture,
not ethnicity, anyone can 'tap into' Celticity. Some look to geography,
some to language, some to ancestry to establish Celtic credentials, but
increasingly there are what I have referred to elsewhere (Bowman,
1995) as 'Cardiac Celts' – people who feel in their hearts that they are
Celtic. We shall thus examine some of the ways in which Celticity is
constructed and construed in the contemporary milieu, the effects of
commodification and globalization, and why, in the wake of the most
recent Celtic revival, people should want to self-identify as Celts.

Making a song and dance

If we look at some of the markers and measures of Celticity expounded by the Pan-Celtic Association, we can see the extent to which there is both continuity and change. We saw, for example, that festivals to promote Celtic performance arts such as poetry, music and dance had been started in the nineteenth century, and these Celtic festivals continue to flourish in Ireland, Wales, Scotland, France, America, Canada, Australia and many places besides. In line with the stress on traditional pastimes, highland games are also popular in Scotland, America, Canada and Australia. Particularly in the Celtic diaspora, playing bagpipes, learning highland or Irish dance, participating in highland games, or simply attending Celtic music festivals are important not simply in reflecting but also in establishing and expressing Celtic identity. (See Hale and Thornton, 2000 and Curtis, 2000 for American examples.)

A fine example of the commodification and globalization of traditional music and dance is the highly successful stage show *Riverdance*. Developed from a short dance routine devised for the interval of the 1994 Eurovision Song Contest, hosted by Ireland (and watched by a European audience of 300 million people), it features spectacular dance routines based upon 'traditional' Irish dance. *Riverdance* self-consciously traces its roots back to the *Feiseanna* (festivals) established by the Gaelic League in the 1890s and the resulting growth of interest in Irish dance in Ireland and beyond, the latter reflected in the London *Feis* inaugurated in 1907 and the World Irish Dancing Championships (*Oireachtas Rince na Cruinne*) established in 1969 (see O Se, 1997–8, p. 27; and the *Riverdance* website). The growth of competitions necessitated increasingly fixed and regulated standards for performance to assist judging, so that what started as a 'national pastime' became increasingly formalized and formulaic, and correspondingly less spontaneous. (Highland dancing and Scottish country dancing underwent a similar fate.) The stage show *Riverdance* is not only a celebration and virtuoso display of Irish dance, it also presents a broader critique of prehistoric Irish culture, the mass emigration of Irish people to America and their encounters with different cultural traditions there. It is a triumphal celebration of contemporary Irishness.

Celtic music is a flourishing but ubiquitous industry (see Thornton, 2000). However, these days Celtic music can be anything ranging from plainsong and 'Celtic harp', through Irish, Scottish and Breton folk revival (including music from groups such as the Chieftains, Ossian, Silly Wizard and the contemporary Breton bagpipe ensemble Bagad Kemper), to 'inspirational' music such as Terry Oldfield's 'Illumination: a Celtic Blessing' or Medwyn Goodall's 'Druid'

('Cascading rivulets of ancient sounds ... evoking the powers of ancient standing stones'). In March 2002 there were two 'Celtic chill-out' albums in the top fifty album chart: these contained tracks by popular 'Celtic music' groups such as Clannad and Runrig; music from *Riverdance;* the theme tunes of the films *Rob Roy* and *Braveheart;* and Simon and Garfunkel's 'Scarborough Fair' and 'Sounds of Silence'. There are various crossover forms, including Afro-Celtic, Celtic-salsa, acid croft and techno ceilidh. Celtic music thus now encompasses the old, the new, the inspirational and the 'feel good'; it is often found in the 'world music' section of music shops, reflecting its vaguely ethnic status and eclectic content.

At the 1997 Celtic Connections Folk Festival (an annual event held in Glasgow), in addition to workshops on fiddling and traditional dance there was one on 'How to decorate your didgeridoo'.

The tartan trail

The Pan-Celtic Association's concerns with costume may have seemed amusing to some people, but the ways in which tartan has been used to express a variety of political and national identities provides an interesting case study. Pittock comments that in Scotland,

> the use of tartan to signify national antiquity and authenticity can be dated back at least to the marriage of James VI to Anne of Denmark in 1596, and by the end of the succeeding century tartan had become conflated with the symbols of Jacobite nationalist patriotism.

(Pittock, 1999, p. 86)

In the Jacobite rising of 1745, as far as possible all pro-Stuart factions were attired in tartan – even the Manchester Regiment. After the suppression of the rebellion, the Disclothing Act 1747 forbade the wearing of highland attire, although this was repealed in 1782 after the political rehabilitation of the highlanders. In the British army the tartan of the highland regiments became 'a token of Celtic derring-do against all odds' (Pittock, 1999, p. 86). With the visit by George IV to Edinburgh in 1822, tartan was firmly re-established as a respectable and desirable symbol of Scottish (that is, not simply highland) identity, and the tartan 'industry' really took off. The contemporary custom of bridegrooms wearing highland dress at weddings is not only a colourful alternative to a boring suit, but an expression of 'Scottishness'. The increasing numbers of Scots of Asian and other ancestry who have taken to wearing the kilt underlines tartan's continuing role as a measure and marker of Scottish identity. Since 1999 there has been a Singh tartan.

Although from Jura to Japan tartan *can* be simply a fashion item, it has Celtic cultural resonances which in some contexts are increasing rather than diminishing in scope. The creation of the Cornish tartan, for example, was an important assertion of both Cornish and Celtic identity, and for some people the possession of a kilt, a coat, a purse or other small item in that material has great significance. Irish tartan seems to be growing in popularity. In 1998, 6 April was declared National Tartan Day in the USA, the date being linked to the Declaration of Arbroath (1320), which contains the stirring lines: 'For it is not glory, it is not riches, neither is it honour, but it is liberty alone that we fight and contend for, which no honest man will lose but with his life' (quoted in Pittock, 1999, p. 87). Liberty, Celticity and tartan were thus conflated and celebrated.

Writing on the new pan-Celticism of Australia, where Australians of Irish, Welsh, Cornish and Scottish descent are articulating a *common Celticity* within a context of increasing multiculturalism, Philip Payton includes this quote on the role of the Australian tartan:

> The recently-created Australian tartan is a move ... to achieve a Celtic unison. Based on the colours of Central Australia and a variation on the sett of Lachlan Macquarie [governor of New South Wales, 1810–21], this 'tartan for a Sunburnt Country' is intended to cater for those proud of being both Celtic and Australian. It is intended for all Celts.
>
> (Alexander quoted in Payton, 2000, p. 122)

Perhaps predictably, should Euro-Celts desire a pan-Celtic costume these days, there is the European Union tartan. Developed in 1997–8 in Scotland, the tartan's design includes a white line ('for peace on the Continent of Europe and the world') and a red line ('to commemorate those who lost their lives in the many conflicts on our Continent') on a base of gold and blue ('the colours of the European Union Flag'), with small gold squares representing the stars on the flag (see Kilsyth website).

Tartan, claims Pittock, is 'the most widespread, most recognizable, and most central of Celtic artefacts' (Pittock, 1999, p. 88). It can be 'merely' a fashion choice, available to a global market, but it also has a history of being a flexible, multivalent symbol of Celticity, pressed into service for a variety of causes.

Commodifying Celticity

By the late twentieth and early twenty-first centuries, the Celts had come to enjoy high status in some contexts. It became clear at an early stage in my fieldwork on Celtic spirituality, for example, that being a Scot (albeit a lowland, non-Gaelic-speaking Scot) was to some extent an advantage. An American I met in Glastonbury confided that when he had first visited Scotland a few years previously he had suddenly realized that this was his spiritual home, and that he felt sure he had been a Scot in some previous life. Later that same day, when I was talking to another Scot, this American stopped us in mid conversation to say that he just wanted us to know how thrilled he was to be 'in the presence of two Celts'.

Having some sort of Celtic or quasi-Celtic ancestry is frequently used to help establish credentials in both secular and spiritual circles; the co-organizer of a workshop during a Festival of the Celtic Spirit, for example, was described as 'a Northumbrian Irish Celt exiled in London'. Rhiannon Evans, maker of 'designer Celtic jewellery' and T-shirts, drops these words into her advertising copy:

> All our jewellery is handmade by Welsh-speaking craftsmen at Tregaron in Wales – one of the last remaining corners of Britain where the Celtic heritage is still very much of the present time.

Undoubtedly, in the present climate, Celtic sells. A spokesman for the bookstore chain Waterstones commented in a radio interview that books with the word 'Celtic' in their titles simply 'fly off the shelves'. In addition to the ever-increasing literature relating to contemporary Celtic spirituality, there are many lavishly illustrated books about Celtic art, archaeology and locations. As Chapman has commented,

> any picture of Early Celtic Europe is necessarily based upon a rather comprehensive ignorance. I make this point, since one could be forgiven for thinking, after reading one of the many illustrated books on the Celts, that the authors had been round pre-Roman barbarian Europe with camera and tape-recorder.

> (Chapman, 1992, p. 6)

Shops such as Wilde Celts provide 'Pan Celtic Art inspired by the Golden Age of Celtic Creativity' in the form of books, cards, crafts and Celtic jewellery. When it comes to commodifying the Celtic, the usual option is to take otherwise ordinary objects and make them Celtic by adding knotwork or tartan or some Celtic connection; thus we find Celtic mousemats, Celtic ties, Celtic notepaper and so on. The 'Celtic Art' section of the 'Past Times' (2000) catalogue, for example, included the 'Boudicca Bracelet Watch':

> The legend of Boudicca, the defiant Celtic queen of the Iceni who battled valiantly against the Romans, was the inspiration for this silver-plated watch. The bracelet has knotwork panels echoing designs from the large 9th-century 'Cadboll' brooch.

The Celts play an important part in the heritage and leisure industry. Have you ever noticed how much Celtic paraphernalia there is for sale in the gift shops of cathedrals, historic sites and museums? There are open-air museums (of the type described by Tim Benton in Chapter 4 of this book, 'Architecture and identities: from the Open-Air Museum Movement to Mickey Mouse') in Scotland, Ireland,

Wales, Brittany and elsewhere, a fine example being the Museum of Welsh Life at St Fagan's, Glamorgan, where on a 100-acre site there are reconstructed buildings gathered from all over Wales; here, increasingly, the celebration of 'Celtic' calendar customs are featured among the visitor activities. There are also various 'Celtic' museums or 'Celtic experience' attractions which often function as 'wet weather' activities in regions not celebrated for the clemency of the climate.

At the Story of Mann on the Isle of Man, you can 'Explore the language and landscape of a kingdom at the heart of the Celtic world'. In Wales you can 'Experience the mysterious and magical world of the Celts' at Celtica, in Machynlleth, Powys:

> Welcome to Celtica, a new visitor centre presenting the history and culture of the Celts – people whose culture has influenced European history over 3000 years. A great place for an enjoyable and informative day out, Celtica reflects Wales' distinct Celtic inheritance; a magical blend of myth and music, landscape and language, reflecting a nation which, in common with the people of the other Celtic lands on the Western Europe [*sic*], is as proud of its past as it is of its present and future.

> Celtica is a unique attraction telling the story of Celtic myths and legends. Here visitors can encounter an exciting, emotive and dynamic presentation aimed at evoking a sense of the Celtic spirit – the very life-blood of Welsh Culture and heritage. Visit Celtica, re-live our Celtic inheritance and feel the kindred spirit of our artistry, traditions and culture. It is not a museum, it is a vibrant, sensual and intellectual experience that expresses the spirit which was and still is 'Celtic'.

> (Celtica website)

Stop and think for a moment about the image of the Celts presented in this quotation. What do you recognize in terms of ideas and assumptions? In such attractions, the conventional picture of the prehistory and spread of the Celts tends to be reinforced, with pan-Celtic assumptions underlying regional specificity, and there is frequently a stress on the romantic Celt and the 'Celtic spirit'.

Celluloid Celts

In previous centuries literature was arguably the most influential purveyor of images of the Celts, and now there are huge numbers of publications relating to Celtic subjects, including Celtic art (old and new), Celtic spirituality and the 'Celtic mysteries' consistently solved by Peter Tremayne's heroine Sister Fidelma (see Sister Fidelma website).

However, in terms of mass audiences, in the course of the twentieth century cinema and television have become paramount in the portrayal of Celticity. (See Piccini (1996) and Jones (2000) for discussions of the portrayal of Celts in film and television.) The film *Local Hero* (1983), for example, confirmed the image of the highlands as an unspoilt and otherworldly location, complete with mermaid, while in the 1990s there were two particularly striking examples of the Celt as noble savage – in the American films *Rob Roy* (1994) and *Braveheart* (1995). The theme music for *Rob Roy* set the scene, being a vaguely native American chant, and the film eulogized such virtues as bravery, loyalty and, above all, honour. *Braveheart* was particularly influential, despite its lack of historical accuracy, its anachronisms and its many bad accents. In *Braveheart* William Wallace is the warrior hero of classical accounts of Celts and Ossian, the noble savage *par excellence*. Pittock comments on the extent to which American projections of Celts influenced the film – such as the introduction of an Irishman who saves Wallace's life and a Scots–Irish alliance at the battle of Falkirk, underlining Celtic solidarity. He also critiques how the portrayal of Wallace has been seen in American survivalist terms: 'living in the open, a man of integrity and a foe to both English and Scottish "big government", which in their turn seek only to destroy him' (Pittock, 1999, p. 5).

The battle scenes involving Scots wearing face paint in the colours and pattern of the saltire (ancient British woad meets native American 'war paint') were to inspire similar face painting at football matches involving Scotland, and at highland games on both sides of the Atlantic. The film had an impact on Scottish politics and self-image, as well as reinforcing images of 'Celtic' qualities such as integrity and honour.

The film also gave rise to '*Braveheart* weddings', inspired by the scene in which Wallace marries his sweetheart Murron in a 'handfasting' ceremony:

> [T]he Most Rev William Mackie, a bishop with the Celtic Church in Scotland, said Braveheart had been instrumental in a growing number of people opting for the handfasting ceremony, after it appeared in the film.
>
> 'There's no doubt that people saw Braveheart and thought "I would like to do that"', he said ... 'Scotland has its own parliament now and our identity is growing stronger. A lot of people want to marry in the traditional Celtic style.'
>
> (*The Scotsman*, 24 May, 2000)

155

On 6 May 2002 the *Aberdeen Press and Journal* reported on the 'Braveheart-style wedding' of a Canadian couple at Cullerlie standing stones. The couple had chosen the venue after seeing a picture of the stones on the internet, and as the bride's grandmother had emigrated from Aberdeenshire they felt it was appropriate to have a 'Celtic wedding' there. While handfasting ceremonies have been common for some time within contemporary pagan circles, the '*Braveheart* weddings' are an example of 'Celtic tradition' being created on screen and 'revived' in its supposed country of origin.

There is thus a huge market for information about the Celts and products which provide people with means of expressing a love of or affinity with things Celtic. That there is a sort of scramble for Celticity provides a fascinating example of 'elective affinity', that is, people choosing how to identify themselves. Identity and ancestry can have an element of fluidity and choice about them. A familiar example might be the American who declares 'I'm Scottish' when what s/he actually means is that one great grandparent was a Scot; in such a case, a particular identity has been selected from a range of possible affiliations. Indeed, recent US census data has revealed a substantial increase in the number of people self-identifying as 'American Scots', and a new television channel, Tartan TV, has been established specifically to cater for this 'market'.

Spiritual Celts

We have already seen how ideas of a Celtic spirit, and the Celts as spiritually gifted people, had started to be articulated in the eighteenth and nineteenth centuries. A significant factor in the current interest in and striving for Celticity is the growth of Celtic spirituality. Celticity is now regarded by many as a spiritual quality, a particularly attractive 'brand' of religiosity, so that many people in Britain, Ireland, Europe, North America, New Zealand, Australia and elsewhere are putting considerable and genuine effort into being restorers of Celtic spirituality, or 'innovators' within it. The Celts are being looked to for inspiration by a variety of spiritual seekers, whether Christian, New Age, pagan or non-aligned (see Bowman, 2002).

For all of these spiritual seekers the Celt seems to be a 'flexible friend' who can satisfy their needs. As historian and theologian Ian Bradley enthuses,

> Celtic Christianity does seem to speak with almost uncanny relevance to many of the concerns of our present age. It was environment friendly, embracing positive attitudes to nature and constantly celebrating the goodness of god's creation. It was non-hierarchical and non-sexist, eschewing the rule of

diocesan bishops and a rigid parish structure in favour of a loose federation of monastic communities which included married as well as celibate clergy and were often presided over by women. Like the religions of the Australian Aborigines and the native American Indians which are also being rediscovered today, it takes us back to our roots and seems to speak with a primitive innocence and directness which has much appeal in our tired and cynical age.

(Bradley, 1993, pp. vii–viii)

Considered more spiritual, more intuitive, more in touch with nature and the unseen realms, less tainted by modernity and materialism, the Celt and the Celtic thus envisaged seem to be the epitome of what is most highly prized in the contemporary spiritual milieu. Inevitably, though, while increasing numbers of people consider their lives to be enhanced by Celtic spirituality, there is a huge variety of understanding as to what that comprises. Some are trying to reconstruct a Celtic past; some are trying to reinterpret a Celtic past to make it relevant to the contemporary situation; some are inventing something about which they know little can be said or proved, but which somehow 'feels' right. The spiritual Celt thus provides a role model of staggering diversity.

To take the example of Druidry, we can find in this continuity in relation to ideas from earlier periods, but we can also determine the influence of the present globalized spiritual milieu. There are Christian, pagan and New Age Druids, even self-styled Zen Druids and Hassidic Druids. Many modern Druids meet 'in the eye of the sun' and use Iolo Morganwg's Gorsedd prayer; some use extracts from *Carmina Gadelica* in their rituals; often Druids try to hold ceremonies in ancient stone circles, or construct new ones for that purpose. Some groups are keen on 'traditional' robes, while for others a Celtic T-shirt or ordinary clothes will suffice. Those who regard Druidry as Celtic 'native religion' feel that it is legitimate and logical to adapt practices from other indigenous traditions. There are thus numerous workshops and books on Celtic shamanism, while sweat lodges, drumming and didgeridoos are also common at Druid gatherings. The groom at a Druidic handfasting ceremony that I attended at Avebury, for example, wore a long white robe with a didgeridoo hung on one shoulder, while at another 'traditional Druidic wedding' in Glastonbury the groom wore a stylized version of highland dress, the bride wore a long white dress with a sash of Royal Stewart tartan and the bridesmaid wore fairy wings.

Caitlin Matthews writes of practitioners of Celtic spiritual traditions that

Celtic ethnicity is not necessarily a prerequisite, as might be imagined. We have entered a phase of maturity wherein *spiritual lineage* transcends blood lineage ... The impulse for joining such groups often springs from exposure to the lands of Britain and Ireland, or from reading stories and myths deriving from Celtic tradition. A sense of belonging is also often felt from perceived memory of previous incarnation.

(Matthews, 1993, p. 7)

Thus being or feeling Celtic is something that can be acquired, either from contact with the land or from encountering some aspect of Celtic cultural tradition – a sort of contagious Celticity. People visiting what are perceived to be 'Celtic' destinations, whether Ireland, Scotland, Wales and Cornwall in general, or more specific locations such as Iona, Glastonbury, Lindisfarne, Newgrange or Avebury, often comment on the 'feel' or 'energy' of such places; there is thus the authenticating nature of the experience of place. Past-life remembrance can confirm Celticity. All this is a far cry from the measures and markers of Celticity envisaged by the Pan-Celtic Association.

Language

We have already seen that Celtic languages, both ancient and modern, have been at the heart of Celtic studies and ideas about Celtic culture. Indeed the Pan-Celtic Association regarded the living language as the major signifier of Celticity. At the popular level, while some Celtic languages (such as Welsh and Cornish) are now enjoying a revival, and many people are learning Celtic languages to enable them to read material in the original or to express solidarity with the Celtic people, for the most part it is the message not the medium which is considered important.

Most people encounter Celtic myth, poetry, prayers and so on in the *same* language, namely English. From Celtic literature appearing in English for an English-speaking audience has emerged a sort of hybrid 'Celtlish', which reflects the style of English to emerge in translations of Celtic literature, involving formulaic – frequently threefold – repetition, metrical forms, short lines and archaic turns of phrase (such as 'Power of storm be thine, power of moon be thine, power of the sun ...'). Thus, to the linguistically uninitiated, Celtic literature comes in a homogenized package, with Irish, Welsh, Cornish and Gaelic writings (which we rarely see in their varied original versions) seeming all the same. Similarly, there is a collapsing of chronology, as translations of early medieval, nineteenth- and twentieth-century texts frequently appear together without differentiation, often with the implication that these are all 'ancient' writings. This genre of 'writing in the Celtic tradition' is frequently found for sale as a 'Celtic prayer' or 'Celtic blessing' on cards edged with knotwork, often with no clue as to its provenance. It is no wonder that Celtic writings seem 'timeless' – they are often presented in a completely atemporal manner. Moreover, because of the pervading 'Celtlish' style, Celtic prayers, blessings and ritual/liturgical speech written now (whether Christian, Druid, New Age or pagan) frequently sound similar – which in turn all feeds back into the impression of pan-Celticism and the pervasiveness of the Celtic spirit.

From Celtic fringe to cyberspace

At a time when Europeans are being urged to reflect on and identify with a Celtic past, based on history and geography (with perhaps some linguistic considerations), and when many people are seeking to construct and consolidate some sort of Celtic identity on the basis of ancestry, language, cultural activity or other markers and measures of Celticity, we see the rise, simultaneously, not only of the spiritual Celt but also of the cybercelt. 'On-line' Celtic communities and cyberclans are appearing on the internet; for example Celt net was

> conceived as a means to help centralize access to resources of interest to the Celtic online community, to fire the minds of the curious, and to help keep alive the rich traditions, history, folklore and legends of the Celtic peoples

> (Celt net website)

Similarly, Clann an Fhaoil-Choin (Clan of the Wolfhound) describes itself as 'a Celtic family, come together from many backgrounds to honour our ancestors and keep alive the Celtic ways' (see Clann an Fhaoil-Choin website).

The cybercelts provide the example *par excellence* of ahistorical and ageographical Celticism. In 1998, for example, Clan Keltoi announced 'the formation of a new clan':

> This is a call to those who cherish the pre-Christian Celtic ways! It is a call to those who are proud to be Celts but don't 'fit in' to the 'established' revisionist description of Celtic society! Please note that the question IS NOT ... 'are you of Scottish, Irish or Welsh heritage'. Celtic heritage does not begin nor end in these places, but rather extends to nearly every corner of the globe. It's not where your family came from ... it is a passion in your heart that makes you a Celt!

> (Clan Keltoi website)

Celts as 'other', Celts as 'us'

> One half of the time, since I left you, has been spent in places quite remote from all correspondence, among the Hebrides, and other highlands of Scotland, with whom their neighbours seem to have less commerce than they have with either of the Indies. They are nothing so barbarous as the Lowlanders and English commonly represent them; but are for what I could find a very hospitable and civil people: and the main reasons for the contrary character I take to be for their adhering too much to their ancient custom, habit [dress] and language; whereby they distinguish themselves from all their neighbours; and distinctions always create mutual reflections.
>
> (Letter from Edward Lhuyd, 12th March 1700)

> There's something there, a wonderful ambience, and we can localize it as no one is sure who the Celts really were. It doesn't matter about strict historicity – it sets up a wonderful warm glow of hope, helps you feel more integrated. What we need in the West is a Celtic renaissance.
>
> (Self-styled 'New-Ager', Glastonbury, 1993)

There seem to have been two main ways of looking at Celts over the centuries – Celts as 'other' and Celts as 'us'. What has been said or written about Celts has frequently come from the outside. For example, have you ever considered the implications of the term 'the Celtic fringe'? That designation only makes sense if you feel you are in some way at a centre from which areas or people considered Celtic are perceived to be on the periphery. Whether seen as savages or sages, the dominant view of the Celts has for centuries been generated by the centre towards the periphery.

That perception of the Celts as lying on the edge of Europe, remote in both time and space, living repositories of old ways, ancient wisdom and native virtues, has contributed to the view of the Celts at various points as noble savages, and of the Celtic period – however reckoned – as a golden age. As we have seen, from the eighteenth century onwards romantic images of and extravagant claims for the Celts were frequently made by those who were removed from the everyday reality of life in the highlands, rural Ireland and Brittany, and industrial Cornwall and Wales. Indeed, somewhat controversially, writers such as Chapman and James have argued that until the eighteenth century there had never been a group of people who self-consciously self-identified as Celts. In the present Celtic revival, there is strong evidence that the Celts are still thought of as the romantic 'other', signifying that which is lost but longed for in contemporary life, whether in terms of community, characteristics or spirituality.

Thus some would argue that the phenomenon of Celts as 'us' – that is, people consciously self-identifying as Celts – is a comparatively recent phenomenon, observable in the eighteenth century, developing in the nineteenth century and really blossoming in the twentieth. As Chapman notes,

> Not only are there large groups of people thought to be Celts by others (as has happened before), but there are also large groups of people that think they are Celts themselves. This is a very modern phenomenon, but is nevertheless real: if people think they are Celts, who is to gainsay them?

> (Chapman, 1992, p. 251)

There are a myriad reasons why people are self-identifying as Celts. For some folk it allows an opting out of mainstream society and history; it allows one to be not mainstream British, not colonizer, not exploiter, or whatever else one desires *not* to be. For example, one American woman told me how liberating it had been for her to discover her Celtic (Irish) roots, for thereafter she was 'not Anglo', 'not oppressor', and was better able to identify and interact with native Americans and other oppressed minorities. More positively, it gives many people a sense of identity and belonging in multicultural contexts. That this identity might be in some cases aspirational or virtual could be seen as an example of 'globalization'.

> Everywhere, cultural identities are emerging which are not fixed, but poised, in transition, between different positions; which draw on different cultural traditions at the same time; and which are the product of those complicated cross-overs and cultural mixes which are increasingly common in a globalized world.

> (Hall, 1992, p. 310)

'Celtic' is now, undoubtedly, an ethonym – an identity of choice – but, as we have seen, an identity which has moved away purely from considerations of history, language, geography, culture or ethnicity to become a *quality*, or set of qualities, to which people aspire. Celticism allows people to draw on a wide variety of images, ideas, artefacts, landscapes and literatures to concoct a Celticity in accordance with their needs.

Although beyond the scope of this chapter, it must of course be recognized that Celticity has had – and continues to have – considerable political and religious overtones. There has been an agenda within Britain of Celtic as not, or other than, English; in Brittany as not mainstream French; and in Ireland as not British. In some parts of America Celticity has been equated with Irishness and with support for the Republican cause. In Northern Ireland increasing numbers of Protestant Unionists are learning Irish and invoking Celtic heroes such as Finn and Cu Chulainn in their cause (see Nic Craith, 2002, especially Chapter 5). One argument is that as the original Scots were Irish migrating to what *became* Scotland, the Ulster Scots in Ireland have simply come home and can rightfully (re)claim and express Celticity. In some areas Celticity has been associated with Catholicism (for instance in Ireland and the Scottish highlands), but elsewhere it is linked with non-conformism (for example in Wales and Cornwall). All this underlines the difficulty of proclaiming what Celticity either is or stands for.

Conclusion

As we have seen, there are different European versions of Celticity and complex histories behind them. In France, for example, there has been a tendency to conflate the ancient Gauls described by Caesar and contemporary Bretons, and thus 'to see the present-day inhabitants of Armorica as the last unmixed descendants of Vercingetorix' (Leerssen, 1996, p. 15). This is undoubtedly incorrect.

> The Bretons are an early medieval colony from Wales and Cornwall, arriving on the scene long after the Gauls had been romanized. But the strength of the conflation (which also takes in the megalithic monument builders of Carnac) persists, so that Asterix le Gaulois has been given his residence in Brittany and his friend Obelix is in the menhir trade.
>
> (Leerssen, 1996, p. 15)

Originally the plot and texts for the Asterix stories were written by René Goscinny (1926–77), with drawings by Albert Uderzo (b. 1927), who also took on the plots and texts after Goscinny's death. The adventures of Asterix and Obelix originally appeared in the young people's magazine *Pilote* between 1959 and 1974, and from 1961 onwards appeared as separate albums which have been translated into many languages with worldwide sales of over 200 million copies (see Maier, 1998, p. 26).

While the French cartoon-book hero Asterix may perpetuate an erroneous image, the **Asterix** stories have become a highly significant symbol of Celticity in Europe. Set mainly in a Gaulish village, with inhabitants constantly pitted against Caesar's legions, Asterix's companions in the stories include a bard and a Druid. Maier goes so far as to claim that 'No other work of the twentieth century has been so influential in determining a popular image of Celtic culture' (Maier, 1998, p. 26), and it is worth noting that there was outrage in France when, in 2001, it was revealed that the American multinational fast-food chain McDonald's was negotiating to use the Asterix characters for publicity purposes. However, to state the obvious, the hero is Asterix the Gaul, *not* Asterix the Celt, and the cartoons constantly play on and poke fun at different national traits through their caricatures of the Gauls (French), the Goths (Germans), the Helvetians (Swiss) and others.

As Leerssen comments,

> Vague and disparate as the 'Celtic' tradition in European culture may be, known almost exclusively from outside reports, its name, by virtue of its very imprecision, can attract all sorts of speculations and prejudices; the Celts can be disparaged as barbarians or praised as Noble Savages; they can fall under the shadow of ethnocentrism or be glorified in the spotlight of primitivism; they can be exoticized or identified with; with different authors at different periods, they can be made to fit any role (the Us or the Them; the Good, the Bad or the Mysterious) in the ethnic pattern of Europe's *dramatis personae*.

(Leerssen, 1996, p. 3)

Folklorist Henry Glassie claims that 'tradition is the creation of the future out of the past', and that history 'is an artful assembly of materials from the past, designed for usefulness in the future' (Glassie, 1995, p. 395). What we are seeing in contemporary constructions of Celticity – and indeed Europeanness – are 'artful assemblies'. The banknotes of the euro are strong on architectural motifs (with underlying images of building on the past, building a future, a project under construction), and make frequent use of bridges, which can be seen in terms of building metaphorical bridges between countries and between past, present and future. For the purposes of consolidating some sort of European identity, Celticity is being used as a kind of existential euro, a common currency. As we have seen in this chapter, however, such Celtic constructions are nothing new.

References

Bowman, M. (1996) 'Cardiac Celts: images of the Celts in contemporary British paganism', in G. Harvey and C. Hardman (eds), *Paganism Today*, London, Thorsons.

Bowman, M. (2002) 'Contemporary Celtic spirituality', in J. Pearson (ed.), *Belief beyond Boundaries: Wicca, Celtic Spirituality and the New Age*, Aldershot/Milton Keynes, Ashgate/Open University.

Bradley, I. (1993) *The Celtic Way*, London, Darton, Longman & Todd.

Carmichael, A., et al. (eds) (1992) *Carmina Gadelica*, Edinburgh, Floris.

Celt net website: http://www.celt.net

Celtica website: http://www. celtica.wales.com

Champion, T. (1996) 'The Celt in archaeology', in T. Brown (ed.), *Celticism*, Amsterdam, Studia Imagologica (Amsterdam Studies on Cultural Identity, no. 8).

Chapman, M. (1992) *The Celts: the Construction of a Myth*, New York, St Martin's Press.

Clan Keltoi website: http://celt.net/Keltoi.home.html

Clann an Fhaoil-Choin website:http://www.flash./net/~bellbook/faolcu

Collis, J. (1996) 'The origin and spread of the Celts', *Studia Celtica*, vol. xxx, pp. 17–34.

Curtis, D. (2000) 'Creative ethnicity: one man's invention of Celtic identity', in A. Hale and P. Payton (eds), *New Directions in Celtic Studies*, Exeter, Exeter University Press.

Glassie, H. (1995) 'Tradition', *Journal of American Folklore*, vol. 108, no. 430, pp. 395–412.

Hale, A. (2000) '"In the eye of the sun": the relationship between the Cornish Gorseth and esoteric Druidry', in P. Payton (ed.), *Cornish Studies Eight*, Exeter, Exeter University Press.

Hale, A. and Thornton S. (2000) 'Pagans, pipers and politicos: constructing "Celtic" in a festival context', in A. Hale and P. Payton (eds), *New Directions in Celtic Studies*, Exeter, Exeter University Press.

Hall, S. (1992) 'The question of cultural identity', in S. Hall, D. Held and T. McGrew (eds), *Modernity and its Futures*, Cambridge/Milton Keynes, Polity/Open University.

James, S. (1999) *The Atlantic Celts: Ancient People or Modern Invention?*, London, British Museum Press.

Jones, L. (2000) 'Stone circles and tables round: representing the early Celts in film and television', in A. Hale and P. Payton (eds), *New Directions in Celtic Studies*, Exeter, Exeter University Press.

Kiberd, D. (1995) *Inventing Ireland*, London, Jonathan Cape.

Kilsyth website: http://www.kilsyth-scotland.co.uk/european.htm

Leerssen, J. (1996) 'Celticism', in T. Brown (ed.), *Celticism*, Amsterdam, Studia Imagologica (Amsterdam Studies on Cultural Identity, no. 8).

Löffler, Marion (2000) *'A Book of Mad Celts': John Wickens and the Celtic Congress of Caernarfon 1904*, Ceredigion, Gomer.

Maier, B. (1998) *Dictionary of Celtic Religion and Culture*, Woodbridge, Boydell & Brewer.

Matthews, C. (1993) 'A Celtic quest', in *World Religions in Education 1993/1994*, London, Shap Working Party.

Meek, D. E. (2000) *The Quest for Celtic Christianity*, Edinburgh, Handsel.

Morgan, P. (1975) *Iolo Morganwg*, Cardiff, University of Wales Press.

Nic Craith, M. (2002) *Plural Identities, Singular Narratives: the Case of Northern Ireland*, New York/Oxford, Berghahn.

O Se, Seamus (1997–8) 'From crossroads to *Riverdance*', in Riverdance: *the Show, Official Programme*, Dublin, Abhann Productions.

Payton, P. (2000) 'Re-inventing Celtic Australia', in A. Hale and P. Payton (eds), *New Directions in Celtic Studies*, Exeter, Exeter University Press.

Piccini, A. (1996) 'Filming through the mists of time: Celtic constructions and the documentary', *Current Anthropology*, vol. 37 (supplement), pp. 87–111.

Piccini, A. (1999) 'Of memory and things past', *Heritage in Wales*, no. 12 (spring), pp. 18–20.

Piggott, S. (1989) *Ancient Britons and the Antiquarian Imagination*, London, Thames & Hudson.

Piggott, S. [1968] (1993) *The Druids*, London, Thames & Hudson.

Pittock, M. G. H. (1999) *Celtic Identity and the British Image*, Manchester, Manchester University Press.

Porter, J. (2001) '"Bring me the head of James MacPherson": the execution of Ossian and the wellsprings of folkloristic discourse', *Journal of American Folklore*, vol. 114, no. 454, pp. 396–435.

Raoult, M. (1996) 'The Druid revival in Brittany, France and Europe', in P. Carr-Gomm (ed.), *The Druid Renaissance: the Voice of Druidry Today*, London, Thorsons.

Riverdance website: http://www.riverdance.com

Said, E. W. (1995) *Orientalism*, Harmondsworth, Penguin.

Shallcrass, P. and Restall Orr, E. (2001) *A Druid Directory: a Guide to Druidry and Druid Orders*, St Leonards on-Sea, British Druid Order.

Shore, C. (2001) 'Nation and state in the European Union', in *Times-Places-Passage. Ethnological Approaches in the New Millennium: Plenary Papers of the 7th SIEF Conference*, ed. R. Kiss and A. Paládi-Kovács, Budapest, Institute of Ethnology.

Sister Fidelma website: http://www.sisterfidelma.com

Sutcliffe, S. and Bowman, M. (eds) (2000) *Beyond New Age: Exploring Alternative Spirituality*, Edinburgh, Edinburgh University Press.

Thornton, S. (2000) 'Reading the record bins: the commercial construction of Celtic music', in A. Hale and P. Payton (eds), *New Directions in Celtic Studies*, Exeter, Exeter University Press.

Tierney, J. (1960) 'The Celtic ethnography of Posidonius', *Proceedings of the Royal Irish Academy*, 60c, pp. 189–275.

Tierney, J. (1976) 'The Celts and the classical authors', in J. Roftery (ed.), *The Celts*, Dublin/Cork, Mercier.

University of Aberystwyth website: http://www.aber.ac.uk/aberonline

4

Architecture and identities: from the Open-Air Museum Movement to Mickey Mouse

TIM BENTON

Introduction

What part did architecture play in giving form to European, national or regional identities in the twentieth century? Monumental and representative architecture has been on the whole an insensitive medium for expressing national identities over the last 100 years. Most state buildings have been designed either in a stripped classical style or in the Modernist international style which had its origins in Europe in the 1920s and swept the continent after the Second World War. There was little to distinguish any of these buildings from each other, except for the representational art which decorated them (frescoes, sculptures and ornamentation). For example, there is little on the outside of Johan Sirén's parliament building in Helsinki (dating from 1937) to alert the viewer to the fierce patriotism of a Finnish nation celebrating emancipation from Russia. On the other hand, national and regional identities were often expressed in the conservation of vernacular architecture and, more specifically, in the creation of open-air museums of vernacular buildings in city centres. The mission of such museums was defined at an ICOM (International Council of Museums) conference in Geneva on 9 July 1956 as 'the selection, dismantling, transportation and reconstruction ... of buildings characteristic of threatened lifestyles, dwelling types, peasant and craft skills and cultures' (Zippelius, 1974, p. 31).

In this chapter, I shall explore the idea that national and subnational identities have frequently found architectural inspiration in buildings that are physically, culturally and temporally remote from the actual circumstances of the target audience. Far from seeing the industrialized administrative capital as the heart and soul of a nation (as, for example, Paris had always been represented by the French),

Figure 4.1 League of Nations Building, Geneva, 1928–32. Photo: Tim Benton

Figure 4.2 Johan Sidgrid Sirén, parliament building, Helsinki, 1937. Photo: Tim Benton

many people looked to the 'authentic' rural and primitive to capture a sense of identity. Of course, these things are never simple. A Parisian may think of herself also as a Gascon, while a farmer in Burgundy may also see his French identity properly symbolized by Parisian buildings and artefacts. Commonly associated with the Open-Air Museum Movement was research into and proselytizing for diversity of languages, the recovery of folk tales and legends, the recovery of older and more primitive forms of life and labour, and even the conservation and cultivation of old breeds of wild and domesticated animals. Paradoxically, the search for national roots in primitive and 'old' vernacular buildings from remote regions often turned out to demonstrate that climate, geology and patterns of cultivation mattered more than national boundaries in determining built form. A certain homogeneity can be seen in many of the European open-air museums. And just as urban elites looked to the rural periphery to construct myths of 'authentic' and 'pure' identity, Europe as a whole was seen as a source of 'authentic' inspiration in the United States of America. Many Americans searched for a sense of their identity in the simple American rural communities of their youth (Abraham Lincoln and Walt Disney are two famous examples), but others yearned for a remote identity in 'old' Europe. Here, too, American memories of the 'old countries' tended to homogenize European vernacular architecture. Linking these two *topoi* are the fairy stories and children's yarns – almost invariably set in primitive and remote peasant communities – that were given an increasingly global form in the animated features and theme parks of Walt Disney. After tracing some of the history of the open-air museums in Europe, therefore, I shall turn to the representation of European architecture in the films and theme parks of Walt Disney's various enterprises, notably Euro Disney near Paris (later renamed Disneyland Paris). Perhaps these highly developed products of global capitalism can offer as real a reflection of what 'Europe' means today in built form as any other. But I shall argue that, with the passing of the enthusiasm for the primitive past as expressed in the early open-air museums, neither their successors nor the Disneyland type of attraction captures most people's sense of identity. Mass tourism has brought an increasingly large number of people into direct contact with European towns, cities and countryside which have themselves been prepared to receive them by a mixture of conservation, pastiche and commercial packaging. It is not uncommon to find European cities compared to Disneyland.

The Open-Air Museum Movement

The Open-Air Museum Movement proper was founded in the 1890s in Scandinavia, spread slowly to Holland and north Germany before 1914, expanded in central Europe during the 1920s and 1930s and then flourished all over the continent after the Second World War, particularly in the central European territories of the old Soviet Union (see Appendix). The characteristic method of these museums was to exhibit actual buildings transported from remote areas, complete with native people from these regions, in their original costumes, practising their crafts and industries, tending their animals and performing dances, poetry and songs on special occasions. The idea was expressed in utopian form by the founder of the first open-air museum, the Swedish linguist and ethnographer Artur Hazelius (1833–1901). Not content with exhibiting collections of ethnographical objects from outlying regions of Sweden and Norway, he dreamed of re-creating the living world of the fast disappearing peasant communities.

> We shall rebuild the old farmsteads ... People shall behave in these houses as they did before, the cat shall lie and purr by the stove, the dog shall sun itself in front of its kennel, the animals shall graze on the meadow.
>
> (Quoted in Edenheim, 1995, p. 8)

The keynote of the open-air museum is authenticity: everything is 'real' and the visitor is prompted to contemplate both the hardships and the beauty of life in the wild – the life which forged the heroes of legend and the ancestors of the urban dweller. But, from the first, open-air museums also had a pedagogic and entertainment function which went beyond allowing the visitor to 'see for herself' how things were in the past. It was a small step from the genuine peasant in costume, demonstrating their craft, to the employment of amateur or professional museum guides (born and reared in the cities), also in costume, explaining the life of yore. And from the start there has been a progression from the performing of poetry, songs and dances by people from remote regions who learned them as children, to folk displays put on by professional performers. The ethnographic purists never accepted the legitimacy of any folk performances. For example, a group of specialists in Holland around 1914 were unanimously of the opinion that

> To make people wear costumes which in reality are no longer worn, to satisfy the curiosity of the public, is the equivalent of staging a banal historic review and will finish by making ridiculous local costumes which really are still part of a living tradition.
>
> (Quoted in De Jong and Skougaard, 1992, p. 153)

From the start, tensions existed between the authenticity of architectural and design conservation, the desire to make the life behind these artefacts live and the financial need to provide entertainment and instruction to a large public. In a very different context, similar debates between imagination, populism and authenticity preoccupied the 'imagineers' (image engineers) employed by Walt Disney to design the theme parks in California, Florida, Tokyo and Paris. Disney conceived his theme parks in the idioms of film and advertising: his staff were 'cast members', the parks were laid out as a succession of 'scenes'. The 'imagineers' used 'inspirational' paintings and renderings to explore the fantasy world of the theme parks, but they also carried out meticulous research into real locations and cultures as part of their preparation. In even this, the most cut-throat and price-sensitive end of the entertainment business, 'authenticity' had marketable values which were at the core of Disney's dream. The 'guests' in a Disney theme park are to be transported into another world, and this world must be as 'real' as it is 'fantastic', like a dream. Of course, the interest in the buildings of the past is expressed in countless other forms, in mass tourism, in visiting town centres, churches and country houses and in TV programmes recreating the lifestyles of the past. We shall see that this new cultural tourism has had an impact on both the open-air museums and the theme parks.

Eclecticism and regionalism

The Open-Air Museum Movement was in part motivated by cultural, ethical and patriotic emotions, but also in part by archaeological, architectural and art historical research. Before looking at the origins and spread of the open-air museum, we should briefly examine the architectural context. During the nineteenth century, Eclecticism allowed architects to choose different historic styles to express different functions and associations. Thus Sir Charles Barry and A. W. N. Pugin were required to design the new British Houses of Parliament in 1840 in an Elizabethan style, to reflect the importance of the Tudor period in the evolution of the 'mother of parliaments'. Victorian churches were usually designed in a gothic style and banks and club houses often in a Renaissance palace manner, evoking the origins of modern commerce, while senate houses (as opposed to parliament buildings) were almost invariably planned in a Greek or Roman style.

A number of reactions against Eclecticism developed during the nineteenth century, of which one key movement was Regionalism. Regionalist architects, all over Europe, shared certain assumptions (Vigato, 1994). They believed that Eclecticism had gone too far in allowing architects to pick and choose architectural styles. They held that the best buildings are those which respect their topographical context, in terms of the materials used, cultural traditions and architectural history. People from a particular region feel comfortable, so the theory runs, with buildings which look and perform like the traditional buildings in the area. These structures serve to perpetuate and reinforce group memories. Urban people, contaminated by the 'devil's darkness' of industry, are unfavourably compared with the 'timeless peasant' who appears to retain the basic values and stylistic expression of an age-old vernacular. Architects, trained in the cities, lose contact with the local crafts of building and the emotional needs of their rural counterparts and become deracinated cosmopolitan intellectuals. As the Polish painter and critic Stanisław Witkiewicz said in 1903 of the Polish regions of the Austro-Hungarian empire,

> Even knowing nothing of [John] Ruskin and [William] Morris we may find that their theories and that one of their dreams can be realized in real life. [Here] the heads of both the mighty and the poorest are protected by roofs of a single style: churches, salons and chambers, and the poorest cottages gleam brilliantly with the same beauty. The civilising foundations for all ranks of society lie in this instance in the 'lowest classes', a source that Morris and Ruskin, who did not encounter the peasantry, sought in the art of the middle ages.
>
> (Quoted in Crowley, 1995, p. 9, n. 20)

Open-air museums were intended to present the urban masses with living demonstrations of this lost innocence. A close parallel can be found in the construction of nationalist cults around epic poems, sagas, fairy tales and folk culture in general, stimulated in the early nineteenth century by Romanticism but continued into the twentieth century, not least in the film industry. A necessary feature of this kind of yearning was a sense of loss, whether for the heroes of days gone by (from Beowulf to the American cowboy), for dying ways of life, language and customs or, more literally, for 'lost' territories under foreign domination.

While English writers explored Icelandic sagas, Polish intellectuals such as Stanisław Witkiewicz in Russian Warsaw during the 1890s looked to the vernacular architecture of the Górale people (highlanders) in the Tatra mountains (around Zakopane, then in the Austro-Hungarian empire) as inspiration for a 'national' Polish architectural style (Crowley, 1995, p. 11). In fact, J. Baranowski and A. Scholtze, who founded the Tatra Museum in Zakopane, contemplated the establishment of an open-air museum there as early as 1888 (Zippelius, 1974, p. 205). And in 1894 six vernacular buildings were

Lemberg is now L'tit in the Ukraine. As Lemberg it was the capital of Galicia in Austria in 1894. It was part of Poland between 1919–39, and invaded by the Soviet Union in 1939.

transported to the Jubilee Exhibition site in **Lemberg**. Polish nationalism was also expressed in two small open-air museums in Wdzydže (1906) and Nowogród, near Łomža (1909).

Finnish patriots, such as the painter Akseli Gallen-Kalela or the composer Jean Sibelius, explored the remote forests of Karelia, in the Russian Grand Duchy of Finland, crossing the frontier into the Russian empire to seek the heartland of Finnish culture: the homeland of the heroes of the Kalevala epic poems (see below). And many German and Scandinavian writers began to undertake northern tours, notably above the Arctic circle to visit the Laplanders (Sami), considered by many to be the last truly 'primitive' people in Europe.

Another strand of Regionalist thinking was Structural Rationalism, the theory that every architectural form should reflect the structural properties of the materials of which it is made. In a sense the origins of Structural Rationalism go back to the Roman architect Vitruvius, who in the first century CE traced the origins of the classical temple to a 'primitive hut' made of simple tree trunks in the forest. He explained, convincingly, the details of the Doric temple as a translation into stone of the structural forms necessary to keep out the rain in the 'original' wooden hut. The primitive wooden hut, then, could be seen as the 'authentic' original of the later stone copy. The habit of tracing back the logic of architectural style to primitive structural principles became increasingly important in the nineteenth century. Open-air museums presented examples of simple but solid constructions which could be admired for their ingenuity, durability and aesthetic purity.

National Romanticism

Towards the end of the nineteenth century, under the pressure of nationalist hopes and frustrations, many architects in Scandinavia and Germany developed a version of Regionalism known as National Romanticism. The origins of this movement can be traced to the writings of Johann Gottfried Herder (1744–1803) and German Romanticism, in which a myth of 'northern peoples' and their culture could be contrasted with the French culture that dominated most European cities at the time. Herder and his many followers believed that a study of Germanic and Scandinavian languages, archaeology, architectural history and literature would show a common heritage and tradition. Privileged witnesses to this heritage were those primitive peoples, typically living on the fringes of Europe, from Scandinavia to Transylvania, who had not yet been 'spoiled' by civilization. The open-air museums founded in Scandinavia and north Germany between 1891 and 1914 were therefore a means of capturing their experience and making it visible to others.

One strand in this thinking made the racial argument explicit. People, according to this theory, are formed by their racial origins and their attachment to particular places. For example, in 1897 the German medieval architectural historian Friedrich Seesselberg (1861–c. 1926) published an important book on the origins of German and Scandinavian medieval architecture in which he asserted that the 'northern peoples' shared the same 'race experience' that explained the similarities in architectural forms in the area. After the First World War such ideas were developed in Germany into a full-blooded racial theory of architecture by Gustaf Kossinna (1858–1931) who, after joining the Nazi party, stimulated an official policy, promoted by high-ranking figures such as Darre, Rosenberg and Himmler, of venerating archaeological sites and vernacular buildings which preserved a 'true German' spirit. This prompted the foundation of a new wave of open-air museums in the 1930s. For example, Heinrich Ottenjann founded a large museum in Cloppenberg in 1934 (opened in 1936). In a bizarre example of the use of vernacular architecture in the service of *Realpolitik,* the buildings in the East Prussian open-air museum at Königsberg (founded by Richard Dethlefsen in 1909–13) were transported to Hohenstein (Polish Olsztynek) in 1940 as a sign of the cultural unity of 'greater Germany'. Seriously damaged during the war, they were rebuilt and now form part of the large Muzeum Budownictwa Ludowego (museum of vernacular architecture, covering 34 hectares).

A number of postwar open-air museums sprang up in the Warsaw Pact countries. For instance, during the 1950s and 1960s several were founded in the Baltic regions (Estonia, Lithuania and Latvia), following the example of Riga in 1932. In Poland open-air museums were founded in Zubrzyca Górna (1955), Sanok (1958), Chorzów (1961), Opole-Bierkowice (1961), Torún (1966) and Nowy Sacz (1968). Between 1966 and 1970 many museums were also founded in Hungary in Zalaegerszeg, Szentendre, Szombathely, Bugac and Nyiregyháza, while a similar enthusiasm gripped Romania and Czechoslovakia too. The Village and Folk Art Museum in Bucharest, whose origins go back to a series of ethnographic exhibitions in the 1930s, was significantly enlarged after the war and retained a memory of Romanian vernacular architecture throughout the Ceauşescu regime.

Many of the postwar open-air museums 'reunited' vernacular cultures divided by the Iron Curtain. For example, in West Germany five large open-air museums were founded in the north of the country between 1953 and 1961 (in Hamburg, Kommern, Hagen, Detmold and Kiel), while the first such museum in the south was opened in 1963 in Gutach (Schwarzfeld). In East Germany, meanwhile, the existing museum in Diesdorf (founded 1911) was enlarged after 1951, while new foundations followed in Lehde (1954), Landwüst (1960), Alt-Schwerin (1962) and Klockenhagen (1969). Most of these were promoted and sponsored by state or regional funds. Many of the new open-air museums, however, were private institutions, reliant on entry fees and research grants and thus dependent on people's increased mobility and the growing tourist industry. This trend accelerated in the 1980s, when many previously public open-air museums were driven into the private sector by governments whose officials were no longer motivated by the 'scientific' conservation principles and the nationalist yearnings of the founders. Open-air museums therefore exist at the intersection of leisure and political forces, and both factors profoundly reflect attitudes of identity.

Origins of the Open-Air Museums Movement

The first open-air museum to be officially opened to the public was Skansen, in Stockholm, inaugurated on 11 October 1891. Artur Hazelius, who had carried out fundamental research into Nordic languages, had begun to form an ethnographical collection in 1873, which he exhibited at the Universal Exhibition in Paris in 1878, and in 1888 he embarked on the foundation of the Nordic Museum in Stockholm. Travelling all over Sweden in his study of Swedish languages and dialects, he had been struck by the rapidity with which certain customs, costumes and practices were disappearing. Over the years, he had watched local people putting out their church boats on the lake to attend the church at Leksand in the picturesque Dalarna region, and had noticed how the old costumes and material objects were being replaced by new ones. He therefore began to collect clothing and artefacts, just as he had documented and regularized local dialects. The next step was to put these objects into a realistic setting. Hazelius experimented with using painted backdrops and wax figures of peasants in costume, but at the Paris exhibition he introduced into his scenes live women from the Dalarna region, in traditional costume, practising their crafts.

In the series of world exhibitions which began with the Great Exhibition in London of 1851, it was common to exhibit exotic peoples from the colonies or the provinces alongside reconstructions of buildings and animals from their homelands. For example, in the Colonial Exhibition in Amsterdam held in 1883 a highlight of the show was a reconstructed Indonesian *kampong* (settlement), complete with native Indonesians playing their music, demonstrating their crafts and working their water buffalo. In many cases, peasants from outlying European areas were also put on show, partly for their picturesque value, partly to demonstrate the 'internal empires' of subject peoples and partly to demonstrate the economic cycle of production and consumption of modern industrialized capitalism. This kind of approach was coming under fire from many of those who were trying to assert their regional independence. For instance, at the Vienna *Weltausstellung* of 1873 many Saxons, Ruthenians and Transylvanians took exception to the exhibition of peasants and their crafts and buildings as 'primitive' and backward. At the Paris *Exposition Universelle* of 1867, on the other hand, both Sweden and Norway had exhibited replicas of old wooden buildings, and this time the intention was to take pride in the age-old heritage of Nordic culture. Artur Hazelius knew of these buildings, because in his plan for Skansen, drafted in 1890, he proposed to reconstruct the Swedish building on the site of his open-air museum. He claimed that he had been inspired to create Skansen by the French colonial pavilions at the Paris Exhibition of 1878 (De Jong and Skougaard, 1992, p. 152). These reconstructed buildings served really as shop windows for the display of colonial products. Bernhard Olsen, the founder of the Danish Open-Air Museum of Lyngby (1906), on the other hand, was more impressed by a Dutch exhibit at the Paris Exhibition of 1878, a complete house from the small Friesian village of Hindeloopen, where the public could freely penetrate all the rooms, and where each object was in its 'natural' place. This wasn't precisely a question of 'authenticity', since parts of the house were reconstructed in new materials, and all the furniture and objects came from different locations. It was the psychologically important factor of entering into the house, as if you lived there, which fuelled Olsen's imagination. At the Colonial Exhibition in Amsterdam (1883) and the Jubilee Exhibition in Lemberg (1894), however, actual buildings were transported and reassembled in the exhibition grounds.

Stave churches: wooden churches made of vertical planks, common in Norway in medieval times.

From 1881 to 1888, King Oscar II of Sweden and Norway began to have some famous Norwegian wooden buildings, which were in danger of destruction, transported to and reconstructed on his estate at Bigdøy. **Stave churches** and farm buildings of this kind were brought from all over Norway over the next decades and formed the basis for an open-air museum which was formally opened in 1894. This seemed to be the logical extension of a long process of surveying medieval buildings, carrying out digs on Viking remains and restoring old castles and churches, which had been promoted by art historians like Nicolay Nicolaysen (1817–1911) and the German architect Hermann Major Schirmer (1845–1913). In the culture of National Romanticism these old buildings were seen as important not just to the region or country they were in, but to a wider understanding of the 'Nordic spirit'. German art historians and architects played a major role in this conservation drive.

Figure 4.3 Replica of Swedish fifteenth-century farmhouse from Ornässtuga at the 1867 exhibition, Paris. Photo: Nordic Museum, Stockholm

It was just a short step to link this kind of conservation with Hazelius's cultural programme. Hazelius began to acquire buildings, and indeed groups of buildings such as the farmstead complex from Mora in the Dalarna region, complete with all their contents, livestock and even the people themselves. He also set about purchasing the land for Skansen on the island of Djurgården in Stockholm to set them up. From the inauguration of Skansen buildings from all over Sweden could be seen from the tents of the Laplanders in the Arctic circle to the well-equipped Kyrkhult farmhouse from Blekinge in southern Götaland in the south. In some ways, this idea is similar to the motivating spirit behind various collections of miniature architecture, where model buildings from all over a country are exhibited in one place. A characteristic example is the 'Suisse Miniature' village outside Lugano in Italian Switzerland (colour plates 3 and 4). Here the blend of traditional vernacular and historic buildings and modern technology is revealing: an artificial hillside of chalets is juxtaposed with a suspended jet plane, for instance. The political purpose of Suisse Miniature is clear: to show the Italian Swiss of the **Ticino** all the varieties of architecture and culture in French and especially German Switzerland across the Alps. Similar miniature villages exist all over Europe, and one of them, Madurodam in the Netherlands, made a big impression on Walt

The Ticino is the Italian-speaking region of Switzerland around Lugano

Disney when he visited it in 1935 with his colleague Bill Cottrell, influencing the conception of Disneyland in Anaheim, California, twenty years later (Allan, 1999, p. 228).

The difference at Skansen, of course, is that the buildings are full-size, 'authentic' and contain people. A group of women from the Dalarna region lived permanently on the site from the outset and worked the farm (colour plate 6). The paintings of Anders Zorn give an evocative image of the kind of culture preserved at Skansen. One shows a midsummer dance in 1897 in Mora, where Zorn lived, complete with a maypole (colour plate 5). Not only did Zorn paint the Dalarna people, he began to collect wooden houses from the area and reconstruct them himself. The Mora farmstead was the first to be moved to Skansen (complete with a maypole, as in the Zorn painting) and captures the picturesque but hard life and culture of the Dalarna people and a building style full of robust good sense and fine detailing. Another painting, this time by Carl Schubert (colour plate 1), shows one of the Mora farmhouses in 1894, with a woman in traditional costume spinning and examples of her work on display.

From the first half-dozen buildings at the turn of the century, Skansen grew steadily to include over 100 buildings, including whole streets, workshops and light industries. A great effort was made to include buildings of every type, evoking every ethnic group in Sweden. For example, a group of primitive wooden buildings was brought from the forests of northern Värmland (colour plate 7).

Figure 4.4 Mora farmhouse, Skansen. Photo: Tim Benton

These houses came from the area known as Finnbygden (Finn territory) and derived from the encouragement given by the Swedish government to Finnish immigrants in the sixteenth and seventeenth centuries to colonize the uncultivated forest areas on the Norwegian border.

Skansen was conceived as a microcosm of the whole country, in a literal sense. The site was laid out to mimic the geography of Sweden, from the balmy pastures of Danish-speaking Skåne in the south to the frozen forests of the north. The range of cultures represented at Skansen varies widely. On the north side of the site were the primitive spring and autumn encampments of the nomadic Laplanders (Sami), their reindeer and even a collection of wild animals from above the Arctic circle. The Lapp encampment shows the kinds of dwelling built in the province of Jämtland and the Gällivare parish of Lapland at the turn of the century, in between the local people's winter quarters in the valley forests and the summer grazing on the higher slopes. The herd of reindeer at Skansen, for which an artificial mountain was constructed, was a popular attraction.

A very different style of building is shown in the Kyrkhult farmhouse, a little further north, with its turf-covered roof and picturesque beehives. The interior shows fine workmanship in the furniture and a set of beautiful tapestries painted by Clement Håkansson in 1727–95 (colour plate 2). The son of the house described the family's surprise when Artur Hazelius visited them in 1890, the year before the opening of Skansen.

> Hazelius came to us late one evening at about eleven o'clock ... Bengta opened the door and Hazelius handed her a card with his name on it .... Inside the house, he started talking to my father, and Father and Bengta followed Hazelius through the downstairs and upstairs rooms of the building, and you could tell he was surprised at this old way of building, because he kept clapping his hands as he went about in all the corners. In the end Hazelius asked my father if he wanted to sell the house, and that was done in the winter of 1891.
>
> (Quoted in Edenheim, 1995, p. 69)

An interesting contrast is provided by the Finnish National Open-Air Museum on the island of Seurasaari, in the vicinity of Helsinki. Founded in imitation of Skansen in 1909 by ethnologist Axel Olai Hekel, it had a strategic purpose in aiming to develop a sense of national consciousness during a period of oppression by the Russian state. Although the Russian empire had allowed the Grand Duchy of Finland a real measure of autonomy throughout most of the nineteenth century, Russian control was considerably tightened in the 1890s and especially after 1899. Hekel worked for the State

Figure 4.5 Kyrkhult farmhouse, Blekinge, Skansen. Photo: Tim Benton

Archaeological Commission of Finland. It was part of his aim to show not only that Finnish vernacular architecture shared distinctive characteristics (very different from Sweden's, despite a similar range of climates) but that it provided an age-old example of Nordic culture from which all the Nordic peoples could learn. Just as Finnish vernacular housing was seen in Swedish Skansen as 'primitive' (but also 'authentic'), the Finns looked to the eastern province of Karelia as the heart of their primitive consciousness.

Karelia had been, in remote medieval times, a prosperous and extensive power, stretching from the Arctic circle to the Baltic. Throughout the medieval and modern period Karelia was fought over by the Russian empire and Sweden, and then by the Soviet Union and Finland. Since the foundation of St Petersburg at the eastern end of the Baltic, all Russian regimes have viewed the adjoining Karelia as a security issue. Indeed, since 1944–5 a large section of eastern and southern Karelia has been closed to Finns, as a militarized buffer zone protecting St Petersburg. In the nineteenth century, however, when Finland was a semi-autonomous grand duchy of the Russian empire, access to Karelia was easier and many intellectuals explored the beautiful remote landscape of forests, lakes and jagged hills on both sides of the border. An important stimulus for this came with the publication in 1835 of a collection of Karelian poems known as the Old Kalevala. This 12,000-line epic was compiled from first-hand research in eastern Karelia by Finnish-Ugric language specialist Elias Lönnrot and soon afterwards was translated into Swedish (in 1841) and French (in 1845). A subsequent, extended edition, the New Kalevala, followed in 1849 and was translated into German in 1852, in which form it influenced the poet Longfellow, whose *Song of Hiawatha* owes much to it. By 1900 one or other edition of the Kalevala had been translated into virtually all the European languages and joined the corpus of sagas and epic poems which represented to Europeans a sense of origin and identity.

The association between myths of national consciousness, the vexed question of boundaries and a search for a national architectural style can be seen in the career of the painter who is often described as the 'Finnish national artist' (Martin and Sivén, 1995). Axel Gallen, like many Swedish and Finnish artists, was trained in Paris (in 1884–9). Following his marriage to Kaarle Slöör, the daughter of a Finnish nationalist and herself a Kalevala specialist, he took his honeymoon, like the young Sibelius, in Karelia and began to develop a militant Finnish nationalism. He changed his name from the Swedish Axel Gallen to Akseli Gallen-Kallela in 1907. By the 1890s Gallen-Kallela was obsessed with the Kalevala epics, illustrating them in wall frescoes, books and magazines. Following the clampdown on the Grand Duchy of Finland by Tsar Nicholas II in 1899, the Finnish architects Gesellius, Lindgren and Saarinen collaborated with Gallen-Kallela to build a Finnish 'national' pavilion at the Universal Exhibition of 1900 in Paris in defiance of the Russian authorities. Gallen-Kallela's frescoes of the Kalevala legends filled the dome. They were later redone for the dome of the National Museum in Helsinki.

Meanwhile, Gallen-Kallela had built himself a wooden studio deep in the forests overlooking Lake Ruovesi, northwest of Helsinki. Although not located in Karelia, the house – which he called Kallela – attempted to recreate the simple but noble wooden architecture of Karelia. In this, Gallen-Kallela was following the example of a number of other Finnish intellectuals who built rustic retreats as a nationalist gesture. The successful Arts and Crafts architects Gesellius, Lindgren and Saarinen established an artists' colony called Hvitträsk near Helsinki, incorporating simple log cabins, based on Karelian buildings, into an increasingly elaborate sequence of spaces (colour plate 8). This house (widely publicized in books and articles) became well known in international Arts and Crafts circles for its fine craftsmanship, bold decoration and rich colours. Later Gallen-Kallela built a rather more comfortable home in the outskirts of Helsinki, complete with a castellated octagonal tower. It's important to note the characteristic mixture of intense local patriotism and cosmopolitanism here. Akseli Gallen-Kallela was a well-travelled man, who was feted in Budapest, Paris and London. Like many European artists and intellectuals who had been fascinated by 'primitive peoples' in their own countries, for him a logical next step was to seek out primitive but noble peoples elsewhere. Gallen-Kallela duly

Figure 4.6 Finnish pavilion, 1900, Universal Exhibition, Paris. Photo: Museum of Finnish Architecture, Helsinki

Figure 4.7 Akseli Gallen-Kallela's studio, overlooking Lake Ruovesi, 1895. Photo: Gallen-Kallela Museum, Tarvaspaa

went on safari in British East Africa during the 1920s, painting the hunters he encountered there as well as the animals.

In Seurasaari, therefore, it is not surprising to find examples of vernacular buildings from Karelia and other outlying areas. The Pertinotsa farmhouse (some 100 kilometres on the Russian side of the current border) is characteristic of the self-sufficient working buildings of the Karelian region, with spaces for the animals on the upper floor during the winter months and a number of cottage industries for all members of the family during the long days and nights of enforced enclosure.

But Karelian buildings can also be found in the museum of wooden buildings in Moscow and in the open-air museum of Malye Korely, not far from Arkhangelsk in Russia. Another Russian open-air museum celebrating Karelia is at Petrozavodsk and the island of Kizhi (some 200 kilometres to the east of the current Finnish–Russian border). In the early part of the nineteenth century Elias Lönnrot had travelled throughout Russian Karelia in his search for the old songs and poems, visiting Petrozavodsk, as had Gallen-Kallela and other Finnish nationalists. Russian scholars, such as Pavel Rybnikov (1831–85), added to the corpus of sagas collected by Lönnrot, while the Russian architect Lev Dal began to record and restore old vernacular buildings in the 1870s. The Russian equivalent of Akseli Gallen-Kallela, Ivan Bilibin, also visited Russian Karelia and found there the peasant costumes, log cabin buildings and brightly coloured decoration which he used to illustrate folk tales and modern children's stories. Bilibin travelled widely in north Russia, seeking out primitive wooden buildings, which he photographed, and works of arts and crafts, which he collected avidly. Bilibin was aware of current

Figure 4.8 Pertinotsa farmhouse, Karelia from Suojarri, 1880s, interior, showing byre on upper floor, Seurasaari. Photo: Tim Benton

Architecture and identities: from the Open-Air Museum Movement to Mickey Mouse

TIM BENTON

1 Carl Schubert, painting of interior of Östnors farmhouse (Mora region) 1894. Photo: Skansen (Skala Books) 1995

2 Kyrkhult farmhouse, from Blekinge, interior with painted tapestries, one by Clemet Håkansson (1729–95). Photo: Skansen (Skala Books) 1995

3 Suisse Miniature, Lugano. Photo: Tim Benton

4 Suisse Miniature, Lugano. Photo: Tim Benton

5 Anders Zorn, Midsummer Dance, 1897. Photo: © National Museum of Fine Arts, Stockholm No. 1063

6 Dalarna women, c.1890. Photo: Skansen (Skala Books) 1995

7 Finn Settlement from Lekvattnet and Gräsmark, Skansen. Photo: Skansen (Skala Books) 1995

8 Gesellius, Lindgren and Saarinen, Hvittrask, near Helsinki 1901–23. Photo: Tim Benton

9 Main Street, Euro Disney. Photo: Tim Benton

10 European Square, Euro Disney. Photo: Tim Benton

11 Sleeping Beauty's magic castle, Euro Disney. Photo: Tim Benton

12 The fairy tale, inside Sleeping Beauty's castle. Photo: Tim Benton

14 Disney vernacular cottage, Euro Disney. Photo: Tim Benton

13 Urban children posing with a Disney 'cast member', Euro Disney. Photo: Tim Benton

graphic art in Paris and Germany, but his search for the primitive and bold was characteristic of the time.

It can be seen from this example that Karelian arts and crafts and vernacular buildings could feed both Finnish and Russian yearnings for national identity. Paradoxically, the Karelian language has survived better in Russian Karelia than in the Finnish region, where state nationalism has imposed the Finnish language in schools. According to Karelian nationalists, 300,000 Karelians from the Russian side of the border fled to Finland after the Second World War, while Russian sources claim that most of the Karelian and Finnish people were content to stay in the Karelian Autonomous Soviet Socialist Republic (formed in 1923). You only have to consult the internet, however, to see the passion with which people who think of themselves as Karelian, and who emigrated to Finland after the Second World War, view their 'homeland' in Russian Karelia. Clearly, a visit to Seurasaari, and participation in the various folk festivals staged there to celebrate the life of the different regions, could be a very moving experience. The Kizhi island open-air museum has one of the finest collections of wooden architecture in Europe. Ivan Bilibin marvelled at the sweep of constructive fantasy in the villages and churches originally on the island, which gave him the impression of being on the threshold of a fairy-tale land at world's end. The house of the peasant Sergeyev (dating from 1908–10) in the village of Logmoruchei, for instance, belongs to the same type as the slightly earlier Pertinotsa farmhouse in the Seurasaari open-air museum (see Figure 4.8). The presentation of these buildings, and the reverence associated with them, must be placed in the context of the area's history of violent events, contested borders and massive displacement of populations.

The Danish Open-Air Museum of Lyngby was opened in 1901 by Bernhard Olsen, who had followed developments in Sweden, Norway and Finland closely. His aims were specifically nationalistic.

> In the choice of buildings at Lyngby, I have tried to follow the evolution of the house from the open hearth to the brick fireplace; in addition, I wanted these buildings to come from provinces which Denmark has lost, because this is where the most primitive buildings survived and because young people must be taught everything about Denmark's history, to consolidate the memory of lost provinces and to open the way to their intellectual and spiritual restoration – the only kind of restoration I can envisage – in order to put back together that which has been dispersed.
>
> (Quoted in De Jong and Skougaard, 1992, p. 155)

It's noticeable, however, that Olsen was also an excellent showman: he directed the Tivoli Gardens' funfair in Copenhagen, which was famous as a tourist destination and which was to influence Walt Disney in the conception of Disneyland in 1954–5.

In 1909 a Flemish philologist, Henri Logemann, produced the first scholarly account of the Scandinavian open-air museums, and a wave of foundations followed in the Netherlands and north Germany. It is interesting that, although a passionate interest in local monuments, cultures and languages existed all over Europe, it did not, to begin with, express itself in the form of open-air museums, except in the north. Neither Catalan nationalism (which inspired the architect Antonio Gaudí and many artists, including the young Picasso), nor the Breton revival (which had provided subject matter for the Pont Aven group, including Gauguin), nor the well-developed revival of Provençal culture and literature (including, in 1899, the founding of the Arlatan Museum by the poet Frédéric Mistral) produced open-air museums before the First World War. It is true that wooden and half-timbered buildings are much easier to disassemble and transport than the stone structures of Catalonia, Brittany and Provence. In Russia open-air museums consist almost exclusively of wooden buildings, as if wood were a material with particularly strong peasant (and therefore historically resonant) credentials. In medieval times 'wooden markets' existed where prefabricated houses and even churches could be acquired and transported to their remote sites. But there is also something in the shared culture of 'Northern Romanticism' which found particular value in contemplating the noble simplicity of the peasant life of its ancestors as expressed in their buildings.

Open-air museums and the leisure industry

Despite the high-minded principles of the early open-air museums, these institutions could never completely escape the realities of the entertainment and tourism business. Nevertheless Skansen retains its high idealism concerning authenticity. Only a few buildings are copies; most have been carefully disassembled and rebuilt. In many cases people from the region, with their characteristic dialects and accents, can still be seen at work in this museum.

Visiting many of the smaller and more remote open-air museums in Scandinavia can be a very moving experience. Hundreds of them exist all over Norway, Sweden and Finland. Coming across a little group of houses in the forest, miles from anywhere, you can still feel that you have stumbled into the past. But, as time has passed, the living cultures of the remote areas have evolved and no longer really match the buildings in the major open air museums. The young men and women in costume performing their crafts are effectively actors, who have learned their roles. Concern has been expressed over the need to capture a more recent vernacular culture: reconstructing an apartment of the 1950s, for example. Skansen is effectively in the leisure business; it has to offer people a day out. There have to be wild animals and swings and roundabouts, as well as ice creams and sweets. Many open-air museums began as 'scientific', educational establishments and have had to adapt to the exigencies of the leisure industry.

In many ways the public exhibition of wild animals in zoos and circuses presents a similar history to that of open-air museums. One of the pioneers of the modern zoo was **Carl Hagenbeck**. His first enthusiasm for animals was awoken when his father picked up a barrel of live seals from the harbour in Hamburg. Young Carl soon learned how to buy all sorts of exotic creatures from the sailors in this busy harbour and make some money with a travelling circus. As soon as he started travelling to India, Africa and the Far East in search of bigger and rarer animals, he became fired with a missionary zeal to teach urban people about the beauty of life in contact with animals. So he tended to collect the people who went with the animals and exhibit them together, either in his travelling circus or in the zoo he established in the suburbs of Hamburg in 1907. He followed a similar development to that of Hazelius. To start with, he created simple dioramas and backdrops to provide a setting for the animals. But after the success of his 'Polar World' (originally at Hamburg Zoo and then travelled) he began to build full-size landscapes in concrete, carefully planted, and present the animals to the public at eye-level, separated from them by cleverly concealed moats. This 'natural' display method was later adopted in the 1930s by the Vincennes Zoo in Paris, for which Hagenbeck's firm was a consultant. The Hagenbeck Zoo took on a form similar to Skansen's, with the different regions of the world represented as zones, planted in appropriate ways, with the animals and people of the regions displayed together. But although Hagenbeck's aims contained a lofty educational purpose, he was always a shrewd businessman who needed to make significant income from receipts if he was to be able to continue to develop his collection and breed animals successfully in captivity. In fact he became very successful, after the First World War, in selling large numbers of animals to the crowned heads of Europe, at a time when colonial competition was at its height. At the same time, he established a successful foothold in the United States with a touring circus. Combining a sense of the authentic with a Barnum and Bailey **three-rings showmanship** was the secret of Hagenbeck's success.

Gottfried Clas Carl Hagenbeck first exhibited some seals in Hamburg St Pauli in 1848 and began a business importing live animals in 1863. His son Carl Gottfried Heinrich Hagenbeck opened the present 'fenceless' zoo in Hamburg-Stellingen in 1907.

The Barnum and Bailey three-rings circuses had three circus tents in one, with lots of things going on at once.

Although, by the nature of things, Hagenbeck's Zoo and circus focused on the exotic – animals and people remote from urban Europeans – the impulse to visit zoos, which he helped to popularize, serves an important function in European societies. The idea that 'civilized' people, and especially their children, need to keep in touch with the natural world derives in part from notions of lost innocence and instincts but also from an impulse to reassert the distance which separates urban people from the wild world of fierce or disturbing creatures. Like a dream, a visit to a zoo reassures us that normal life can go on. The spread of eco-museums, common in many European countries (especially in France), results from a comparable desire to educate urban dwellers into the realities of sustainable life on the planet, particularly in the countryside.

Zoos and open-air museums usually began as scientific and educational establishments, with a mission to 'improve', but increasingly came under pressure to transform themselves into self-reliant, money-making entertainment businesses. A Europe-wide crisis of open-air museums was experienced in the 1970s and 1980s, when several were privatized. A special conference of the Association of Open-Air Museums was held in 1993 to discuss the situation (Open-Air Museums Association, 1993). Most of the museum directors present agreed with Peter Lewis, director of the Beamish open-air museum, who asserted that open-air museums are 'mission-driven' rather than 'market-driven'. And the president of the Open-Air Museums Association, Christopher Zeuner, saw the crisis in these terms:

> Open-air museums are especially exposed to a misunderstanding by those who do not value the cultural heritage presented to them. Because our Museums have so successfully used the needs of modern society for leisure and recreational activity and have as a result become associated with the tourist industry, it is easy to undervalue or indeed reject the need for a scholarly basis, and the role in the extension of understanding, that is so essential to the concept of our Museums. Without this role the Museums would become theme parks and little by little they would lose their ability to make a contribution to the cultural life of our communities.

(Association of European Open Air Museums, 1993, pp. 28–9)

But a study of contemporary open-air museums in Europe shows that there is a wide spectrum of establishments, ranging from the most 'scientific' approaches of the 'mission-driven' museums to the 'market-led' enterprises which come close to theme parks in their methods.

Two contrasting examples of open-air museums in Ireland show the range of intention and practice involved. The Bunratty Folk Park was founded in 1964 for explicitly commercial reasons, to boost tourism in the Shannon area after the big jets stopped visiting Shannon Airport to refuel (Sheed, 1995, p. 91). A private company, Shannon Development (founded in 1959), supervises and encourages the tourist industry from County Clare to north Kerry. Following a successful scheme to stage medieval banquets in various castles in the area, this company established a permanent open-air museum in a pleasant valley in the grounds of Bunratty Castle near Shannon Airport. The buildings re-created in the village street area aim to give the impression of Irish rural life towards the end of the nineteenth century and visitors are offered a 50 per cent reduction on the entrance charge if they dress up in period costume (for which prizes are awarded). Costumed staff play music, drive cattle through the village street or drive a donkey cart. The director's aims are realistic:

> Authenticity is extremely important. Nevertheless, I believe that finding a good balance between both reality and fantasy is necessary, provided that the story-line is authentic. At Bunratty we try to achieve a balance between authenticity and commercialism.
>
> (Sheed, 1995, p. 92)

By contrast, the Ulster Folk and Transport Museum near Belfast has as part of its explicit brief the aim of trying to bring the Protestant and Catholic communities together, reconstructing Protestant chapels and Catholic churches side by side and clearly 'typing' the domestic buildings with appropriate decorations. 'An important feature of the museum's work to heal the worst features of the conflict between Catholic and Protestants has had little to do with religion as such, but is concerned with social interaction' (Buckley, 1995, p. 129). The museum has collaborated with the EMU (Education for Mutual Understanding) group, which organizes visits by religiously mixed groups of children. The belief that visiting replicas of old buildings from different 'cultural traditions' can produce a healing process in a context of bitter sectarian conflict is revealing. Surprisingly, the museum has achieved some success in providing one of the relatively few zones in the city where Protestant and Catholic children can meet regularly and peacefully to consider their cultural traditions.

There is a pattern in the different fortunes of the open-air museums. In parts of Scandinavia, Germany and much of central Europe their original educational mission is usually respected by national and state governments. In these museums, the public purse pays all the staff fees and sometimes more, allowing the management to use entrance fees and profits from shops for special activities (such as exhibitions, publications and research projects). In the areas closest to the impact of 'Thatcherization' (Britain, the Netherlands, parts of Denmark), however, open-air museums have had to fend for themselves, and this process has put to the test the 'seriousness' of the experience they offer. At the same time, the 'new museology' has been working through museums of all kinds, privileging participatory spectatorship. There is a tension between encouraging 'participation' by persuading spectators to 'do things' (such as weave, spin, make bread or plaster walls) and the original belief in absorbing information by entering 'real' domestic environments.

There are hundreds of open-air museums in Europe today. A selection can be found in the Appendix to this chapter. Many were founded in the 1960s in eastern Europe, during the long process of awakening national consciousness which led to the dismemberment of the Soviet Union. Looking at the map of Europe, it is tempting to say that, wherever there have been disputed cultural boundaries and borders, there you will find at least one open-air museum (often one on both sides of the boundary).

As an example of this, we can look at the Finns and Hungarians, who share a remote common ancestry, as reflected in the Finnish-Ugric language group. Akseli Gallen-Kallela frequently lectured in Hungary, spreading the taste for 'primitive' arts and crafts from Finland to central Europe. In Hungary and Romania interest was focused on the disputed territories of Transylvania, where ancient lifestyles and vernacular buildings survived alongside fairy-tale castles. In 1861 a Transylvanian association for the literature and culture of the Romanian people was founded in Sibiu (formerly Hermannstadt), just north of the Transylvanian Alps, where a large open-air museum was established in 1967. In the same year an open-air museum with similar interests was opened in Hungary at Szentendre, near Budapest.

There are interesting exceptions to this rule. The ambitious plans to establish a national open-air museum in Yugoslavia never overcame local rivalries. Moreover, in Spain Catalan nationalism, which in short order revived the use of Catalan as the official language in offices, schools and universities, seldom looked to vernacular architecture for a site of identity. As far as I know, there are no Basque open-air museums either. But they do exist in Turkey, Greece and Cyprus, in the Middle East and all along the east–west watershed.

In mainland Britain a distinction can be made between collections of buildings, such as Singleton in West Sussex or Avoncroft near Birmingham, and the more emotionally charged North of England Open-Air Museum in Beamish, County Durham. The urban and rural buildings at Beamish have been drawn from an area of over 400 square miles, but they have been set up in such a way as to give a sense of 'community'. In Singleton, the buildings are largely left in isolation to tell their mute story of what it must have been like to live in smoke-filled houses without glass in the windows. At Beamish, every effort is made to stimulate nostalgia for and understanding of a threatened Geordie culture. Actors and local people explain to the visitor what life was like in the industrialized and agricultural northeast.

Open-air museums and eco-museums have shown that they can attract very large audiences. In 1974 Skansen boasted 2 million visitors a year, in a country of 7 million inhabitants. But mass tourism and large attendances have created new problems.

> [The] new fleeting experience of life in the modern urban world demanded that the past be held onto, but as with all processes of modernization, the past became something which emerged as yet another form of institutionalised discourse, often articulated through the Museum and the academy ... This process has been one which has steadily intensified to the point where, during the late twentieth century, the past has emerged as a reservoir of shallow surfaces which can be exploited in the heritage centre or on the biscuit tin.

> (Walsh, 1992, p. 3)

In the United States of America the strong desire of immigrant European people to be reunited with their 'old' cultures triggered the establishment of a series of museums which, in different ways, attempted to re-create life in the recent past in Europe. In the 1930s Henry Ford founded Greenfield Village (in Dearborn, Michigan), which included transported and reconstructed American and European buildings. In the Frontier Culture Museum of Virginia, an Irish cottage from County Tyrone sits next to an English homestead, a Virginia farm building of 1850, a Rhineland village house and various other buildings from America and Europe. Although great attention to detail and 'authenticity' in materials can be seen in these museums, and although every effort is made to transmit correct historical information to visitors, the effect on the viewer is to create a somewhat arbitrary and homogenized spectacle of exotica.

Any attempt to dramatize local cultures was transformed by what took place in 1954–5 at Anaheim, California. When Walt Disney opened Disneyland, in the face of scepticism by even his brother Roy and on a mountain of debt, he had in mind a new concept, something between the open-air museum, the traditional fairground and a three-dimensional version of an animated film. Unsatisfied by the amusement parks he had visited with his children, and looking for a new venture during a lull in the fortunes of his animated films, Walt began to visit open-air museums and parks in Europe and America. Fascinated by the miniature village at Madurodam in Holland which he visited in 1935, Disney also began to make miniature furniture and objects for his personal pleasure, stimulated by the doll's house interiors exhibited by Mrs James Ward Thorne at the New York World's Fair of 1939. Disney's first ideas for a theme park revolved around miniature buildings and interiors from America and round the world. Another ingredient, however, was the fashion for building miniature railways or actually buying full-sized steam engines. Disney built his own 1:8 scale locomotive and train, while one of his associates, Ward Kimball, restored a full-sized train and length of track which he named the Grizzly Flats line (in 1948). Meanwhile, Disney became engrossed in the live-action movie *So Dear to My Heart* (1949), based on sets lovingly created around the memory of the short period he had spent in Marceline, Missouri, as a child. One of the houses constructed for this film, Granny Kincaid's cabin, was first meticulously recreated in miniature for his Disneylandia project (the miniaturized version of Disneyland). Later, versions of the house would appear full-size in many of the Disney theme parks. The very close relationship between 'old' vernacular buildings and childhood memories, always a motivating factor among the founders of open-air museums, is demonstrated here in exemplary fashion. In 1940 Disney's friend Walter Knott had begun assembling a 'ghost town' in Buena Park, California, from frontier buildings collected from all over the 'wild west', and demonstrated that people in large numbers would visit a site containing atmospherically arranged buildings which they could associate either with the relatively recent past or with western movies. Finally, Disney drew on the American open-air museum tradition, visiting Henry Ford's Greenfield Village in 1948 at a crucial moment in the conception of Disneyland.

Disneyland was conceived as a mixture of 'authentically' re-created 'lands' (including a nineteenth-century American Main Street, a wild west frontierland, a reconstructed train and an adventureland), all of which were more or less based on real buildings or things. The 'magic' was added by the central castle and a fantasyland based on the completely fictitious world of the Disney animated features. Seeing Mickey Mouse 'in the flesh', and being photographed shaking his hand, has always been a central plank of Disney reality. Originally designed to occupy part of the Disney Burbank film lot, the project was transferred to a greenfield site located near the Stanford Research Institute at Anaheim, selected for its motorway access and pleasant climate. Disneyland opened in 1955, but not before Walt had secured a weekly TV show with the ABC channel which would guarantee its success by providing nationwide coverage year in, year out. This show allowed Disney to set alongside each other the animated features, the cartoon shorts, and stars and scenes from his live-action movies and features on animals and people located in Disneyland. The Disney brand therefore worked tirelessly to promote trips to Anaheim until, in 1971, the 100 million-visitor mark had been passed. The internal tourist market to Disney theme parks was further boosted in that year by the opening of the 27,400-acre Walt Disney World in Florida. Disneyland Tokyo opened in 1983 and Euro Disney near Paris in 1992.

What needs explanation about the Disney theme parks is why they need historical reference at all. Why not just focus on the rides and the shopping, basing the imagery firmly in the fantasy world of Disney-animated and live-action films? One answer is that Disney had been very impressed by the cleanliness and propriety of Tivoli Gardens in Copenhagen, which he visited in 1950. It seemed that re-creating a well-designed and 'authentic'-looking place would encourage visitors to be tidy and well-behaved. The metaphor for the Disney theme parks is not therefore the funfair but the historic centre. The Disney visitor is a respectful tourist.

Walt Disney had always been concerned with historical detail as a powerful stimulus of fantasy and nostalgia (Marling, 1997, passim). In his animated feature films, his artists meticulously researched vernacular buildings, castles and historic objects, in an attempt to make the fairy tales ever more effective. Disney based most of these features on European fairy tales, from those of the brothers Grimm to those of La Fontaine, and it was important to him that as much as possible of the 'old world' atmosphere should be carried into the finished productions. European illustrators of fairy tales and nursery rhymes such as John Tenniel and Arthur Rackham in England were highly influential and some, such as the Scandinavians Gustaf Tenggren and Kay Nielsen, went to work for Disney. All these artists were very sensitive to European vernacular architecture, informed by the open-air museums they had seen in their youth. In *Snow White and the Seven Dwarfs*, the film which swept Europe in 1937 and marked a breakthrough for Disney, much care was taken to make the domestic details believable. The design of *Pinocchio* (1940) is even more immersed in the detail of north European architecture, thanks to the Swedish Tenggren, who joined Disney in 1936. Tenggren's sketches of the Bavarian town Rothenburg ob der Tauber informed the interior and exterior scenes in the film. Although these animated features are for the most part thoroughly American in characterization and dramatic style, the settings do reflect strong European vernacular roots. With eleven of the Disneyland attractions (in 1985) based on animated feature films (mostly set in Europe), the pressure to create a reasonably convincing representation of Europe was clear.

When it became known that Disney proposed to open a European theme park near Paris, attempts were made to set up 'European' dream factories instead. A *Schtroumph* (Smurph) theme park was opened in short order, and plans were made in France for an Asterix park. The call went out in the French media to humiliate the American invaders with their incomprehensible values. On the face of it, Albert Uderzo's and René Goscinny's Asterix and Obelix cartoons should have made ideal references for a theme park that combined a strongly nationalistic flavour with a location in a mythical remote region (Brittany) under Roman occupation (see also Chapter 3). In fact the idea behind the Asterix cartoons, first published in the magazine *Pilote* in 1959, was precisely aimed at resisting the invasion of American and Belgian cartoons in France, and the choice of the fiercely independent Gauls as the subject matter was deliberate. Interestingly, Uderzo's first idea was to take on Disney directly, by using animal characters based on the traditional French **Roman de Renart** characters, only to find that someone else had done it already.

These were a collection of stories, using animals as characters, from the late twelfth century, some attributed to Pierre de Saint-Cloud.

In the end, Parc Asterix simply copied the Disney formula, replacing Main Street with a Via Antiqua, leading to a central Gaulish village surrounded by different 'lands' (such as Greece, Rome and Paris). The Disney brand was simply too strong to be resisted, not because the Asterix cartoons lacked resonance in France but because the Disney theme parks themselves had become the benchmark for an expensive outing. It's the park itself which is the 'real thing'. After a difficult start, Parc Asterix focused on the adventure rides, building its rough and violent wooden ride *Le Godurix* in 1989 and, more recently, scoring a hit with its terrifying Towers of Zeus roller-coaster and its *Trace de Hourras* rides – considered among the biggest and most frightening in Europe. Subsequent theme parks, such as Europa Park near the town of Rust in southern Germany, have focused on the raw sensations of the rides with a token tribute to national theming. Europa Park has German, Greek, Italian, French, Spanish and Swiss zones, all with their pastiche vernacular buildings, but the emphasis is on the rides, manufactured by the owners of the park, the Mack family.

By contrast with more recent theme parks, Disneyland Paris is sedate, as far as the rides go, and culturally rich. Above ground, almost everything in the Disney theme park is referenced, and not just to Disney films but to the fables or novels which underpin them, to actual landscapes (and flora), actual buildings and, at least in a token way, actual people. The Main Street, which in all the Disney theme parks leads to the centrepiece castle, is lined with plausible reconstructions of American mid west Victorian buildings (colour plate 9). The upper storeys are reduced in scale, to make children feel less oppressed by the buildings. But behind the fantasy architecture lies the absolute reality of the day out: sugar and thrills. Here is an architecture actually made out of sweets, the fundamental currency of parental relations and a public sense of fun. The 'culture' (or at least the simulacra of historic buildings) is above ground and visible. Even the most fantastic of fairy-tale images, such as Jack's giant beanstalk, is presented in full matter-of-fact detail in an architectural setting recognizable as French domestic architecture. The rides are almost invariably hidden, mostly underground, so that each one creates its effects cut off from the real world. Even the Thunder Mountain roller-coaster is disguised as a Colorado mountain

Figure 4.9 Candy shop on Main Street, Euro Disney, Paris. Photo: Tim Benton

and you wait your turn in a plausible reconstruction of a miner's cabin, with as many 'real' nineteenth-century artefacts as any open-air museum.

Even Sleeping Beauty's magic castle is precisely referenced, both to fact and fantasy. Inside, an architecture of branching trees, recalling the Roman architect Vitruvius's description of the origin of architecture in a natural avenue of trees, frames stained-glass windows which represent scenes from the now classic cartoon films on which the Disney myth resides (colour plate 11). The original artist for the film *Sleeping Beauty* (1950), Eyvind Earle, was called out of retirement to design these windows. Every care, therefore, was taken to make the magic mountain 'authentic' to its source – the Disney film. And yet the 'imagineers' have driven the point further. Around the upper storey of the castle are opened books, displayed like the Book of Kells or the Bible, representing the 'text' of which the fairy tale is the copy (colour plate 12). (Most of the Disney animated features begin with a leather-bound book which opens to reveal the story.) The 'text' brings together the fairy tale and an image of Sleeping Beauty's castle, as constructed in Disneyland Paris, but coloured to show its dependency on the ***Très riches heures du duc de Berry***, the illustrated manuscript which provided one of the references for the building (along with various castles in France and Germany). Sleeping Beauty's castle (the third variant of the original Disneyland castle) perfectly captures a generalized impression of Europe as tradition and fantasy combined.

Behind Sleeping Beauty's castle is an urban townscape incorporating houses from a range of countries in Europe (colour plate 10). What do the Dutch make of the windmill teahouse, with the windmill transformed into a ride for young children? Do the British smile at the Toad of Toad Hall mansion (or is it meant to be a pub?) selling Disney-licensed soft drinks? And yet this architecture of reassurance, with the Victorian American Main Street leading to the familiar four zones, surrounded by an American railroad, provides a kind of literal metaphor for arrival in Europe from America. The tourists come straight off the plane and RER rapid subway (or the TGV express train if they're coming from elsewhere in Europe) into the Disney version of Europe. All the guides ('cast members') will speak some English; all the products will be recognizably American; all the rides will be versions of Disneyland and Walt Disney World. The exotic will be present and real. 'Cast members' (Disney staff), from different ethnic origins, in traditional costume, pose for photographs, reassuring visitors from multi-ethnic American and European cities (colour plate 13).

The *Très riches heures du duc de Berry* was a Book of Hours painted between 1412–16 by the Limbourg brothers (Paul, Hermann and Jean) from Nimwegen. Jean Duc de Berry was a wealthy French nobleman, brother to King Charles V, the Duc d'Anjou and the Duc de Bourgogne.

What adds complexity at Disneyland Paris is that the 'originals' of the settings for the Disney fables and film sets are just round the corner. As American mass tourism has been developing a taste for European historic towns and countryside, and as the tourism industry moves to meet the new visitors, the standard of 'authenticity' within the entertainment industry has been rising, just as standards of building conservation in historic centres and open-air museums have been eroded by the need to entertain and inform. Architectural critics and conservationists complain about the conversion of historic sites into theme parks (Moos, 1998), while for the first time the Disney theme parks are all in crisis (in 2002). Disneyland Paris (formerly Euro Disney) has never escaped from the biggest debt in the history of European private financing. At any rate, in both the theme parks and the open-air museums, the acute sense of identity with remote and distant ancestors is giving way to a more reassuring, generalized and homogeneous sense of recognition of European identities.

It is instructive to compare a Disney version of a vernacular cottage at Disneyland Paris (colour plate 14) with a scene from the ride 'It's a small world'. This is a water-borne ride in fantasyland for the very young, through a series of settings representing the nations of the world personified by audio-animatronics dolls and the most abstract of identifiers (a double-decker bus, Tower Bridge). As all the dolls sing to the same hypnotic melody, the viewer is bathed in the warm glow of global harmony (at the expense of the trivialization of cultural difference). When this ride was first opened in 1966 (designed by one of the most abstract of the Disney artists, Mary Blair) it might have seemed a reassuring response to the terrors of the cold war and entanglements in Vietnam. In our century, neither 'It's a small world' nor the blending and blurring of regional characteristics visible in Disney's 'authentic' built reconstructions seem acceptable to most Europeans. Presented with the twin dangers of globalization and the revival of blood-and-soil nationalism and ethnic cleansing, it is hard to see how architects can adequately represent aspirations to national identity.

Appendix: List of selected open-air museums (OAMs) in Europe

Open-Air Museum	Opening	Description
Skansen, Sweden	1891	Museum in Stockholm including buildings from all over Sweden, as well as a zoo and funfair
Bigdøy, Norway	1896	A collection of transported wooden buildings, begun by King Oscar II in 1884
Lillehammer, Norway	1904	Large collection, begun in 1894 by a private collector
Lyngby, Denmark	1906	Near Copenhagen, influential in promoting the Skansen model in northern Europe
Park der Burg, Turku/Åbo, Finland	1906	The first OAM in Finland, destroyed in the Second World War and partly rebuilt, consisting of an entire town quarter featuring local crafts
Wdzydze, Poland	1906	Private OAM (also Nowogród near Łomża, 1909), stimulated, like the Tatra Museum in Zakopane, by Polish nationalism during the period of the partition up until the Treaty of Versailles in 1918
Bunge, Sweden	1907	One of many small OAMs founded in Sweden before 1914
Königsberg, Germany (now Kaliningrad, Poland)	1909	Founded in what was then East Prussia, the 19 peasant houses were transported to Hohenstein (now Olsztynek in Poland) in 1940
Seurasaari, Finland	1909	Large collection of buildings from all over Finland and Karelia, set on an island near Helsinki
Trondheim, Norway	1909	Most northerly OAM in Norway
Arnhem, Holland	1912	The national Dutch OAM
'Den gamle by', Aarhus, Denmark	1914	Collection of town houses added to an existing set of old town houses in Aarhus
Mora, Sweden	1914	Collection of houses from the Dalarna region assembled by the painter Anders Zorn
Kolomenskoje, Russia	1923	5,000-hectare OAM near Moscow, representing all the regions of the former USSR
Cluj (originally Klausenburg), Romania	1929	OAM added to the Ethnographic Museum for Transylvania, founded in 1922
Balassagyarmat, Hungary	1932	Small OAM, the first to be built in Hungary, despite the success of the ethnographic village exhibited at the Millennium Exhibition in Bucharest in 1896

Riga, Latvia	1932	The first of the Latvian, Lithuanian and Estonian OAMs, founded in 1924
Bergen, Norway	1934	Collection of town houses
Cloppenberg, Germany	1934	Houses from west Münsterland and Lower Saxony
Bucharest, Romania	1936	Large OAM prompted by a series of ethnographic exhibitions in the 1930s
Olsztynek, Poland	1940	Moved from Königsberg (q.v.). Restored after the war and enlarged
St Fagans, Wales	1948	The Museum of Welsh Life in the grounds of St Fagan Castle, near Cardiff
Bokrijk, Belgium	1953	The Flemish OAM, near Genk on the eastern border of Belgium
Zubrzyca Górna, Poland	1955	First of a series of postwar Polish OAMs
Talinn, Estonia	1957	One of a number of OAMs in Lithuania, Latvia and Estonia
Holywood, Northern Ireland	1958	Ulster Folk Museum, near Belfast
Kommern, Germany	1961	Large museum specializing in buildings from the province North Rhine and Westphalia
Alt-Schwerin, Germany (formerly GDR)	1962	On Lake Tauchow, with a focus on social and economic activity
Škofia Loka, Slovenia	1962	One of the few OAMs to be built in former Yugoslavia. OAMs were also planned in the 1960s for Croatians, Bosnians and Serbians
Kizhi, Russia	1966	Island OAM (begun in 1951) on Lake Onega, dedicated to conserving wooden churches and houses from all over Karelia. Inscribed on the ICOMOS international list 1990 (International Council for Monuments and Sites linked to UNESCO)
Szentendre, Hungary	1967	National Hungarian OAM, built on a 47-hectare site
Nowy Sącz, Poland	1968	Large OAM
Valtimo, Finland	1969	Near to the Russian border, dedicated to conserving and celebrating north Karelian architecture
Beamish, England	1970	Dedicated to preserving cultural traditions in the northeast of England
Stübing, Austria	1970	National OAM for Austria. A project for an OAM in the Steiermark region was first proposed in 1908, on the Scandinavian model. Includes buildings from all over Austria

References

Allan, Robin (1999) *Walt Disney and Europe: European Influences on the Animated Feature Films of Walt Disney*, London, John Libbey.

Buckley, Anthony (ed.) (1995) *Seventeenth Annual Conference of the Association of European Open-Air Museums*, pp. 127–34.

Crowley, David (1992) *National Style and Nation-State*, Manchester, Manchester University Press.

Crowley, David (1995) 'The uses of peasant design in Austria-Hungary in the late nineteenth-and early twentieth centuries', *Decorative Arts*, vol. II, no. 2 (Spring), pp. 3–28.

De Jong, A. and Skougaard, M. (1992) 'Les premiers musées consacrés aux traditions populaires', *Museum*, 175, XLIV, no. 3, pp. 151–7.

Edenheim, R. (1995) *Skansen Traditional Swedish Style*, Stockholm, Scala.

Lane, Barbara Miller (2000) *National Romanticism and Modern Architecture in Germany and the Scandinavian Countries*, Cambridge, Cambridge University Press.

Marling, Karal Ann (ed.) (1997) *The Architecture of Reassurance: Designing the Disney Theme Parks*, Montreal, Canadian Centre for Architecture.

Martin, Timo and Sivén, Douglas (1995) *Akseli Gallen-Kallela: National Artist of Finland*, Helsinki, Wattikastannus.

Moos, Stanislas von (1998) 'Het Disney-syndroom: Luzern van stad tot attractie' (The Disney syndrome: Lucerne: from city to attraction), *Archis*, 3, pp. 30–9.

Open-Air Museums Association (1993) *Privatisation and Commercialisation of Open-Air Museums: Opportunity or Threat?*, Arnhem, Netherlands Open-Air Museum.

Sheed, Tom (1995) 'The village in Bunratty Park', in *Seventeenth Annual Conference of the Association of European Open-Air Museums*, pp. 91–7.

Vigato, Jean-Claude (1994), *L'Architecture regionaliste en France 1890–1950*, Paris, Norma.

Walsh, Kevin (1992) *The Representation of the Past Museums and Heritage in the Post-Modern World*, London, Routledge.

Zippelius, Adelhart (1974) *Handbuch der europäischen Freilichtmuseen*, Führer und Schriften des Rheinischen Freilichtmuseums und Landesmuseums für Volkskunde in Kommern, no. 7, Cologne, Rheinland Verlag.

5

Cars, contexts and identities: the Volkswagen and the Trabant

COLIN CHANT

Introduction

How do artefacts acquire identities? In order to explore this issue, this chapter takes as its subject the motor car, surely the twentieth century's prime object of consumer desire. It starts with an examination of the range of identities that can be associated with motor cars in general. The chapter then focuses on two small German economy cars with common origins and remarkably prolonged production histories. Despite their similarities, they acquired distinctive identities, at times contested between producers and consumers, and developed within markedly divergent political, economic and cultural contexts.

The motor car: technology, design and identity

Which invention had the biggest impact on European society during the twentieth century? A wonder of electrical communication, such as the telephone, radio, television or personal computer? Some application of electric power that revolutionized home life, such as the incandescent light bulb, the washing machine or the vacuum cleaner? A medical breakthrough, such as antibiotics or the contraceptive pill? All of these items, and others, will have their advocates, but many, perhaps most of you, would plump for the internal combustion engine, or its principal application, the motor car. Car production, after all, drove the European economy for much of the second half of the twentieth century and so was a major source of direct and indirect employment. As car ownership rose, so residential patterns, journeys to work, shopping and leisure activities radically changed, and in consequence so did the shape of towns and cities and their relationship with the countryside. Motorization became indelibly stamped on the built environment as a whole, as houses, streets and workplaces were reworked to accommodate the car, and mile upon mile of tarmac and reinforced concrete unrolled throughout the lands of Europe. Reactions to all these changes tended to polarize. Enthusiasts celebrated not only particular triumphs of design and technology enshrined in favourite European marques, but also the personal freedom that motorized private transport extended to so many strata of modern European society. Only some fifty years after the very first 'horseless carriages' chugged along the roads of Germany in the mid 1880s, and at a time when car ownership still remained well beyond the reach of most European households, one enthusiast declared that the automobile 'has revolutionized the whole face of human existence as perhaps no other scientific invention in this or in any other age' (Nixon, 1936, p. 17). For their part, critics of the car bemoaned the congestion that it engendered, as well as the seemingly endless toll of death and injury, the destruction of traditional communities and street life, and the pollution of the atmosphere (Kay, 1998).

The paragraph above deliberately deploys the kind of discourse that is common in debates and writing about technology in general and the car in particular. Technophiles and technophobes alike have tended to present the car as some kind of exogenous technological given, impacting upon society like a meteorite, or as a *deus ex machina*, or perhaps as a *machina ex deo*, visited upon a passive populace. More considered analyses have ascribed active roles to an elite of visionary inventors, entrepreneurs of flair, designers of genius, vote-grubbing politicians, or latterly the directors of multinational corporations with some plan of global economic domination. This chapter does not deny all validity to such discourses, or to the top-down producer-led causal models that they imply. However, it takes the view that they are at best one-sided as the authors of a cultural history and of a psychological study of the motor car suggest.

> The automobile is much more than a mere means of transportation, rather, it is wholly imbued with feelings and desires that raise it to the level of a cultural symbol ... A technological history, setting one type of automobile next to others and singing a devotional hymn to increasing perfection, is blind to human needs and cultural significations; it fails to consider that every technology is the product of a historical period, in which it rises to prominence and then disappears.
>
> (Sachs, 1992, pp. vii–viii)

The idea that car-obsession can be explained in terms of mobility and cost is quite inadequate. To understand the car properly, and particularly why it is used as such a powerful means of self-expression, we have to look at the inherent symbolism of this otherwise purely mechanical object.

(Marsh and Collett, 1986, p. 26)

In the pages that follow, I shall seek to redress an imbalance in much of the previous literature about the car, first by examining the influence of the wider social, economic and political environment on the technology and design of two selected cars, and secondly by considering whether the consumer can be ascribed a more active, shaping role in the history of these artefacts. This second line of enquiry has been opened up by historians of the automobile in the United States: they have focused on its early history, when its design was more open to negotiation and more technical intervention was required of drivers to keep their car running, or to bend it to their specific needs (Scharff, 1991; McShane, 1994; Kline and Pinch, 1996). Their lead has since been followed in a pathbreaking study of British motorists before the Second World War (O'Connell, 1998).

This chapter considers the roles of the producer and the consumer in the construction of the identities that become invested in cars and that can be the most decisive consideration in their success or failure. The debate about the possible role of the consumer in the shaping of technological artefacts is thereby extended into the period when the engineering design may be reckoned to have reached closure and to be firmly under the producers' control. It is by no means clear whether the consumer or the producer is more influential in the construction of such identities – as you will see, in different contexts there is a different balance of power between the various actors involved. Nor is it clear either whether the identities are in some sense built into or constrained by the technological and design features of the artefact, or whether the artefact is a neutral matrix capable of bearing an infinite range of identities according to changing historical circumstances. These are questions that will be addressed, and space will be left for you to form your own views about them.

Critics of conventional ways of thinking about technological innovations will insist that the motor car did not simply emerge from the brains and workshops of inventors and mechanics as an objectively superior mode of transport – one that was bound through its inherent qualities to become the dominant way chosen by people to get from place to place. This is not to deny that the technological heart of the motor car had much greater potential than other power units to drive forms of personal transport. It transpired that the internal combustion engine had a more favourable power-to-weight ratio than other mechanical alternatives to the horse: a unit producing a given amount of energy from ignited petrol vapour could be significantly lighter than one producing the same amount from expanded steam, or from the electrical potential of a battery. But this is to a great extent a judgement of hindsight after a great deal of development and refinement of the rival power units; it should not be overlooked that it was by no means certain at the time when the petrol-engined vehicles of Gottlieb Daimler and Karl Benz first took to the roads of Europe in the mid 1880s. After all, the first mechanical mode of land transport was a steam-powered road vehicle that Richard Trevithick tried out in south Wales in 1801. Although, again with hindsight, this innovation is usually presented as the first step towards the railway locomotive, there was another line of development leading to other steam-powered road vehicles. Some of these carried fare-paying passengers on British roads during the 1820s and 1830s, and steam-powered goods vehicles and road rollers would trundle on into the twentieth century. There remain steam-carriage aficionados who play down the hazards of boiler explosions and the propensity of such heavyweight machines to destroy the surfaces of roads and frighten the horde of horses that laboured on them; instead, they insist that it was punitive taxation and legislation blatantly favouring the interests of stagecoach proprietors that denied the steam carriage its rightful place in the annals of mechanical road transport (see, for example, Beasley, 1988). Be that as it may, it was not until the early years of the twentieth century that petrol-engined cars began to show clear advantages over vehicles powered either by electric batteries or by lighter, more efficient steam engines fuelled by oil rather than coal. The course of technological developments is apt to look much more orderly and predictable in retrospect than it would have appeared in prospect.

Transport is assuredly one of the most important subdivisions of the history of technology. There is certainly a story that has been told and retold about the invention and subsequent refinement of the major technological items that drivers can now take for granted in today's motor vehicles, which are relatively secure, weatherproof and comparatively easy to start, run and stop. The historical significance of some of these developments extends beyond the purview of the petrol-head; the electric self-starter, for example, has often been portrayed as opening the way for women to take the wheel, although Virginia Scharff insists that it made petrol-engined cars more attractive to men as well as to women (Scharff, 1991, p. 60). But cars are not only *technology*; they also exhibit *design*. By one definition, technology means the practical means that humans fashion from their environment to meet their various purposes in life and the principles underlying them, while to the layperson design is probably associated above all with the appearance of things. According to this distinction, technologists or engineers are concerned with making things work as well as possible and designers with making them look as good as possible. Any successful commercial product will involve some balance between these two (often conflicting) aims. In the case of the car, the engineer's quest is for functional efficiency – for example, the search for an engine that strikes an affordable balance between power, reliability and economy and, increasingly, for a body shape that reduces drag to the minimum. The designer, however, wants to produce a car that will attract the buyer: with a pleasing shape and range of colours, and comfortable and attractive seats and other internal fittings. The formal structure of the modern motor-car industry reinforces a division of labour between the engineers who develop the power-train that produces, transmits and controls the movement fundamental to this and any other mode of transport, and the designers who are responsible for the body shell and internal fittings that not only protect and accommodate people and possessions within the vehicle, but make it most easily identifiable.

Despite this apparently clear demarcation within the modern car industry, the technology/design distinction is actually quite difficult to make with any precision on the conceptual level, as the domains of each term overlap. Both terms are notably ambiguous, but perhaps design is the more so, as it has both functional and aesthetic connotations. Take the example of a carburettor. This can be seen in principle as one of a series of ancillary technological mechanisms needed to enable the internal combustion engine to turn the chemical energy of the petroleum fuel into the rotary motion of the car's wheels. The carburettor is a distinctive way of vaporizing the liquid fuel and introducing an appropriate fuel–air mixture into the cylinders of the engine, where it combusts, releasing energy that moves the enclosed pistons up and down alternately. Rods and bearings attached to the pistons convert their up-and-down motion into the rotary motion of the engine's crankshaft, and this is conveyed by the car's transmission system to the wheels, usually in contemporary cars by way of the front wheel-bearing axle. The carburettor is an essential component of this energy system, but its function can be realized in different technological ways. It started out as a large pot in which fuel evaporated from the surface, usually assisted by heat from the car exhaust (the surface carburettor). Two other types emerged in the 1890s, one using a wick to assist evaporation and another, conceived by Wilhelm Maybach, in which a jet turns the liquid fuel into a fine spray. Maybach's mechanism became standard, but there are several different *designs* of this type of carburettor, which would not feature in a general technological history of the car. Such a work would normally move on from Maybach's float-feed spray carburettor to its displacement in recent years by more efficient electronic fuel injection systems. These involve a different technological principle, where an unmixed spray of fuel enters through a series of nozzles fitted to each cylinder of the engine. This principle would be of note in a general technological history of the car, even if, again, the various proprietary *designs* of such systems would not.

An essay about the identities ascribed to motor cars might appear to be almost wholly about their design, in the aesthetic sense of their external shape and appearance. Since such features make a car readily identifiable, one might reasonably infer that they contribute most to the construction of a car's identity. But you will see from the discussion of the two German marques chosen as case studies in this chapter – the Volkswagen Beetle and the Sachsenring Trabant – that this is not quite so. Different makes of car have technological features and functional as well as aesthetic design characteristics that can be defining elements in the identities that consumers, as well as producers, have forged for them. This is not to say, however, that such identities are *determined* by the car's technological and/or design features; the purposive *selection* of some of these features as definitive of the car (and therefore to some extent of the car owner) can also be interpreted as exhibiting the role of human agency in the process.

Issues of identity are as rich and ambiguous as those surrounding technology and design, and only a few can be explored in one chapter. In choosing to focus on the Volkswagen and the Trabant, I can note certain identity issues only in passing. Selecting two motor cars – rather than, say, the Italian Vespa scooter or the London omnibus – necessarily limits the discussion of identities and motorized transport to one particular realization of the potentials of the internal combustion engine: the four-wheeled, private form. Choosing two small, mass-production cars also closes off a fruitful area of debate in which different designs of cars can be seen to embody or reflect the characteristics of the specific, usually better-off sections of society targeted by the producers. This is not to say, however, that the cars examined in this chapter really are 'classless', even if this is often claimed for the Beetle in particular (Meredith, 1999, p. 7). Limiting the main case studies to cars from West and East Germany, at any rate as the countries of production if not of consumption, might also seem to limit discussion of the question of car designs and national characteristics, at least in a more broadly comparative way than by considering only the temporarily disunited parts of one country. Not that attention to one country precludes discussion of national identity: the point has been made that one of the main reasons for the qualified support within the East German leadership for an indigenous motor-car industry was its importance in constructing an identity for East Germany (GDR) both within the Soviet bloc and in relation to capitalist West Germany (FDR) (Zatlin, 1997, p. 368; Stokes, 1997, p. 222).

EXERCISE

We might pause here to think about the issue of national identities in a more comparative way. Suppose that the case studies in this chapter had been selected from a range of marques with strong national associations: for example, a Swedish Volvo estate, a German BMW executive saloon, a British BMC Mini, a French Citroën 2CV and an Italian Fiat 500 Cinquecento. Have the designs of these cars been shaped by national identities? Do they reflect, or embody, national characteristics?

DISCUSSION

This is not an easy question to answer off the cuff, especially if this isn't an interest of yours or if some of these models are a bit before your time. Perhaps you made some of the connections seen by two contemporary commentators on the symbolism of car design: the 'safety and security of Swedish welfarism' and the sturdy structure of the Volvo; the German engineering efficiency and even 'Prussian militarism' embodied in cars like the BMW; British 'swinging Sixties' confidence and cultural leadership captured by Alec Issigonis's Mini; Gallic chic and alternative Left Bank culture expressed in the 2CV; Italian design flair realized in the Cinquecento (Holden, 1998, pp. 31, 33–6; Bayley, 1986, pp. 47, 73, 83, 86). You may also have reflected upon other national features, such as climate and topography, the layout of cities and so on. Yet even if you are into car design, you might not have considered another possibility: that car designs may not only in some sense incorporate national characteristics, but that they are so ubiquitous in contemporary life that they are actually *constitutive* of national identity. Thus the vision of an outstanding designer such as Alec Issigonis or Dante Giacosa (who designed the Fiat 500) may partly shape contemporary perceptions of nations, as well as reflecting national identities.

Focusing on specific marques also constrains the exploration of a fascinating range of identity issues to do with the psychological relationship between the motor car and its occupants. The car is the 'most psychologically expressive object that has so far been devised' (Marsh and Collett, 1986, p. 26); these expressions include the car as an extension of the driver's personality, sexuality, dress, family, home and territory. Though it would be impossible within the confines of a short chapter to investigate these issues fully, some of them will perforce arise in the ensuing discussion of artefactual identities; for example, the 'animistic' tendency to attribute personalities to cars and to give them nicknames (Marsh and Collett, 1986, pp. 13–14).

Not only do consumers have a part to play in the construction of the car's identity, a role that is the main focus of this chapter, but the consumption of cars, the great consumer durable of the twentieth century, has much to do with the construction of the consumer's identity, whether it be that of nation, region, class, subculture, gender, occupation or generation.

> [T]he driver of the rusty Beetle and the one in the gleaming turbo-charged Porsche both make equally powerful statements about themselves. They declare themselves to be particular kinds of people, and so define themselves socially. They are what they drive, and so are we.
>
> (Marsh and Collett, 1986, p. 4)

The people's car of the west: the Volkswagen Beetle

'Germany gave birth to the automobile, and France was its cradle' (Angelucci and Bellucci, 1975, p. 48). But although the motor car was a European invention it remained a luxury item until the watershed of the First World War, which served to spread the experience of motoring beyond the wealthy classes and their hired chauffeurs. For social and economic reasons, the aspiration to design an affordable car for the masses was first realized by Henry Ford in the United States: his Model T or 'Tin Lizzie' was first manufactured in 1908. By 1927, when production ceased, 15 million cars had poured out of Detroit, spearheading the development of the world's first motorized society. In the case of the Model T, technological innovation and favourable social and economic circumstances were mutually reinforcing. The size and purchasing power of the American market encouraged investment in mass-production plant and machinery. Ford introduced flow production methods based on the moving assembly line as early as 1913 at his Highland Park factory in Detroit.

Ford's mass-production technology, as well as the cars themselves, were exported to Europe, but demand conditions were initially less conducive to their spread. The first home-grown European mass-produced economy vehicles included the British Austin 7 of 1922, but none of these came close to matching Ford's worldwide success. The car that was to surpass the Model T as a mass-produced economy car, both in numbers manufactured and in global success, emerged from the motor car's German homeland during the Third Reich. The Volkswagen (people's car) is an especially apt choice of vehicle for a discussion of producer and consumer identities, as so many diverse actors were involved in its production and as it has appealed to many diverse groups of consumers. The contest for ownership of the car's identity is reflected in uncertainty about its name: the title of

There are various accounts of the origin of the car's best-known nickname. Some attribute it either to Adolf Hitler or to the car's designer Ferdinand Porsche. There are published references as early as 1942, both in Germany and in the USA (see Mantle, 1995, p. 4; Hodges, 1997, p. 9; Sloniger, 1980, p. 65). It was first popularized in Britain by an enthusiast who set up a VW Owners' Club in 1953; the club magazine was called *Beetling* (Davies, 1996, pp. 178–9). There have been variations on the insect theme beyond the choice of 'Beetle' in Britain, Germany (*Käfer*) and other European countries: 'Bug' came to be preferred in the USA, *Coccinelle* (ladybird) in France and *Maggiolino* (maybug) in Italy.

'Volkswagen' was by no means uncontested among its producers, and the nickname '**Beetle**' was until very recently representative only of the car's unofficial European consumer identity.

The Volkswagen is sometimes seen as a specifically Nazi creation, but in fact the car's roots lay rather deeper in the history of the German motor industry. The vehicle's designer, Dr Ferdinand Porsche (1875–1951), was born in the German-speaking part of Bohemia in the Austro-Hungarian empire. He began his career in Vienna at the very beginning of the twentieth century by designing electric cars, before moving on to luxury petrol-engined touring cars and sports cars with various Austrian and German manufacturers such as Austro-Daimler and Daimler-Benz. Despite his success with the large-engined vehicles that dominated the European motor-car market, Porsche aspired to design a small, cheap car. This ambition was a source of conflict with his employers, and in 1928 he decided to go freelance. It was in 1930, as head of his independent design consultancy based in Stuttgart, that he started work in earnest on a people's car, intended as a 'spiritual successor to the Model T Ford' (Boddy, 1999, p. 13).

A motor-cycle manufacturer, Zündapp of Nuremberg, produced the first people's car prototype for Porsche in 1932 (see Figure 5.1), though the company soon decided to return to motor bikes. The next year another German motor-cycle manufacturer, NSU, collaborated with Porsche on a *Volksauto*, with all the main Volkswagen design and technology features: an air-cooled engine, mounted at the rear of the car and directly driving its rear wheels, Porsche's own patented torsion-bar suspension system and a characteristic streamlined body shape (see Figure 5.2). However, the Italian manufacturer Fiat had a prior agreement with NSU on car manufacture, and the German company was obliged to revert to motor-cycle manufacture for the remaining pre-war years, producing a low-cost 'people's motor bike', the NSU Quickly (Davies, 1996, p. 22). These early details are worth noting: it was the motor-cycle manufacturers, who already catered for the popular end of the market, who were more interested in producing a mass, economy car than were the motor-car companies themselves. Demand conditions in Germany were such that motor cycles outnumbered motor cars until 1957 in the Federal Republic, where levels of car ownership attained uniquely in the United States as early as 1920 were not seen until 1960 (Abelshauser, 1995, p. 276).

Development of the people's car in the form of the early Porsche prototypes was therefore well under way in Germany before the national socialists were voted into office in 1933. There is no doubt, however, that Nazi sponsorship was necessary to the eventual fruition

Figure 5.1 Prototype Porsche people's car designed for Zündapp in 1932. The front of the car was conventional, but the streamlining at the rear that would later characterize the entire Beetle body is evident from this side view. Photo: Das Volkswagen AutoMuseum

Figure 5.2 Prototype Porsche people's car designed for NSU in 1933. The main Beetle characteristics were now in place: rear-mounted, air-cooled flat-four engine, torsion-bar suspension, and fully streamlined profile. Photo: Das Volkswagen AutoMuseum

of Porsche's design concept after the Second World War (see Figure 5.3). Adolf Hitler was 'the first chief of state to welcome the vision of the German people rolling on wheels and the German land covered with streets' (Sachs, 1992, p. 48). His commitment to the car was manifest in his backing for the construction of the *Autobahnen*, a national system of roads designed to extend motorization throughout German society. Like Porsche, Hitler was an admirer of Henry Ford; soon after his election he made his own support of the 'people's car' idea public at the 1933 Berlin Motor Exhibition (Hopfinger, 1971, p. 64).

Porsche initially made contact with his fellow Austrian Hitler to secure state support for what were to prove spectacularly successful Auto Union rear-engined Grand Prix racing cars. Hitler was receptive to this idea, being only too keen to exploit the propaganda value of German technological prowess. But he also wanted to break the middle-class monopoly on private motor cars, and so took seriously a subsequent paper from the designer called '*Exposé* on the construction of a German people's car'. At a subsequent meeting with Porsche in 1934 the Führer issued his own set of specifications, which included a seemingly impossible price limit of 1,000 reichsmarks, a mere half the cost of the Morris Minor, the leading cheap British model of the 1930s. A reluctant Mercedes-Benz company was coerced into building further prototypes in 1936 and submitting them to the most rigorous testing, before the time was

Figure 5.3 Ferdinand Porsche demonstrating a model people's car to Adolf Hitler. Photo: Das Volkswagen AutoMuseum

Figure 5.4 VW's Wolfsburg factory alongside the Mittelland canal. Photo: Das Volkswagen AutoMuseum

judged right for the vehicle to go into production. Hitler announced the state-funded people's car project at the 1937 Berlin Motor Exhibition. The project included a scheme allowing workers to obtain a car once they had bought sufficient weekly savings stamps, a notably consumer-unfriendly alternative to hire purchase.

The German Führer used his power to force the German aristocracy, in the person of the reluctant Count von der Schulenberg, to provide most of the land for the factory where this democratic car would be mass produced. The count's Wolfsburg Castle estate was situated not far from Hanover in Lower Saxony and, more important, was right by the Mittelland canal, and close to the Hanover–Berlin *Autobahn* (see Figure 5.4). Its ancient oak trees were cleared and a state-of-the-art car factory sprang up, built around imported American mass-production equipment. When the foundation stone of the Wolfsburg factory was laid in 1938, it was clear from the Führer's speech for the occasion that Porsche's people's car concept had been reshaped ideologically, if not aerodynamically. To Porsche's apparent dismay, Hitler renamed the car the *Kraft-durch-Freude-Wagen* (KdF-Wagen), after the Nazi 'Strength through Joy' movement (Hopfinger, 1971, p. 121; see also Figure 5.5). This was the car's first real identity crisis, and it is noteworthy that this awkward, politically inspired name failed to stick, the cars being generally referred to as Volkswagens. The next

Figure 5.5   Three models of the Kraft-durch-Freude Wagen – standard saloon, convertible cabriolet and saloon with full-length sunroof – at the opening of the Wolfsburg factory by Hitler, who is on the podium. Photo: Das Volkswagen AutoMuseum

crisis was soon to follow, as preparation for war rapidly assumed priority over domestic consumption of motor cars. With only some 210 peacetime KdF-wagens produced, 'hand-tooled by Daimler-Benz as show and display vehicles and toys for the Nazi elite' (Ludvigsen, 1996a, p. 2), the Wolfsburg plant, which made increasing use of foreign slave labour as the war took its course, turned over to military production. This time Porsche literally reshaped the people's car and it entered combat in a number of guises, including the *Schwimmwagen*, an amphibian vehicle, and, above all, the *Kübelwagen* (bucket car, so called because of its seat design), a rugged multi-purpose vehicle that turned out to be especially suited to desert warfare, partly because its rear-wheel drive gave effective traction in sand (see Figure 5.6).

In the end, over 336,000 aspiring German Volkswagen-owners had made their weekly contributions of a minimum 5 reichsmarks to the state savings scheme, but because of the war none of them saw a car in return for their investment. After the cessation of hostilities, the Russians seized the accumulated RM267 million from what had become an East German bank as war reparations (Davies, 1996, p. 45). Meanwhile the Wolfsburg plant, badly damaged by Allied bombing in 1944, found itself just inside the British occupation zone, a mere 4 kilometres from the Soviet sector border. The British army's Royal Electrical and Mechanical Engineers (REME) recommended production of military vehicles. REME officer Major Ivan Hirst proceeded in August 1945 to revive Porsche's original saloon design for the benefit of the occupying forces (see Figure 5.7). Now Hitler's

Figure 5.6 The Kübelwagen, one of the wartime adaptations of the Volkswagen. It coped particularly well with military operations in the Sahara Desert: according to Field-Marshal Erwin Rommel, his 'Kübel' could go wherever a camel could go. Photo: Das Volkswagen AutoMuseum

Volkswagen was inscribed with the national identities of his victors: maroon for the Russians, blue for the RAF, light grey for the French and dark grey for the Americans (Davies, 1996, p. 61). The subsequent direction of the enterprise was influenced by an adverse report on the 'ugly', 'noisy' and 'uneconomic' Volkswagen by a commission headed by Sir William Rootes, head of the British Humber motor company (Davies, 1996, p. 57). The report concluded:

> Looking at the general picture, we do not consider that the design represents any special brilliance, apart from certain of the detail points, and it is suggested that it is not to be regarded as an example of first class modern design to be copied by the British industry.

(Ludvigsen, 1996b, p. 10)

Hirst went on in 1948 to appoint a former executive of the German Opel motor company, Dr Heinz Noordhoff (1899–1968), as director-general. Hirst formally handed over the plant to the German authorities in September 1949, though for some years the ownership of the company was a matter of dispute between the two shareholders, the federal government and the *Land* government of Lower Saxony: 'In those days it was said that in France the government owned Renault; in Italy Fiat owned the government; and in Germany nobody knew who owned Volkswagen' (Nelson, 1970,

Figure 5.7 The thousandth Beetle to come off the reactivated postwar Wolfsburg assembly line, with Major Ivan Hirst at the wheel. Photo: Das Volkswagen AutoMuseum

p. 267n.). The status of the company was only clarified in 1960, when it was privatized as Volkswagenwerk AG, with the federal and *Land* governments retaining substantial minority shareholdings (Nelson, 1970, pp. 267–9).

After the war Ferdinand Porsche was accused of war crimes and imprisoned in France, but before his death in 1951 he was able to return to Germany and see the *Autobahnen* abundant with his Volkswagen design. The fact that the postwar car was faithful to Porsche's developed pre-war concept says much about the nature of the British stewardship of the plant. It also reflects the accord between the western Allies that the main point of rescuing the plant was to support the creation of a stable, prosperous Germany, rather than to use it to exact war reparations. In this way the British authorities contributed to the creation of the postwar identity of the Volkswagen as a prime symbol of the German *Wirtschaftswunder* (economic miracle). But despite his initial scepticism about a 'miserable duckling' that was 'tarred with the brush of political trickery' (quoted in Davies, 1996, pp. 67, 70), it was Noordhoff's strong commitment to the design, technology and 'personality' of the Volkswagen that underpinned the remarkable success story both at home and abroad that unfolded under his patriarchal leadership. His British predecessor, Major Hirst, categorized as 'Americanization'

Noordhoff's main design changes: a softer ride, bigger engine, synchromesh gearbox and hydraulic brakes (Parkinson, 1996, p. 120). The revamped Volkswagen proved to have universal appeal: some 40 per cent of the first million produced by 1955 were exported to a total of 103 countries (see Figure 5.8). More than a million Volkswagens were produced in all bar one of the years 1965–73 and, although Noordhoff did not live to see it, overall production surpassed the world record of the Model T Ford in 1972, reaching 21 million in the 1990s (Davies, 1996, pp. 77, 92).

The technological heart of the *Wirtschaftswunder* car remained its rear-mounted, air-cooled engine, with its characteristic 'flat-four' layout, devised by Porsche's engine designer Franz Reimspreiss. This arrangement of the car's four cylinders in two opposing horizontal pairs yielded volume and weight savings that suited the engine's position over the rear driving wheels. It mitigated the inherent tendency of such a configuration to 'oversteer', meaning that the rear of the car swung out when cornering. These features of the power unit became Porsche's design trademark, and it is no accident that the classic Porsche sports cars developed by Ferdinand's son Ferry also had air-cooled, rear-mounted engines, as well as torsion-bar suspension.

An obvious question is raised as to why the technological heart of the world's best-selling car failed to displace the standard water-cooled, front-mounted power unit. The principal advantages of air-cooling

Figure 5.8   The millionth Beetle, manufactured in 1955. The small split rear window had given way to a larger oval one. Flashing direction indicators were built into the wings of US models from this year, but the old semaphore indicators in the window columns persisted in European models like this one until 1960. Photo: Das Volkswagen AutoMuseum

were self-evident: no freezing of water in winter, no boiling over in the heat of summer. There were also no water hoses to perish and leak. However, air-cooled engines are noisier, and the Volkswagen's version struggled to keep pace over the years with the gains in power and fuel economy, and reduced emissions of waste gases, attained by rival water-cooled units. Another innovation already mentioned in passing was the car's method of suspension, used to reduce the vibration and jolting caused by uneven road surfaces. Porsche had obtained a patent for this novel suspension system, first fitted to the NSU prototype of his people's car; it used torsion bars, which worked by twisting and so was more responsive than the traditional leaf-spring system (see Figure 5.9). But the most immediately apparent feature was the car's design, in the sense of its overall appearance: its distinctive aerodynamic shape, which was to inspire its nickname, was evident from Porsche's very first prototypes.

Figure 5.9 Volkswagen torsion-bar suspension, as fitted between 1950 and 1953. Apart from the mechanical advantages over traditional leaf-springs when the system was introduced in the 1930s, enclosing the springs protected them from impact damage and corrosion. Volkswagen persisted with torsion bars while many other companies were switching to systems of coil springs and shock absorbers. These were fitted after 1970 to the 'Super Beetles', but cheaper models retained torsion bars, and they still feature in current Mexican and Brazilian Beetles. Photo: Das Volkswagen AutoMuseum

There was relatively little change in the overall appearance and basic technological specification of the Volkswagen saloon throughout its long European production history. Porsche had increased the original engine capacity of 985cc to 1131cc during the war and this gain in power was retained for the immediate postwar private cars. It rose again to 1192cc in 1954 and further increases followed between 1965 and 1970, when two 'Super Beetle' models were launched. One of these had a 1584cc engine, as the company sought to keep up with the growing power of the dominant water-cooled, front-mounted engine. A range of engine sizes was now available, but the definitive rear-mounting and air-cooling features persisted. The company also kept pace with other less definitive technical developments, for example in transmission, electrical, heating, ventilation and braking systems. Brand fetishists make much of various styling changes, such as the replacement in 1953 of the original small split rear window by a larger oval shape (there is even an enthusiast group called the Split Rear Window (Beetle) Club of Great Britain), and the replacement of the oval shape by a rectangular window in 1957. Esoteric predilections only reinforce the point that the styling was remarkably constant. Just as there were minor variations on the Model T Ford, there were versions of the Beetle other than the dominant saloon-body type, most notably the convertible cabriolets, though these have accounted for fewer than one in sixty of all Beetle sales.

Despite other departures, such as the VW Transporter van and the roomier, more upmarket Type 3 and Type 4 saloons and estates of the 1960s and early 1970s (all of which retained the Beetle engine and suspension technology, if not the body styling), Noordhoff's strategy for Volkswagen was essentially to concentrate on one model. Was the relative stability of the Beetle's technology and design therefore the result of producer rather than consumer choice? Producers have always had to strike a balance between familiarity and novelty of design in the quest to anticipate and manage the vagaries of consumer taste. 'Car buyers are essentially conservative people. They want cars with a degree of individuality, but also with features common to other cars on the road and with a well-known name' (Marsh and Collett, 1986, p. 49).

The producers will want to have their cake and eat it, both by encouraging loyalty to a well-defined brand and also by encouraging their devotees to trade up to the latest model. It may be that there are groups of consumers who value continuity of design above novelty, perhaps for the sense of affiliation that attaches to a constant but instantly recognizable type, affirmed in the case of the Beetle and some other marques by the mutual flashing of headlights. VW, perhaps, saw its greatest market return in nurturing such loyalty and in encouraging long-term brand identification. In the 1950s the company gave certificates and gold wristwatches to owners whose engines and transmissions achieved 100,000 kilometres without major repair (Davies, 1996, pp. 115–16). Subsequently, artful advertising campaigns sought to make a marketing positive out of the vehicle's continuity of design, though whether this amounts to manipulation of the consumer is open to debate:

> Technical and stylistic innovations ... can never be sufficient in themselves to revamp either corporate or model images. Such changes come about not through rational but through emotional appeals. It is here that the copy-writers of the big advertising agencies have the potential to endow a car with qualities that give it cult status. Equally, they can turn the car into an unsaleable lemon.
>
> (Marsh and Collett, 1986, p. 52)

The Beetle's unprecedented success notwithstanding, it may be too much to attribute it all to a robustly constructed producer identity and a marketing strategy that effectively exploited this. When the European consumer began to tire of the saloon, sales fell quite dramatically, and very soon after the car's glory years the decision was taken to end indigenous Beetle production at Wolfsburg in 1974, and subsequently at Emden in 1978. The manufacture of Beetle convertibles by the Karmann coach-building company in Osnabrück ceased in 1980. Most of the other manufacturing and assembly plant that opened throughout the world during the Beetle's heyday closed down in the 1970s and 1980s, though production has continued at Puebla in Mexico (where the cars now have electronic fuel injection, and catalytic converters fitted to their exhausts). The assembly of *Fuscas*, some of them running on alcohol fuel derived from sugar cane, resumed in Brazil in 1993 after a gap of seven years.

The latter history of the Beetle indicates a variable role for the consumer. On the one hand, a general shift in taste forced the VW company to ditch the Beetle and invest in water-cooled, front-engined Golf and Polo hatchbacks. On the other, the persistence of diehard Beetle enthusiasts, as well as the car's continuing suitability for certain non-European environments, has kept the marque alive and has also engendered yet another identity shift. This latest crisis has arisen from the company's decision in the 1990s to produce a New Beetle. It is ironic that when the German company for the first time officially called a model by the popular name 'Beetle' – a case of a producer appropriating a consumer-constructed identity – some aficionados of the marque refused to accept that it was the genuine article, dismissing it as a retro-styled Golf in Beetle's clothing (see Meredith, 1999, p. 9). Indeed, the car that first appeared in 1998 is built upon a fourth-generation Golf platform, and has a standard

It also reveals something about European identities and Americanization that the car is marketed in Germany as 'Der New Beetle'.

water-cooled, front-mounted engine. Its relationship with the old Beetle now resides wholly in its mimicry of the original aerodynamic body shell, though, as one sympathetic enthusiast notes, the bonnet is a bit more bulbous to accommodate the front engine (Boddy, 1999, p. 126). It could indeed be argued that the distinctive aerodynamic shape and the rear mounting of the engine were much better matched design partners, though repositioning the engine at the front has allowed the modern desideratum of a lift-up hatchback. It may help explain initial European resistance to the new model that the idea originated from VW's new design studio in California, and that the car, which is assembled at the Mexican Puebla plant, was at first intended only for the North American market.

There are some intriguing lessons to be drawn from this embryonic contest over the identity of the new car. First, it supports the view that the consumer, as well as the producer, decides the identity of a car (though it remains to be seen whether the New Beetle is accepted as a continuation of the Beetle saga). It is unlikely that Ferdinand Porsche intended to design a car which would inspire the consumer loyalty that had so much to do with its success:

> Some cars are 'cute', and thus have an immediate popular appeal. In this category we might include the old VW Beetle, the Citroën 2CV and the now defunct Morris Minor. What makes them so immediately attractive is that their form is reminiscent of a young child or animal ... They are objects demanding loving care and devotion, and not surprisingly it is these kinds of cars which are most often given pet names and treated like one of the family.
>
> (Marsh and Collett, 1986, p. 58)

Secondly, it shows that questions of identity are by no means confined to the appearance of a car, important though that undoubtedly is. The Beetle enthusiast's fundamental objection is that the new model imitates the shape of the old classic, but lacks its distinctive air-cooled, rear-mounted engine technology.

The people's car of the east: the Trabant

The Trabant has been described as 'the most loved and loathed of Eastern Bloc cars' (Nowill, 2000, p. 119). On the negative side, it features in a selection of the world's worst cars, has been likened to a 'collision between a mailbox and a lawnmower' (Jacobs, 1991, p. 101; Mantle, 1995, p. 143) and has been the butt of numerous other jokes, not least from its lugubrious owners. Before the Berlin Wall came down, west European observers disparaged it as the epitome of outdated east European polluting technology. The BBC's Berlin correspondent Caroline Wyatt, for example, looked back on her first taste of the east as follows:

> As I went through Checkpoint Charlie just a few minutes away, the smells of freshly baked bread and real coffee from the last western café were rapidly replaced by the unmistakable odour of communism. A sour, tainted smell, tinged with noxious fumes from the sputtering Trabant engines. Out of the first café in the east – on Unter den Linden – wafted the smell of overcooked cabbage, disinfectant and drains.
>
> Even the air was a choking yellowish colour – from the brown-coal heating, and a thousand factories busily pouring out waste, as East Germany sought to become *the* communist success story.
>
> (Wyatt, 2000)

For a while, the Trabant was one of the most potent symbols of the end of Soviet hegemony in eastern Europe.

> With a cloud of blue smoke and a high-pitched whine, the Trabant, powered by its two-stroke engine, carried many an East German westward after the fall of the Berlin Wall in 1989. The car's 1950s design, its obvious environmental incorrectness, and its all-plastic body had made it a symbol of the technological limitations of communism in the German Democratic Republic (GDR). The famous photographic image from the early 1990s of the rear of a 'Trabi' (as they were called) protruding from a dumpster ... seemed to suggest that the car, like the system that produced it, had been consigned to the dustbin of history.
>
> (Stokes, 2000a, p. 1)

Compared with the Volkswagen the Trabant underwent even fewer technological or design changes throughout its similarly long production history. It has nevertheless been inscribed with a surprising range of identities, not all of them negative. When the car first appeared in the late 1950s its 'futuristic design and all-plastic body attracted worldwide attention' (Stokes, 2000a, p. 48). Within the boundaries of the GDR there was a contest between the upbeat authorities and the downbeat people about the way the car should be perceived. In a Germany officially reunited in October 1990, the car took on further symbolic meanings. On one level it could be portrayed simply as 'a poor man's Beetle, affordable transport with a certain amount of character' (Nowill, 2000, p. 119). But its range of inscribed meanings has transcended its market appeal: the Trabant has acquired the identity of a cult car, with regular rallies of owners and dedicated internet websites on which aficionados can indulge their passion for the artefact.

Like the even longer-lived Volkswagen, the Trabant has roots deep in the history of the German motor industry. The car was manufactured in the city of Zwickau, where August Horch, who learned his craft with Karl Benz, founded the Saxon motor industry as early as 1904. Horch was sacked from his own company in 1909. In the same year he set up a second car factory in the city under the name Audi, a latinized version of his own name, the commercial use of which was blocked by his original company (Schiebert, 1997, p. 9). A sign of increasing demand for the Horch and Audi products was the introduction in Zwickau during the 1920s of the assembly-line production methods pioneered by Henry Ford in the United States for his Model T. But not long after this investment the German economy plunged into severe depression, and as a result in 1932 Horch and Audi agreed to integrate with two other Saxon motor manufacturers, DKW and Wanderer. They formed Auto Union, a merger still symbolized by the four interlocking rings of the Audi badge. It was DKW (*Das Kleine Wunder,* meaning 'the little wonder'), a manufacturer of motor cycles and then of small economy cars, which had the most direct technological and design link with the Trabant. The DKW F1, first seen at the Berlin Motor Show in 1931, prefigured the Trabant as a small economy car with a two-stroke engine and front-wheel drive. There is also in this story an early genealogical connection with the Volkswagen, other than Porsche's own experiments with economy cars – it was at Zwickau that his renowned 1930s Auto Union Grand Prix racing cars were built.

> *Horch* is the command 'dare' in German, and *audi* its Latin equivalent.

During the Second World War, like the fledgling Wolfsburg factory, the Zwickau factories switched to military production. Using forced labour, they turned out lorries and armoured personnel carriers, until in 1944 they too were bombed by the Allies. After the war the stricken factories found themselves in the Soviet occupation zone, which became the new German Democratic Republic. The East German Communist party (Sozialistische Einheitspartei Deutschlands (SED), or Socialist Unity Party of Germany), nationalized Auto Union, and Audi duly transferred its operations to Ingolstadt in the Federal Republic, where it was taken over by VW in 1965. The residual eastern enterprise became known from 1948 as the IFA (Industriewaltung Fahrzeugbau, or Industrial Department for Vehicle Building). The refurbished Zwickau plant initially manufactured heavy lorries and tractors, but returned to car production with the IFA F8, a revival of the pre-war DKW F8 (see Figure 5.10). This model, the last of DKW's interwar economy cars, had a small 690cc

Figure 5.10 The IFA F8. Photo: Julian Nowill, *East European Cars*, Sutton Publishing, 2000

two-stroke engine, and because of steel shortages it also boasted wooden bodywork covered with artificial leather.

The IFA continued to investigate alternatives to steel as a material for car bodies and eventually came up with Duroplast, a composite material (like fibreglass) consisting of phenolic resin, an East German plastic, reinforced with Soviet cotton fibres. The new material, it should be stressed, need not be dismissed as a mere inferior substitute in the German wartime *ersatz* tradition. As owners of elderly steel-bodied cars can readily attest, the propensity of the metal to rust is often the main cause of their demise, and for this reason the Ford Motor Company in the United States experimented with plastic car bodies in the 1940s. The East Germans boasted that, compared with steel, Duroplast was lighter, more elastic, more resistant to vibration (and therefore quieter) and possessed superior weatherproofing and heat-insulation qualities (Schiebert, 1997, p. 23). Its introduction can be seen as anticipating General Secretary Walter Ulbricht's policy of the 'chemicalization' of the East German economy, announced in the autumn of 1958. The aim of the policy was to use a mixture of traditional German coal-based chemicals and modern petrochemicals derived from imported Soviet oil, to demonstrate the superiority of the socialist over the capitalist system and to provide a bridge from the prevailing emphasis on heavy industrial production in the economy to a greater role for consumer goods (Stokes, 2000b, pp. 70–1). The policy anticipated the so-called refrigerator socialism of the 1960s.

Duroplast body panels, screwed on to a wooden frame, were first used in the P70, a version of the IFA F8 (see Figure 5.11). Only some 36,000 were built, between 1955 and 1959, though there were estate and coupé models as well as saloons, implying some responsiveness to consumer demand. The even smaller successor to the P70 was first known as the P50, until a workers' committee was empowered to select a name for the car – an attempt, one might say, on the part of the East German authorities to establish a popular identity for the vehicle. The chosen name, 'Trabant', meaning 'satellite', was inspired by the recently launched Russian Sputnik space satellite. Although the choice perhaps had unintentional undertones of East German deference to Soviet power, the intentional connotations were of cutting-edge east European technology. 'In projecting its potent message encompassing competence, confidence, pride and progressivism, the Trabant relied primarily on its design, and most importantly, its futuristic, all-plastic body' (Stokes, 2000b, p. 72).

The minimalist technology and austere lines of the Trabant were in line with the GDR's official espousal of functionalist industrial design, which in the simplest terms required that the design of an artefact should faithfully represent its practical purpose.

Figure 5.11 Fifteen employees at the Zwickau car factory vouch for the strength of the P70's Duroplast body panels in 1955. Photo: Jürgen Schiebert, *Duroplast in Pastel Colours: the Trabant*, MIXX, Berlin, 1997, p. 20

> From the state's perspective, functionalism was uniquely well suited to socialism ... Its emphasis on austerity, rationality and use-value was viewed as the perfect aesthetic expression of the larger GDR effort to create a controlled socialist consumer culture ('each according to his needs') that would not fall victim to capitalist decadence and fetishism ... [T]he SED's championing of modern design went hand in hand with the regime's new belief in the miraculous powers of science and technology to transform GDR culture and society.
>
> (Betts, 2000, pp. 755–6)

It was therefore with a robustly constructed producer identity that the first of what were to become more than 3 million Trabants rolled off the assembly lines at the old Zwickau factories in November 1957 (see Figure 5.12). The chassis was built at the old Horch plant and the body was constructed at the Audi installation, where final assembly of the vehicle also took place. In 1958 the two factories were united and renamed VEB Sachsenring Automobilwerke Zwickau (Schiebert, 1997, p. 32). The essence of the design and technology choices made during the relatively innovative period between 1957 and 1964 was simplicity, reliability and economy. As with the Volkswagen, air-cooling was soon adopted for the P50's little 500cc two-stroke engine: a simple, maintenance-light system, albeit not a clean one, as a mixture of oil and petrol is required to fuel the relatively straightforward, rugged and reliable **two-stroke** version of the internal combustion engine. In 1962, after some 130,000 P50s had been made, the model was replaced by the P60 (also known as the Trabant 600), the main feature of which was a slightly bigger 600cc two-stroke engine. Some 150,000 P60s were produced by 1964, when the final version of the Trabant, the 601, made its first bow. The encores were to last for the next twenty-six years (see Figure 5.13). Dr Werner Lang, the 601's chief design engineer, had a very limited development budget, but managed to include some inexpensive improvements, including better noise insulation and wind deflectors in the upper part of the rear windows, affording draught-free insulation.

After 1964 stagnation set in, and despite the claims of Trabi enthusiasts the 601's design history lagged well behind developments in the global motor industry, partly because of political pressures within the east European Comecon trading bloc. The Soviet Union insisted on its monopoly of powerful engines within the framework of Comecon cooperation and repeatedly quashed attempts by the East Germans to build their own (Naegele, 1999). Sachsenring's public relations director during the 1980s recalls the way the two East German weekly motor magazines treated the minor improvements to home-produced vehicles that were possible under these circumstances:

The two-stroke engine operates as follows: one stroke of the piston serves both to admit the fuel-air mixture to the cylinder and to compress it; the spark then combusts the fuel, initiating the opposite stroke of the piston, which also serves to evacuate the cylinder of the exhaust gases. In the four-stroke cycle, each stroke is associated with only one function: intake, compression, combustion and exhaust. Although the two-stroke engine is cheaper and simpler to build and generates more power per weight, it requires a mixture of petrol and relatively expensive oil, is more prone to wear, generates more pollution and is less fuel efficient.

Figure 5.12 Some early Trabants leaving the factory in Zwickau in 1958. Photo: Bundesarchiv: Koblenz, Bildsammlung Bild 183/52061/23

Figure 5.13 The millionth Trabant at Zwickau in 1973. Photo: Bundesarchiv: Koblenz, Bildsammlung Bild 183/M1122 22N

> every screw, every door-handle that was different and every
> series part that had been developed further was presented as
> a major innovation. Admittedly those in the know found a
> suitable helping of sarcasm and self-irony between the lines,
> and were perfectly aware of what was going on.
>
> (Schiebert, 1997, p. 41)

During the last few years of the GDR under Erich Honecker's
leadership, after the end of the Brezhnev hegemony in eastern
Europe, the East German authorities were more receptive to
modernizing their car industry. A four-stroke engine was approved for
the Trabant as early as 1984, even though it never went into
production. The apparent stasis in design for most of the 601's
production history concealed some conflict between the car's
designers and the authorities. Among Dr Lang's prototype Trabants
was a model with a four-stroke engine, automatic transmission and a
fastback body. But because of political opposition this and other
prototypes were hidden in a cellar, and are only now on display at
Zwickau's Horch car museum (Nowill, 2000, p. 126).

How powerful was the consumer in shaping the Trabant? On one
level, it was the affectionate diminutive 'Trabi' that was to represent
the people's positive construction of the car's identity; the name is
analogous to the nickname 'Beetle' on the other side of the Iron
Curtain. But a cleavage soon opened up between the official
presentation of the car, and an increasingly critical consumer
estimation of it. There were other nicknames representing a more
negative side of the East German consumer experience, such as
'cardboard racing car' (*Rennpappe*) and 'plastic bomber'
(*Plastikbomber*). Customers usually had to wait many years to receive a
car after they had placed their order. In 1989, for instance, Trabants
were being delivered to customers who had placed their orders in
1976, and there could be a queue of sixteen years for the even more
expensive Wartburg (Zatlin, 1997, p. 369). When the car was finally
available for collection it was not unusual for the whole family to
dress up and go to the distribution centre, following a send-off from
their envious neighbours. After their long wait for the vehicle, owners
were faced with similar problems in obtaining spare parts (the social
historian Ina Merkel has reminisced about an acquaintance who kept
three complete Trabant exhaust systems in his cellar; see Merkel,
1998, p. 298). The official hyping of the little passenger vehicle has to
be set against a popular strand of black humour among the East
Germans – for example, 'Why is the Trabant called Luther? Because
Luther once said, "Here I stand; I can do no other".' Another quip
targeted the vehicle's innovative choice of construction material:
'How many workers does it take to make a Trabant? Two – one to
fold, one to paste.' And another: 'Is it true that the Trabant can

reach a top speed of 200 kph? In principle, yes; it depends what height you drop it from' (quoted in Holden, 1998, p. 28; Schiebert, 1997, p. 47).

The following reading is an extract from the American historian Jonathan Zatlin's essay on the consumption of the Trabant within the political context of the GDR.

The Vehicle of Desire: the Trabant, the Wartburg, and the End of the GDR

In early June 1989, shortly before East Germans began pouring into Hungary, Czechoslovakia, and Poland in search of an exit from the German Democratic Republic, the Ministry for State Security put together a report for the leadership of the Socialist Unity Party (SED) on popular attitudes towards the economy. Like many of these accounts written during the last year of the GDR's existence, this one noted with alarm the increasing inclination of the East German population to link economic performance, as measured by the supply of consumer products, to questions of political legitimacy. The quantity and quality of consumer goods in the GDR, the report claimed, 'is increasingly becoming the basic criterion for the assessment of the attractiveness of socialism in comparison to capitalism'. The report went on to warn that the political stability of the GDR risked becoming dependent upon the availability of one consumer good, the automobile. 'Many citizens', the Stasi [secret police] wrote, 'view the solution of the "automobile problem" as a measure of the success of the GDR's economic policies' ...

Despite the warnings of the Stasi, the planning apparatus, and technocrats at the Central Committee, however, the leadership of the SED was unable to do the one thing that might have dampened popular discontent – make more consumer goods available, and more cars in particular. Instead, the quantitative and qualitative inadequacies of the SED's economic strategies found their concrete expression in the Trabant and the Wartburg, the two domestically produced automobiles. The Trabant's plastic chassis, for example, was a creative response to a shortage of sheet metal, presented to the public as a statement of modern design. To the population, however, who referred to the Trabant as the *Rennpappe*, or cardboard race-car, the dangerously pliable body was an excellent example of the SED's tendency to try to meet needs the population did not have while ignoring the ones it did have. To a large extent, popular expectations regarding the quality of consumer goods were shaped by perceptions of western abundance culled from West German television and radio. The quality of the Trabant was the butt of many a bitter joke, such as the following: 'How do you double the value of a Trabant? Fill it up with petrol.' The perceived contrast between western plenty and eastern penury, combined with insufficient quality, politicized discontent; desire intensified by its frustration drove the East German population to insurrection ...

Under these conditions, the Trabant became a symbol of the shortcomings of the SED's economic policies and the concomitant political lack of the freedom to travel. With its plastic chassis and two-stroke engine, it came to epitomize the regime of want created by the failure of the Marxist–Leninist moral economy.

The 'automobile problem' to which the Stasi rather obliquely referred in 1989 was in reality nothing less than the paucity of cars manufactured, although the tendency of the SED to conflate causes with effects led the Stasi to focus on the consumer behaviour induced by the shortage of cars rather than on production levels. According to GDR figures – which were often slanted to represent the reporting authority in the best possible light – the roughly 17 million East Germans seem to have had at their disposal the largest number of cars in Eastern Europe, with a total of just under 3.6 million automobiles registered to private persons as of October 1988. The majority of these cars were Trabants, but there was a goodly portion of Wartburgs, as well as Soviet Ladas, Moskvitsches, Zaporozhets, and Volgas, Czechoslovak Skodas, Romanian Dacias, and Polski Fiats. There were even some Volkswagen Golfs, Citroëns, Mazdas, and Volvos. Of course, in comparison to its West German neighbour, which was the standard of measurement for most East Germans, things looked a bit different. The Federal Republic dwarfed the GDR in the density of automobiles proportional to population: in 1988, the last full calendar year before the Berlin Wall came down, there was one car for every two West Germans compared to one car for every 4 East Germans. According to internal GDR figures, some 50 per cent of East German households owned cars in the late 1980s. A more realistic estimation lies probably under 40 per cent, but either way it compares poorly to the rough figure of over 70 per cent for West Germany. The main reason for this disparity was the low level of production, which by the late 1980s had stagnated at just under 220,000 annually. Car production for the Federal Republic in 1988 totalled 3.98 million, or 18 times East German production.

Worse still, not all of the cars manufactured in the GDR were made available for domestic consumption. This was less because of international demand for the Trabant, which was quite limited. Rather, the political constraints of economic co-operation with the Soviet bloc promoted an inequitable trade structure for the transportation sector, requiring that the GDR export more than it imported. The plan for the year 1989, for example, foresaw the retention of about two-thirds of the automobiles actually produced for domestic consumption. Even when we add the 21,700 imported cars to this sum – for the most part Soviet Ladas and Czechoslovak Skodas – the total number of cars the SED planned to make available to the populace amounted to a mere 150,100, far less than total domestic production.

The wave of automobile purchases soon after German monetary union in July of 1990 provides ample evidence of the pent-up desire for automobiles in the GDR. Why, then, did the party decide to produce so few automobiles, especially given the political headaches the shortage caused? Almost all of the reasons refer back, directly or indirectly, to the Federal Republic. The need to keep a dissatisfied population in check, epitomized by the Berlin Wall, made the SED suspicious of private travel and provided little incentive for the party to satisfy the desire for individual mobility as represented by the automobile. Another, more important answer lies in the moral critique of capitalism which served to justify the planning apparatus. In Marx's writings, production in capitalist economic orders is presented as excessive and therefore morally compromised, while the logic internal to the subsystems upon which classical liberal theory is based, such as efficiency or supply and demand, is exposed as proceeding from irrational, and therefore unpredictable, sources. In particular, Marx argues that the profit motive and the time lag in producers' response to market signals are responsible for the crises of over- and underproduction periodically experienced by capitalist economies. This irrational allocation of resources leads in turn to material waste and the attempt, via advertising, to manufacture desire for the surplus produced and to sell it as a need. In addition, the production methods specific to capitalism lead to a form of alienation Marx termed 'commodity fetishism', or the false attribution to products of the power to gratify human needs. Based on this important insight into the workings of capitalism, the SED went so far as to suggest a distinction between 'real' and 'false' needs. 'Real' needs, whether of physical or spiritual nature, it argued, are generated by the material conditions of a given society in history. In contrast, 'destructive, parasitical, and false (illusory) needs' consist of 'needs [that] are deformed, manipulated, and in part artificially manufactured to suggest illusions to working people about their real situation in society'. Through this dichotomy, the SED established an equivalency between desire and commodity fetishism ...

In order to eradicate these false needs, the party sought to inhibit the temptation toward social differentiation through a didactic restriction of the objects of desire. In a society where desire did not exist, so the argument ran, there was no need to manufacture and sell people goods they did not require. Instead, the SED was able to plan correctly to satisfy people's real needs, which the party was able to recognize because it enjoyed a privileged position in that it could determine the truth by virtue of its capacity as the vanguard of the working class ...

Following the abstemious maxims central to Marxism–Leninism, the SED proclaimed that everyone had the right to essential material needs at just prices, which led to the policy of subsidizing employment, housing, and basic foodstuffs. On such an ethical scale, cars appeared as a luxury and thus enjoyed a low priority in the apportioning of funds for production ...

Finally, the balance of payments deficit created by the policy of subsidizing goods rather than people introduced a fiscal factor into the equation. Increasingly, the SED found itself confronted by the dilemma of having to export more in order to pay for the increasing cost of the subsidies for basic needs. Consequently, the party encouraged the growth of sectors, such as heavy industry and microelectronics, that it believed to have the greatest export potential. Where possible, consumer goods of sufficient quality and value – such as washing machines and furniture – were exported rather than made available to the domestic market so as to help reduce the crushing foreign debt. Little was invested in the Trabant and Wartburg because they were not considered exportable or as having an exportable future in the West.

The relative lack of importance the SED attached to automobile manufacture is attested to above all by the small number actually produced. The near-complete neglect of the cars' design and engineering, however, and the pricing structure devised for them also testify to the low priority placed on developing technologies in this sector. The antecedents of Trabant, which were assembled in the old Horch plant in Zwickau, were three-cylinder, two-stroke engines with 28 horsepower and front drive. The Trabant itself, with its plastic body, was introduced in 1958, and by the time the GDR began with mass production, it had a two-cylinder, two-stroke engine with front drive, but only 23 horsepower. In 1964, the engine was upgraded to 26 horsepower. Except for minor cosmetic changes, however, no major improvements were made in the car until 1989. The Wartburg was based on a BMW motor, originally a six-cylinder, four-stroke engine with 45 horsepower. The Wartburg went on line in 1956 with a three-cylinder, two-stroke engine and 37 horsepower; in 1966, the chassis was remodelled and the horsepower increased to 45. Until 1988, it underwent only minor improvements.

As with most consumer goods the SED had decided were non-essential, the price structure of automobiles reflected an attempt to provide a powerful disincentive to those wishing to purchase them. Because they were not directly subsidized, cars were rather expensive for most East Germans. In 1989, the average monthly income was around 800 East German marks. A roll cost 5 pfennigs and a haircut 1.90 marks, but the cheapest two-stroke Trabant cost 12,000 marks. The cheapest version of the last Wartburg, which came with a four-stoke engine, cost 30,200 marks. Such high prices reflected the high production costs of an economy hobbled by ageing fixed capital and a predilection for labour-intensive manufacturing methods, but they also provided a convenient way for the party to recoup some of the money lost in subsidizing basic material needs such as bread.

But if automobiles were problematic ideologically, why bother to produce them at all? Firstly, the inflation spawned by the pricing structure stimulated demand for consumer durables. The party kept prices frozen at levels from the 1950s in order to pretend it had eradicated inflation and so contend that the planned economy was therefore more stable than the market economy. Honecker's strategy of placating the population by increasing wages and salaries, however, created strong inflationary pressures. The fiscal problem caused by too much money chasing goods that were too cheap was exacerbated by the general shortage of durable goods, making those commodities more valuable because of their scarcity and therefore more desirable than their actual utility might warrant. The SED could not overlook this problem, and producing cars was one way of soaking up the extra cash it was throwing at its citizens. Perhaps more importantly, however, the production of automobiles enjoyed a certain prestige in Soviet-style economies, and the GDR's national identity, particularly among SED members, was to a large extent contingent on garnering such prestige in the East Bloc. Moreover, the systemic competition with the Federal Republic placed the GDR in the impossible situation of trying to furnish its population with at least some consumer items, even though the number and often the excellence of those goods ended up angering rather than mollifying disgruntled East

German consumers. Thus, the economic consequences of the SED's social policies, as well as its own desire for power and prestige, forced an irrational course of action upon the party that stood in stark contrast to the more rational elements of its social criticism.

Once the decision was made to manufacture automobiles, the problem remained of how to determine the appropriate level of production. The suppression of market mechanisms – specifically, the refusal to allow liberal standards of measurement such as supply and demand an independent status – closed off one of the most reliable methods of gathering information about the extent of 'need' in the automotive sector. Unwilling to abandon automobile production to the vagaries of the market, the SED devised a bureaucratic system of numeric oversight to cope with the mounting demand for cars. The registration system established by the planning apparatus sought to make the needs of the population, as defined by the party, transparent to planners in the form of mathematical divisions in time. Upon turning 18, every citizen of the GDR was permitted to place an order for an automobile with the local IFA-Distribution enterprise, a subsidiary of the appropriately named Volkseigener Betrieb Industrieverband Fahrzeugbau der DDR Kombinat Personenkraftwagen – in English, the People's Own Enterprise Industrial Association for Automotive Construction Combine Personal Automotive Transport, or IFA-Combine for short. In return, the would-be consumer received a slip of paper recording the date of his or her order. The planning apparatus seems to have believed it could employ the registration system to inhibit the desire for a commodity whose production did not fit into its political priorities, while simultaneously channelling the backed-up demand for cars resulting from the low levels of production into an orderly but delayed gratification. Once visible to the party, people's desires could be kept in line and the order in the line enforced.

Needless to say, this strategy did not come close to solving the basic problem, which was one of production rather than registration. In fact, the registration system degenerated into little more than a glorified queue which continued to lengthen as production fell behind ever-increasing demand. In 1989, the IFA-Combine was just beginning to deliver Trabants to people who had ordered them in 1976. People who had ordered Wartburgs, which were somewhat more desirable than the Trabant because their chassis were actually made of metal, had to wait a bit longer – an average of sixteen years depending on where one lived. The waiting time for Ladas and Skodas was eighteen years. As of April 1989, the IFA-Combine had registered a total of 6.2 million orders for cars. In other words, for each person who received an automobile there were forty-three times that number waiting for a car.

In addition, the registration system seems to have had quite the opposite of its intended effect. In the first place, it not only failed to provide an effective substitute for market mechanisms, but as the planners themselves admitted, even introduced inaccuracies into the collection of data. Because of the shortage of automobiles and the long waiting periods, there was an incentive for everyone to order cars even if they had no immediate use for them, which meant that demand as recorded by registration was inflated. Unfortunately, planners had no means of establishing precisely how large this variable was. Neither could the qualitative aspects of consumer demand be ascertained by registration in the aggregate: the mass of orders disclosed nothing about consumer preferences because there were no alternatives to the cars people were waiting for anyhow.

Most problematic for a party that tirelessly trumpeted its ability to dispense social justice, however, was the way that lining up encouraged social inequities. The Section for Mechanical Engineering and Metallurgy at the Central Committee of the SED concluded that 'with the current ordering system, the financial, health, or territorial situation of the person ordering the car is not taken into account'. In practice, however, these factors did play a major role. Berlin and the two party districts where production was located, Erfurt and Halle, enjoyed shorter waiting periods – on the average about two years shorter – than other districts, something that did not escape the attention of the population. Moreover, larger families enjoyed an advantage because grandparents were able to pass the order forms on to their grandchildren, thereby cutting the waiting periods down substantially. The Mechanical Engineering and Metallurgy Section estimated that 'many families can buy a new automobile for themselves inside of six to eight years, while young families and those registering for the first time are affected by the long waiting periods' – as if a six- to eight-year delay did not constitute waiting.

As might be expected, the protracted wait led to various forms of jumping the queue, most of which were illegal. To reduce the lag between ordering and purchasing a car, for example, people began to trade the registration slips, simply ignoring the fact that they were not transferable. The closer to delivery the car came, the more the slip gained in value, rather like a bond. The only hitch was that neither the party nor the company making the cars profited from the slips, which sold for between 10,000 and 40,000 East German marks, depending on their date. Buying registration slips was akin to buying time, moving one closer to the object of desire (despite the fact that the slip did not comprise the purchase of the object to which it referred since the price of the car itself was not included). These and similar transactions illustrate the population's ability to appropriate government regulation aimed at making the population's behaviour transparent and so easier to control.

The thriving black market for used cars was even more problematic for the SED because it threatened the party's control over economic behaviour and challenged the Marxist–Leninist conceptualization of just prices. The SED measured the value of a brand-new product within a moral hierarchy, which replaced market-driven pricing structures with notions of social utility. Officially, the prices of used goods were determined in relation to their cost when sold as new, reduced by the so-called *Zeitwert* ['time value'] to reflect wear and tear, and so could not exceed their official prices as new. Conditions under which used items were sold at rates in excess of their official price as new suggested that pricing mechanisms independent of the SED's theories were at work – pricing mechanisms that restored capitalist relations of profit and exploitation. It is no wonder, then, that the SED labelled the black market for used cars in the GDR 'speculative' and accused people engaged in it of leading 'a parasitic way of life'. The party's vilification of attempts to satiate desire did little, however, to change the fact that a goodly part of the population was engaged in economic behaviour which ran counter to the SED's moral precepts. In fact, it even seems to have elicited mild ridicule in the form of open jokes about how widespread black-market practices were. The procedure for soliciting offers for a used car, for example, was to leave the driver's window slightly open. As the cartoon from the East German satirical magazine *Eulenspiegel* illustrates [overleaf], the number of bids tossed into the car by prospective buyers was often overwhelming.

Of course, the party was not content with mere invective, but also sought to inhibit practices not in line with its definition of ethical economic conduct by outlawing them. According to paragraph 173 of the GDR's penal code, for example, speculation could be punished with fines or a prison sentence of up to two years, in 'serious cases' eight years. Dealing in used cars on the black market became quite a serious business: those who were caught were prosecuted to the full extent of the law, but the penalties constituted no deterrent against the demand for cars ... The

„Da hast du wohl gestern abend das Fenster nicht richtig hochgekurbeit!"

('You obviously didn't wind the window up properly last night!')

prosecution of used-car kings was aimed at making examples of the most visible infractions and deflecting criticism of the party by exciting indignation at wealthy racketeers. At the same time, the party was aware that it could not employ the police to discipline the economic behaviour created by its production system. It is even likely that the planning apparatus was prepared to look the other way and tolerate the parallel economy because it provided partial solutions to problems beyond the purview of the plan ...

The discrepancy between official and illegal prices ensured that the black market would remain the locus of two problems for the SED. Firstly, it intensified the very social divisions the party was devoted to eliminating by creating two classes of people – those who had access to large amounts of cash or, better yet, western currency, and those who did not. Secondly, the black market consisted of an alternate value system, in direct competition with the value system based on moral hierarchies that the GDR tried to impose on its citizens ... [T]he car quickly became a vehicle of social differentiation as limited access led people to attach social status and prestige to possession of it. A peculiarly materialistic mentality developed, in which social station was measured in terms of visible wealth – 'Haste was, biste was', as the popular saying went [literally, 'what you have is what you are']. The fact, for example, that people advertising in newspapers for potential spouses included a list of their material possessions, and their cars in particular, made a mockery of the SED's austere egalitarianism.

Worse, the party itself actively partook in practices that encouraged social differentiation. Driven by its debt problems, the SED set up the Geschenkdienst und Kleinexport GmbH (Genex), a mail-order retailer designed to earn hard currency. People who had relatives in the West could ask them to purchase a Trabant from Genex, which cost 9,000 West German marks in 1989. Even more unpopular were the Intershops, which sold western goods but accepted payment only in western currency. In 1975, the Intershops began selling western cars, such as Fiats, Renaults, and BMWs. The only people who could afford them, however, were those with relatives in the West, artists who sold their work in the West, or those involved in the black market; even retired persons willing to commute and perform manual labour in West Berlin hardly had access to that kind of cash. Like Genex, the Intershops offered most East Germans little hope of satisfying their desires. On the contrary, Genex and the Intershops were nothing less than officially sanctioned forms of the social discrimination carried out by the high prices on the black market. They generated a two-class, two-currency system, a kind of queue-jumping for capitalists and their relatives. These social divisions were greatly resented precisely because of the stark contrast between the SED's egalitarian claims and the social hierarchies it created, a disjunction which rested on equally distributed desire but institutionally rationed gratification ...

To counteract possible resistance to the authoritarian aspects of this arrangement, the party encouraged people to air their grievances in a formal procedure which was presented as a dialogue between the people and official institutions. Private persons were invited to address *Eingaben der Bürger*, or citizens' petitions, directly to party and state organs or the individuals representing them, ostensibly because the party welcomed working people's suggestions about how to improve working conditions and living standards ... The primary purpose of the petition system, however, lay in preventing political fall-out from consumer discontent by preventing individuals with similar complaints from organizing themselves. The system had a distinctly absolutist cast, harking back to the right of subjects to plead their cases personally before the sovereign, which is revealing of the regime's penchant for hierarchy and discipline. The prompt answers given by impersonal institutions to the tens of thousands of complaints written each year by individuals aimed to deflect discontent by imparting a feeling of personal involvement that was intended to compensate for the experience of material want ...

The planning apparatus treated each person *ad hoc*, as an individual case removed from a group context, even if the complaint echoed thousands which had preceded it. The complaints expressed by individual consumers were reduced to their singularity, which allowed planners to respond in a ritualized manner, since the desires of one consumer could hardly form the basis of the entire plan.

For their part, consumers did not treat the petition system as ritualized dialogue, but as adherence to a contractual obligation. Whether complaining about the long queues to buy automobiles, the scarcity of spare parts, or the impossibility of getting anything repaired, people pointed to the disparity between the SED's public rhetoric and actual practice. While the terms of discourse used by petitioners and planners were similar, there was no consensus about the problems and how to solve them. Instead, the petitioners demonstrated an admirable virtuosity in exploiting socialist argumentation to express their desires and improve their material situation. One person who demanded that the manufacturer undertake touch-up repairs on a newly delivered automobile, for example, justified his case by quoting from Articles 21 and 103 of the GDR's constitution. He argued that the manufacturer's refusal to respond to his suggestions abrogated the constitutionally guaranteed right to *Mitbestimmung* and *Mitgestaltung*, or participation in governing, defined as 'a high moral duty for every citizen'. Another man quoted the People's Parliament and the Politburo as promising an increase in automobile production, and tried to hold them to it. 'The need for chassis can be recorded and planned', he wrote, then turned the party's slogan regarding socialism's responsibility to the individual against the SED: 'It really is not in the spirit of the human being as the centre of socialist society when I have to save up for years for a Trabant and then cannot use my car for more than a year because of a shortage of spare parts!' ...

Other petitions addressed imbalances in the distribution system based on residency, from rural versus urban tensions to territorial deviations in automobile allocations. In an open letter to the party leadership, for example, petitioners from the village of Großdeuben complained that the rural population was discriminated against from the outset, since the small number of shops in rural areas made owning a car indispensable for buying food and other provisions. Another person assailed the way in which some party districts received priority, noting that 'those who do not live in Berlin should also have the possibility of buying ... a car'. As with many petitioners, she measured East German consumer articles against West German ones, with a hint of jealousy creeping into her comment that 'the GDR's automotive industry is not going to make a car similar to the [Volkswagen] Golf in the coming five-year plan either. That is regrettable and disappointing, since the retirement of the Trabant is long overdue' ...

There are, however, cases of people, mostly those connected to the party or the mass organizations in its service, whose problems received more attention than a simple form letter ... Seldom, however, did mere membership in the party or mass organizations constitute grounds for intervention regarding a petition. In contrast, the relatives and friends of highly placed party officials enjoyed important privileges, which reinforced the widespread impression that those with connections, or as the East Germans called it, Vitamin B (*B für Beziehungen*) [in English, it would have to be Vitamin C: C for connections], could go to the head of the queue. Such real and imagined social inequities were the target of much sarcasm. One man implied that 'the honourable comrade Minister' of Trade and Supply might not be aware of 'the kind of problems citizens of the GDR with a normal income have when trying to buy such a great "luxury"' as a car. Another fulminated against the 'honourable comrade Volvo drivers' ...

The petitions regarding cars, and for that matter, other aspects of life in the GDR, chronicle with endless variation the way in which people's needs were not met by policies which claimed to do just that. The long queues turned those needs, whether real or otherwise, into longings, and the hypocrisy of the moral regime in which they lived transformed these desires into political as well as economic demand. The anger expressed at what were perceived as unjust economic conditions was clearly on the increase during the 1980s ...

By May of 1989, however, solving the 'automobile problem' seemed impossible. The demand for cars was projected by the regime itself to outstrip production wildly in the coming years because of the continued deterioration of capital stock. The Mechanical Engineering and Metallurgy Section estimated that people ordering cars in 1989 would receive them forty years later ... Within months, televised images of Trabants chugging through the Brandenburg Gate served to point up the way in which frustration with the excessive economic shortages had become the vehicle of pent-up political demands in the autumn of 1989.

Because of its theory of 'real' and 'false' needs, the SED was unable to perceive the threat to its legitimacy inherent in the political discontent arising from shortages of consumer goods. The party viewed desire as a socially mediated wish to acquire status via material objects, thereby reducing it to a 'false' need which could not and should not be satisfied. Moreover, the party justified its power by reference to the truth of the moral claim that it alone was capable of distinguishing real needs from desires. In turn, the plan was the means by which this truth, and thereby the party's power, was socially reproduced. In assuming it could know and plan for society's needs *a priori*, however, the SED made an epistemological blunder which induced it to treat people as if they were unable to decide for themselves what their needs were, while exciting its own didactic inclinations. Both the SED's claims about truth and its concomitant disregard for individual autonomy were carried over into the plan, which committed it to an authoritarian response towards any unplanned behaviour.

The plan, however, simultaneously ensured the creation of conditions which flouted the SED's moral claims to power. The epistemological shortcomings deriving from the distinction between 'real' and 'false' needs, for example, translated into real economic shortages. Confident that it could simply edit out socially counterproductive behaviour, the party refused to devote sufficient resources to the manufacture of goods it deemed 'bad'. In deciding to produce some automobiles, whether to keep up with the Federal Republic [of Germany] or the Soviet Union, however, the SED laid the foundations for precisely those social inequalities it loudly proclaimed it had abolished. The resulting shortage of cars transformed whatever 'need' there might have been for them into a desire, as value was attached to that which was scarce. Thus, the social hierarchies generated by the shortages gained their meaning from the power to circumvent the dearth of cars, and from the car as the site of individual mobility and the prestige this carried. It might be said, then, that the sight of the car in the GDR generated desire for it, whether it was the Trabant itself or images of a Volkswagen Golf in West German television. Just how elusive the satisfaction of that desire was, however, was felt all the more keenly when people saw the relative ease with which highly placed bureaucrats and those with access to western currency could obtain the objects of their desire. The real and unequal distribution of cars led to a growing frustration with the SED's rhetorical insistence on the existence of socialism.

At the same time, the SED's authoritarian response to behaviour which it had not planned for was shaped by its sensitivity to the relation between vision and discipline. The party's ideological criticism of desire, coupled with its aversion to permitting individual agents to interact without government mediation in the economic sphere, led it to respond to the lack of cars and the shortages of parts and patience by trying to keep an eye on consumers and keep them in line. The strategy of observational discipline, however, failed, forcing the party to turn a blind eye to practices which flouted its economic power. On the one hand, East Germans subverted the attempt to regulate their behaviour, as with the registration system, and entered into contractual agreements with each other which circumvented the state, while the SED was forced to turn a blind eye to this behaviour because it helped bridge gaps in production. The alternative ethical and financial value systems exhibited by the black market reflected the way in which consumer desires had shifted from mere economic to political demand, but the party perceived the threat to its power too late. On the other hand, the petitions prompted people to view the SED as the patron of the individual, which encouraged them to hold the party personally responsible for their unfulfilled desires. Yet the criticisms of the party's moral legitimacy expressed in the petitions failed to correct the party's ideological myopia.

The response of the GDR to consumer sovereignty illustrates the failure of Marxism–Leninism to provide a politically stable solution to the problem of consumer desire. If the effectiveness of capitalism lies in its ability to manufacture desire and sell it as need, thereby deflecting much systemic criticism into the activity of consuming the objects of desire, then the ineffectiveness of the planned economy lies in its understanding of desire in terms of need. The SED produced shortages which led to an inflation of desire, and it was the accrual of desire, symbolized by the long waits for scarce goods, which helped undermine the socialist value system financially as well as morally.

(Zatlin, 1997, pp. 358–80)

EXERCISE

Having read the extract from Zatlin, consider the view that 'the dominant tendency in scholarship has been to analyse questions of consumption ... as a function of the political domination of the SED and the Communist state' (Confino and Koshar, 2001, p. 147). Is this 'statist' approach evident in the extract from Zatlin's article, or some evidence of 'human agency' on the part of the consumer?

DISCUSSION

Zatlin emphasizes the role of the state in limiting the production of East German cars, and the strong ideological underpinning for this role. The fact, though, that consumer dissatisfaction is seen as a problem, and that measures such as the petition system are adopted in the attempt to assuage it, indicates at least some state responsiveness to desires and needs as defined by the consumer rather than by the party. But, in this account, the nearest to actual human agency on the part of the consumer is the black market in registration slips and used cars, and perhaps also the elite consumer's patronage of institutions such as Genex and the 'Intershops' in order to bypass the rigours of official egalitarianism.

Trabi humour, of which Zatlin gives examples, is important: it was undoubtedly part of the process whereby consumers constructed an identity that was subversive of that which was promoted by the authorities. It was also a way of sublimating resentment about the inequities of a supposedly egalitarian system under which the people were starved of a people's car, while the elite from 'Volvograd' (as the East Germans dubbed Wandlitz, the government residential district of east Berlin) looked after their own needs: 'they preached water and drank wine' (Merkel, 1998, p. 282). Trabi humour was analogous in its social function to the common habit of 'grumbling'.

> Grumbling illustrates one form of psychic compensation that relieved some of the pressure of everyday hassles and helped people overcome a difficult daily life ... Grumbling constituted the GDR citizens' internal consensus that in being annoyed they were one ... Related to the habit of grumbling was a specific form of humour that revealed an ability to laugh at oneself, one's situation, and the shortcomings of GDR daily life.

(Merkel, 1998, p. 294)

Trabi humour, then, was bound up not only with the popular identity of the vehicle, but also with the self-constructed identity of the East German consumer. But was the Trabi just a joke? Was the condescension of the western consumer justified? Can the car be written off as 'flimsy' and 'loud' (Naegele, 1999)? It could be argued that it was in technological and design terms just what was required to be successful in eastern Europe, where the infrastructure supporting private motoring was meagre by western standards. Both technology and design were geared to economy and reliability. The standard Trabant had only nine moving parts, much reducing the chances of mechanical failure. Duroplast, as noted above in the text before the reading, can be presented as rather more than an inferior, *ersatz* substitute for scarce steel (although, beneath the plastic panels, the wooden frame of the P70 had given way to welded steel in the Trabant). Despite the advantages claimed for the material by its East German producers, it was dismissed as 'out of date' even in its own time, and has been likened to 'a variation of Bakelite, a plastic of the 1920s and 1930s more than the 1960s', one that was 'brittle, cumbersome, and did not take colour well' (Stokes, 2000b, p. 73). The comparison with Bakelite is rather harsh, as this refers to the particular plastic used rather than the more forward-looking composite nature of the material. Nevertheless, even an enthusiast of east European cars has conceded that Duroplast was 'ultimately the factory's undoing: every duroplast panel had to cure within the press, resulting in huge bottlenecks' (Nowill, 2000, p. 125; also see Figure 5.14).

Figure 5.14 Producing Duroplast body panels. The mixed cotton and resin can be seen rolled up on the left, before loading on to the presses dubbed 'waffle-irons' by their operators. The cart in the centre is laden with panels issuing from the presses in the background. Photo: Jürgen Schiebert, *Duroplast in Pastel Colours: the Trabant*, MIXX, Berlin, 1997, p. 30

The polluting two-stroke engine was also a feature of the Wartburg. This was a range of larger vehicles manufactured mainly for the East German elite and for export at Eisenach, J. S. Bach's birthplace in Thuringia, though it derived from the IFA F9 first produced at Zwickau. The Trabants' and Wartburgs' distinctive power unit could also be justified as a rational, durable choice for east European conditions, but it increasingly limited the cars' export potential:

> The real problem ... was that the two-stroke engine was becoming less and less politically correct all over the world. It is possible to sustain a good argument that the infinitely repairable, reasonably economical two-stroke Wartburg is a very environmentally efficient car in many respects. However, more and more countries were legislating against two-stroke use in motor cars. Export markets dried up, one by one.
>
> (Nowill, 2000, p. 132)

Political and economic change in an increasingly globalized market therefore strongly affected both the design of the motor car and its identity. There was an attempt to upgrade the car immediately after reunification, and a new Trabant was produced with a VW Polo 1050cc power unit that was more than twice as powerful as the traditional two-stroke engine – the cynical East German consumer soon dubbed this version 'the mummy with a pacemaker' (Schiebert, 1997, p. 83). The effort was doomed to failure in the wake of 1989, as cheap imports from West Germany and the Far East quickly became available in the Trabant's main east European export markets, as well as in the GDR itself. There was a countervailing westward rush of Trabants out of East Germany, their owners being only too keen to exchange them for second-hand western makes, and Trabants acquired a new identity as cheap student bangers. A banner raised at a popular demonstration in Leipzig shortly after the Berlin Wall came down said it all: 'Mercedes! Buy the Sachsenring factory!' (Garton Ash, 1990, p. 72).

After 1989 all the major east European car producers formed joint ventures with western companies, or were taken over by them. In the former GDR Wartburg was handed over to GM-Opel, after a four-stroke version of the car had been produced in alliance with Volkswagen, while Volkswagen acquired Trabant, together with the Czech brand Skoda. VW's intention had been to mount Polo engines in Trabants. The company duly opened a vast new modern plant 10 kilometres north of Zwickau in Mosel, where the first VW Polos were assembled, alongside the four-stroke upgrade of the Trabant. It was at Mosel in 1990 that the 3 millionth Trabant, with a new 1.1 litre VW engine under its bonnet, rolled off the production line

(Schiebert, 1997, p. 84). A VW spokesman in Mosel, Günter Sandmann, explained the company's changing plans:

> It all began with the Polo, with the idea to give the Trabant a successor. Back then, one believed that the GDR would be able to remain a sovereign, albeit market-oriented state ... We tried to assemble the Polo here. This worked for about half a year. We quickly noticed that people who were used to driving the Trabant for 30 or 40 years really wanted to have something bigger – like a Wartburg, a Skoda, or a Lada. But these models were either unavailable or [their import] could not be financed. People suddenly felt the need to have a classic like the Golf and not merely the Polo.
>
> (Quoted in Naegele, 1999)

So the consumer, it would seem, had the final say in the production history of the Trabant. During the 1990s the Zwickau-Mosel factory, with less than half the employees used to build the Trabant (many of whom had been 'guestworkers' from north Vietnam), produced more than a million VWs: Polos at first, and latterly Golfs and Passats. The last Trabant had rolled off the production line straight into the August Horch car museum, a conversion of Horch's original Zwickau factory, which now competes with the birthplace of the composer Robert Schumann as one of the city's main tourist attractions. The museum today houses an extensive collection of pre-war Horch and Audi vehicles as well as examples of virtually every version of the Trabant: a further, posthumous, identity for the 'cardboard racing car' and, it might be supposed, its final one.

But there is another manifestation of consumer power over the car's destiny. The Trabi, along with the Wartburg and the Schwalbe moped, has become one of those motor vehicles that dedicated bands of consumers refuse to allow to die. It has achieved cult status, an identity that only consumers can construct and through which they typically cock a snook at producer judgements and values. This new identity is partly a facet of the complex phenomenon of *Ostalgie*, defined by two historians of consumption as 'the surprising nostalgia felt by former East Germans for the inferior consumer products of the German Democratic Republic, from Trabant automobiles to functionalist living room furniture' (Confino and Koshar, 2001, p. 138). *Ostalgie* has involved a 'transvaluation' of former East German material culture, whereby the very defects and uniformity of the artefacts have taken on a positive meaning:

> the very lack of product innovation and repackaging assured that these objects – however privately experienced and remembered – would function as transgenerational markers of East German culture and identity ... This is why these

socialist products have played an indispensable role since 1989 in bridging the gap between individual and society, private and public memory.

(Betts, 2000, p. 754)

One manifestation of this phenomenon is that every year Zwickau is overrun by 6,000 Trabis and more than 60,000 visitors to the International Trabant Drivers' Fair at the local airfield, where owners can display their vehicles and trade increasingly scarce spare parts. As well as summer rallies of owners, there are various internet websites, and the newsletters *Du und Dein Trabi* and *Super Trabi* (which also has a website, http://www.supertrabi.de).

According to Rainer Eichhorn, the mayor of Zwickau in 1999,

the Trabant today, as in the past, really is a part of our street life. And every year at the gathering of international Trabant drivers ... one sees that the Trabant is not about to be killed off.

(Quoted in Naegele, 1999)

The mayor of course has a vested producer interest – albeit as a producer of tourist rather than automotive goods – in this final flourish of consumer power in the history of the Trabant. Whether this vogue is simply a temporary, 'transgenerational' phase in the process of German reunification remains to be seen.

Conclusion

There is a circularity in the histories of the Volkswagen and the Trabant, in that they had common roots in the German motor industry of the interwar years, went separate ways on either side of the Iron Curtain and then briefly amalgamated when the country reunited. More than that, it can be argued that the two Saxon cars have recapitulated, as well as participated in, the remarkable history of Germany since the 1930s. The point has been made with a more contrasting east–west pairing:

The difference between, say, a West German Mercedes and an East German Trabant has not been construed merely as alternative automobile styling but seized upon as the very expression of each country's historical destiny.

(Betts, 2000, p. 739)

The fact that that the Volkswagen and the Trabant had a common aim, to provide cheap and reliable private motor transport, and yet had such distinctive and divergent production and consumption histories, amply testifies to the power of economic, political and social structures to shape technologies.

> The superiority of the Golf (or its predecessor the Beetle) over the Trabant, and by extension, of the capitalist economic system over the socialist one, was not predestined ... In fact, the Trabant was seen the world over as the wave of the future when it was introduced. It was the inability of the GDR to improve on the initial design, combined with changes in the international energy and regulatory environment, which condemned the car to the dustbin of history. The qualitative differences we now perceive between the two automobiles – and the two political systems – emerged only gradually over time out of decisions made in specific historical situations.
>
> (Stokes, 1997, p. 237)

This perspective is invaluable for a balanced historical assessment of technologies that we might initially perceive above all as powerful agents of change in their own right.

It only remains to ensure that this contextualist perspective is fully explored. Do the divergent histories and forms of the 'people's car' in the Federal Republic and the GDR simply exemplify the differences between the western capitalist and Soviet communist economic systems, as the East German authorities intended? Is it that simple? The treatment by the producers of the cherished Beetle consumer and the long-suffering, long-queuing Trabi owner could hardly be more different, and this gulf is surely reproduced to some extent in the respective design and technological histories of the cars. But there are some similarities that need to be weighed in the balance. Both cars were the offspring of one-party states, a circumstance that among other things demanded a great deal of patience on the would-be consumers' part, even though, unlike the German communists, the national socialists were never ideologically hostile to consumption as such. An element of authoritarianism continued in the later production history of the Volkswagen, first in the form of the British army, and then in the person of Director-General Noordhoff. Examination of the contexts in which the Volkswagen and the Trabant were produced and consumed might seem to demonstrate producer dominance in the construction of both cars' identities. But the relationship between producers and consumers is complex and variable: you will have noted that both cars have a post-production life and identity principally shaped by enthusiasts.

One of the general issues that this chapter has touched upon is the relationship between artefacts and the culture in which they are produced. Do artefacts simply reflect that culture, or do they also play a part in its formation? Focusing on the specific issue of identity and the motor car helps us to get a purchase on these over-large questions, even if a definitive answer is still elusive. The processes of design and identity formation are shown to be lengthy, contested historical processes, in which a dialogue between various interested actors unfolds. It remains to be decided whether a given design embodies certain cultural assumptions that constrain its subsequent history of identities, or whether the design is an essentially neutral matrix, a *tabula rasa* on which consumers are free to inscribe a wide range of identities that the car manufacturers' design and marketing departments struggle to predict. You need to ponder the range of identities inscribed on both artefacts, and the extent of the design and technology changes, in reaching your own resolution of this issue. The interim general conclusions that I would draw are that the relationship between consumer and producer is essentially reciprocal and highly context-dependent, and that the contribution of the consumer is rather greater than the motoring literature generally suggests.

References

Abelshauser, Werner (1995) 'Two kinds of Fordism: on the differing roles of the industry in the development of the two German states', in Haruhito Shiomi and Kazuo Wada (eds), *Fordism Transformed: the Development of Production Methods in the Automobile Industry*, Oxford, Oxford University Press.

Angelucci, Enzo and Bellucci, Alberto (1975) *The Automobile: from Steam to Gasoline*, 2nd edn., London/Warrendale, PA, Macdonald/ Society of Automotive Engineers.

Bayley, Stephen (1986) *Sex, Drink and Fast Cars: the Creation and Consumption of Images*, London, Faber & Faber.

Beasley, David (1988) *The Suppression of the Automobile: Skulduggery at the Crossroads*, New York/London, Greenwood.

Betts, Paul (2000) 'The twilight of the idols: East German memory and material culture', *Journal of Modern History*, vol. 72, pp. 731–65.

Boddy, William (1999) *VW Beetle: Type 1 and the New Generation*, rev. edn., Oxford, Osprey.

Confino, Alon and Koshar, Rudy (2001) 'Régimes of consumer culture: new narratives in twentieth-century German history', *German History*, vol. 19, pp. 135–61.

Davies, Robert (1996) *VW Beetle: the Complete Story*, Ramsbury, Crowood.

Garton Ash, Timothy (1990) *We the People: the Revolution of '89 Witnessed in Warsaw, Budapest, Berlin and Prague*, Cambridge, Granta.

Hodges, David (1997) *The Volkswagen Beetle*, London, Grange.

Holden, Len (1998) 'More than a marque. The car as symbol: aspects of culture and ideology', in David Thoms, Len Holden and Tim Claydon (eds), *The Motor Car and Popular Culture in the Twentieth Century*, Aldershot, Ashgate.

Hopfinger, K. B. (1971) *The Volkswagen Story*, rev. 3rd edn., Henley-on-Thames, G. T. Foulis.

Jacobs, Timothy (1991) *The World's Worst Cars*, London, Brompton.

Kay, Jane Holtz (1998) *Asphalt Nation: How the Automobile Took over America, and How We Can Take It Back*, Berkeley, CA, University of California Press.

Kline, Ronald R. and Pinch, Trevor (1996) 'Users as agents of technological change: the social construction of the automobile in the rural United States', *Technology and Culture*, vol. 37, pp. 763–95.

Ludvigsen, Karl E. (1996a) 'Introduction' to K. E. Ludvigsen (ed.), *People's Car: a Facsimile of B.I.O.S. Final Report no. 998 Investigation into the Design and Performance of the Volkswagen or German People's Car, First Published in 1947*, London, Stationery Office.

Ludvigsen, Karl E. (ed.) (1996b) *People's Car: a Facsimile of B.I.O.S. Final Report no. 998 Investigation into the Design and Performance of the Volkswagen or German People's Car, First Published in 1947*, London, Stationery Office.

McShane, Clay (1994) *Down the Asphalt Path: the Automobile and the American City*, New York, Columbia University Press.

Mantle, Jonathan (1995) *Car Wars: Fifty Years of Greed, Treachery and Skulduggery in the Global Marketplace*, New York, Arcade.

Marsh, Peter and Collett, Peter (1986) *Driving Passion: the Psychology of the Car*, London, Jonathan Cape.

Meredith, Laurence (1999) *The VW Beetle*, Stroud, Sutton.

Merkel, Ina (1998) 'Consumer culture in the GDR, or how the struggle for antimodernity was lost on the battleground of consumer culture', in Susan Strasser, Charles McGovern and Matthias Judt (eds), *Getting and Spending: European and American Consumer Societies in the Twentieth Century*, Cambridge/ Washington, DC, Cambridge University Press/German Historical Institute.

Naegele, Jolyon (1999) 'Ten years after – the East German Trabant', Radio Free Europe/Radio Liberty website: http://www.rferl.org/nca/special/10years/germany3.html

Nelson, Walter Henry (1970) *Small Wonder: the Amazing Story of the Volkswagen*, London, Hutchinson.

Nixon, St John C. (1936) *The Invention of the Automobile (Karl Benz and Gottlieb Daimler)*, London, Country Life.

Nowill, Julian (2000) *East European Cars*, Stroud, Sutton.

O'Connell, Sean (1998) *The Car in British Society: Class, Gender and Motoring, 1896–1939*, Manchester, Manchester University Press.

Parkinson, Simon (1996) *Volkswagen Beetle: the Rise from the Ashes of War*, Dorchester, Veloce.

Sachs, Wolfgang (1992) *For Love of the Automobile: Looking back into the History of our Desires*, transl. Don Reneau, Berkeley, CA, University of California Press.

Scharff, Virginia (1991) *Taking the Wheel: Women and the Coming of the Motor Age*, New York, Free Press.

Schiebert, Jürgen (1997) *Duroplast in Pastel Colours: the Trabant*, transl. M. Robinson, Berlin, MIXX.

Sloniger, Jerry (1980) *The VW Story*, Cambridge, Patrick Stephens.

Stokes, Raymond (1997) 'In search of the socialist artefact: technology and ideology in East Germany, 1945–1962', *German History*, vol. 15, no. 2, pp. 221–39.

Stokes, Raymond G. (2000a) *Constructing Socialism: Technology and Change in East Germany, 1945–1990*, Baltimore, MD, Johns Hopkins University Press.

Stokes, Raymond (2000b) 'Plastics and the new society: the German Democratic Republic in the 1950s and 1960s', in David Crowley and Susan E. Reid (eds), *Style and Socialism: Modernity and Material Culture in Post-War Eastern Europe*, Oxford, Berg.

Wyatt, Caroline (2000) 'A farewell to Berlin', BBC website: http://news.bbc.co.uk/hi/english/world/from_our_own_correspondent/newsid_924000/924553.stm

Zatlin, Jonathan R. (1997) 'The vehicle of desire: the Trabant, the Wartburg, and the end of the GDR', *German History*, vol. 15, no. 3, pp. 358–80.

6

Making the socialist home in postwar eastern Europe

DAVID CROWLEY

Introduction

This chapter explores ideas about the representation and experience of socialism in the Soviet Union and its so-called satellite states in eastern Europe, focusing on the late 1950s and 1960s when forms of consumerism were encouraged in these societies. The phrase 'refrigerator socialism' was coined to emphasize the increase in consumer goods and the appearance of particular forms of domesticity in the eastern bloc after the repudiation of Stalinism. While an analysis of commonplace items such as open-plan schemes, 'contemporary style' furnishings and kitchen appliances might seem to be a wilfully prosaic theme when eastern bloc states professed to prepare their subjects for the utopia of communism, there are good reasons to reflect on the material and domestic culture of socialism. After all, the communists claimed legitimacy deriving from their promise to improve living conditions by putting all resources into common ownership and all needs under scrutiny.

In making claims for the ultimate superiority of socialist economics, some zealous rhetoricians were led to imagine the fabric of a new world. In 1925, in the slipstream of the October Revolution, Boris Arvatov, a Russian theorist associated with the artistic avant-garde, argued that 'socialist things' could be active agents in the production of a new consciousness (Arvatov [1925] 1997). Under socialism, things would shed the associations with which they were veiled under capitalism, a phenomenon that Marx had described as 'commodity fetishism' (Marx [1867] 1992, pp. 31–40): the true worth of things would be found in their capacity to meet genuine needs rather than stimulating false desires. Later, in the first year of full communist rule in Poland in 1949, one enthusiastic commentator, Andrzej Kulesza, argued that not only would a democratization of consumption follow the overhaul of the economy and production that were then underway, but that a new order would prevail in the design of commonplace objects – that is, that things would be qualitatively or *sensibly* different in socialist Poland (quoted in Crowley, 1999, pp. 68–9). The establishment of a successful and separate socialist material world, and thereby a socialist identity, would distinguish the 'progressive world' from the bourgeois west.

This kind of *relational* understanding of identity (the notion that the socialist world distinguished itself by asserting differences from the capitalist one, and vice versa) shaped many of the debates and practices which are discussed here. Historically, it has been easy to see the world in terms of stark ideological contrasts, divided tidily by political metaphors such as the 'Iron Curtain'. However, you should remember that the east–west divide was far more permeable than such representations would suggest. In a divided city like Berlin, 'western' broadcasts could be watched on 'eastern' televisions in the 1970s, Polish magazine editors poached fashion spreads from French glossies in the 1960s, and (although a predominately one-way flow) increasing numbers of tourists to the eastern bloc constituted a living embodiment of the west. Although less invested with the weight of history and ideology than the images of east–west difference and European division, these commonplace correspondences and connections were important too.

Another line must be drawn between ideology and experience. I hardly need to say that most of the elaborate promises made for socialism in eastern Europe were not met. Nevertheless, it is worth asking whether the eastern bloc states achieved a distinctly socialist identity through the items that their industries produced and their peoples consumed. How might 'socialist things' be distinguished from those produced by other modern societies? As Soviet-style socialism passes into distant history in what was once East Germany, in Poland and Hungary nostalgia for the commonplace things of everyday life under socialism has grown too. Food packaging, cars such as the Trabant and even interiors from cramped public housing have become unlikely memorials (Ludwig and Stumpfe, 1995; Betts, 2000; Gerö and Petö, 1999). What is it about these things that prompts recollection?

The home offers a good opportunity to think about the cold war. In what was predominately an ideological conflict, both east and west produced representations and counter-representations in which not only was 'the enemy' vilified but virtuous ways of living were promoted. We will consider how the 'ideal home' featured in the propaganda and rhetoric of the cold war – both as a site of consumption, where the rewards of capitalism or socialism were to be enjoyed, and as the place where the good citizen (and ultimately the nation) was to be 'reproduced'. In this, I follow the view of architectural historian Gwendolyn Wright, who has written:

> Domestic architecture ... illuminates norms concerning family life, sex roles, community relations and social equality. Of course, architecture itself does not directly determine how people act or how they see themselves or others. Yet the associations a culture established at any particular time between a 'model' or typical house and a notion of the model family do encourage certain roles or assumptions.
>
> (Wright, 1980, p. 1)

Of course the home and its contents cannot be reduced to a motif in the iconography of the cold war. The provision of housing was and is a matter in which all modern states, not least those of the former eastern bloc, make a strong economic and ideological investment. The changing ways in which the home was organized and equipped in eastern Europe after the end of the Second World War has often been characterized as its 'modernization'. One only has to think about the seemingly infinite and monotonous high-rise housing estates dating from the 1960s and 1970s which fringe most major eastern European cities to conjure up one of the more controversial visions of the modernized home. In practical terms the idea of modernization might not seem contentious – for example, a communal laundry with electric washing machines would seem to be an improvement on a mangle and a sad iron. But what might it mean to modernize the patterns of life which are made at home? What, for instance, was the relationship of the 'ideal' arrangement of the new apartment in the high-rise block to older patterns of social life in the countryside from which many new householders had come? How was the idea of the home as a private place of sanctuary, isolated from change and secure as a site of memory, accommodated? And what was the relationship of the idealized image of the home broadcast by the state during the cold war to actual dwellings? Home, after all, was the place where people fashioned their own environment, expropriating resources from the public realm into a private one (sometimes with the support of the state and sometimes illicitly through the so-called second or unofficial economy).

These are, as I am sure you will realize, wide-ranging questions without single or uncomplicated answers. But I hope in thinking about the material below you will develop an understanding of some of the forces – both within and without – that shaped the domestic spaces of those Europeans who lived under socialist authority for a large part of the second half of the twentieth century. Most of the material for our explorations into this subject deals with Poland,

Hungary and the USSR (specifically Soviet Russia). While what Katherine Verdery has called the 'family resemblances' between socialist societies means that many of the patterns I describe are, to some degree, common phenomena across the bloc, it should be remembered that 'local' differences, in terms of culture, history and experience, are important too (Verdery, 1996, p. 28).

To explore these themes in context, let's first visit an exhibition of American culture which was held in Moscow in the summer of 1959: the American National Exhibition.

American homes in a Moscow park

In 1958 the USA and the USSR signed a protocol to promote the exchange of science, technology and culture. This agreement reflected improved relations at this stage in the cold war. Soviet–American exchanges were still marked by intense but, as the Soviet premier, Nikita Khrushchev, would have it, 'peaceful' competition, not least in the hold on modernity claimed by each social system. After the successful launch of the first sputnik in October 1957, the USSR was keen to demonstrate its possession of the latest technology and, under the aegis of the protocol, in June 1959 mounted a display in New York dominated by engineering and machinery. A reciprocal fair organized by the United States Information Agency (USIA) in Moscow's Sokol'niki Park in July emphasized a rather different image of modernity, one that stressed 'personal' consumption rather than 'national' production. This projection of America featured a number of exhibits typical of international expositions of this kind, including a 'Gallery of Portraits of Great Americans', displays of innovative technologies such as an iron lung, and a celebration of modern American architecture. Unusually, however, the American National Exhibition placed more emphasis on the ordinary things of life. Careful to avoid attracting reproach by reproducing fanciful propaganda, the USIA went to great lengths to present a credible picture of American society. Nevertheless, the display was attacked by Russian critics. In fact shrill criticism was voiced by Khrushchev when he was taken on a tour of the exhibition in its opening day by the US vice-president, Richard Nixon. Their exchange on the grounds of a model American home forms the subject of a reading and an exercise below. But before we come to that, let's first follow the path of the 2.7 million ticket-holding Russians who visited the exhibition.

The exhibition was planned by the prominent US architect R. Buckminster Fuller, who designed one of his trademark geodesic domes, clad in gold anodized panels, at its centre. This futuristic structure, 78 feet high and 200 square feet wide, functioned as a processor of both information and visitors. Inside, an IBM computer was programmed to answer visitors' questions about America – for example, 'How much do American cigarettes cost?' and, more abstractly, 'What is meant by the American dream?' Overhead, seven enormous television-shaped screens flashed images of American life. One film, made by Ray and Charles Eames, later entitled *Glimpses of the USA*, projected over 2,200 multiple images in nine minutes, a technique which seemed to echo contemporary fascination with the psychology of perception and 'subliminal messages'. Within seconds the Russian viewer was introduced to dozens of images of supermarkets, freeways, bus journeys and suburban homes. Multiplicity, in this way, suggested not just plurality but also abundance. As the designer George Nelson has stressed,

> the multiple-screen presentation was the one really effective way to establish credibility that the products on view were widely purchased by the American public. An automobile, for instance, might be looked upon, if the Russian public chose to do so, as a prototype made for display purposes. Twenty to thirty shots of the parking lots surrounding factories and shopping centres, traffic congestion in cities, and car movement on express highways could leave no possible doubt in the visitor's mind.

> (Quoted in Abercrombie, 1995, p. 156)

As Nelson makes clear, the function of the first dome was to prove to the viewer that the many things which he or she was about to witness in the 50,000 square foot pavilion that followed constituted the actual material world of ordinary Americans. A frame-like structure inside the larger, second pavilion showcased 5,000 consumer durables such as televisions, state-of-the art kitchen utensils like the Sunbeam mixer and the Pyrex double boiler, and sports equipment. Each day a fashion parade was mounted which included a 'performance' of a wedding ceremony and a rock'n'roll dance, with models wearing the kinds of brightly coloured, casual ready-to-wear clothes found in ordinary stores in the USA. Other displays across the grounds included stands with twenty-two chrome-plated cars, all 1959 models from Detroit, while a model supermarket was filled with the undoubtedly mouth-watering 'heat'n'eat' convenience foods available all over the USA, and sports boats bobbed up and down in a specially constructed lagoon. The shiny, appealing products of American industry were explained to Russian visitors by a small army of exhibition guides who answered the daily deluge of questions and demonstrated the objects in use by re-enacting ordinary domestic tasks such as laundering clothes and rituals such as the backyard barbecue. Combining symbols of egalitarianism and consumerism, the American National Exhibition was a portrait of middle-class America enjoying the benefits of consumerism. It presented a mask of conformity that obscured the extent of poverty in what the economist J. K. Galbraith called *The Affluent Society* (1958). This was an America where civil rights were not a matter of concern or controversy and women, despite their role in the workforce and in public life, were placed in their 'natural' habitat, the kitchen (Marling, 1994, p. 281).

RCA Whirlpool, a manufacturer of electrical goods, installed a $250,000 kitchen, a futuristic exhibit controlled by an electronic brain. This display was equipped with 'push-button' appliances that seemed to turn science fiction into fact. For instance, the Mechanical Maid, an automatic cleaner, washed the floor and then put itself away. The RCA Whirlpool kitchen was designed to be the hub of the house of the future. In its central location in an open-plan home illuminated by large curtain hall windows, it also reflected contemporary American taste in modern housing design for more modest budgets. It was furnished in the 'contemporary style' – a self-consciously modern aesthetic found across North America and western Europe that combined practical utility with visual stimulation. Rejecting traditional tastes, expressive 'industrial' materials such as brightly coloured plastics and fibreglass were employed to produce aesthetic variety in interiors with flowing spaces and curtain wall windows (Jackson, 1994). The 'open plan', it was suggested, encouraged modern, more flexible ways of living. Women could both cook and watch over children, for instance, if the kitchen opened into the living room, while small, portable appliances could be kept out of sight, allowing the kitchen to become a place for entertaining guests. The kitchen could 'move' out from its traditional 'back-stage' location to become a site of display in various ways. In an open kitchen furnished with seamless built-in units and countertops in bright colours, the housewife might demonstrate not only her expertise as cook and mother, but also her possession of fashionable taste. This room, more than any other in the house, was turned into a new showcase for the display of modern possessions.

A model home displaying many of these features was the ideological centrepiece of the Moscow exhibition. It was a six-room, single-storey, flat-roof ranch house – a fashionable housing form that had developed in balmy California and spread throughout the USA in the postwar period following advances in heating technology and insulation. To demonstrate its commonplace character, it was erected by a Long Island builder and furnished by Macy's, the New York department store. The house was filled with the latest domestic devices: the open-plan kitchen contained a cooking range, dishwasher

Figure 6.1 RCA Whirlpool kitchen at the American National Exhibition, Moscow, 1959. Photo: Library of Congress

and upright refrigerator. The model home proved to be the most contentious exhibit on site, at least from the Soviet perspective. Even before the exhibition opened *Pravda*, the official mouthpiece of the Communist party (CPSU), derided plans to showcase such a 'model' worker's home. In an article entitled 'Is this typical?', the newspaper declared that

> such a house can be called a typical home of an American labourer with no more right than, say, the Taj Mahal is a typical house of a Bombay textile worker or Buckingham Palace is a typical home of an English miner.
>
> (*Pravda*, 10 April 1959, quoted in Hixson, 1997, p. 189)

It is therefore perhaps not surprising that this model house became the site of an angry exchange of views for which the exhibition has become famous.

Figure 6.2 Khrushchev and Nixon debating the merits of the American model house at the American National Exhibition, 1959. Photo: Associated Press

After opening the exhibition American Vice-President Richard Nixon took the Soviet premier, Nikita Khrushchev, on a tour. They paused in the kitchen of the model American home. The lively and somewhat irascible discussion that followed has become known as the 'Kitchen debate'. This event became one of the most celebrated exchanges of the cold war, with Nixon drawing much political capital from it in the 1960 presidential election. The two leaders' discussion was not recorded by television cameras but was witnessed by many reporters and widely reported in the press. A journalist writing for the *New York Times* captured their unrehearsed exchanges in the report reprinted in the first reading below.

Nixon and Khrushchev Argue In Public As US Exhibit Opens; Accuse Each Other Of Threats

No Tempers Lost

Both Express Hopes for Agreement in Geneva Talks

By Harrison E. Salisbury

Special to The New York Times

Moscow, July 24 – Vice President Richard M. Nixon and Premier Nikita S. Khrushchev debated in public today the merits of washing machines, capitalism, free exchange of ideas, summit meetings, rockets and ultimatums.

Mr. Nixon cut a symbolic red ribbon and formally opened the American National Exhibition. He said the fair was representative of the American way of life and called for peaceful competition, spiritual as well as material, between the United States and the Soviet Union.

Premier Khrushchev joined Mr. Nixon in expressing hope that the American exposition would promote understanding between the two countries. In a message read by Mr. Nixon, President Eisenhower extended his best wishes to the Soviet people and said he hoped one day to visit them.

'We should be glad if President Eisenhower found it possible to visit the Soviet Union,' Mr. Khrushchev said.

Clashes Mark Day

... Mr. Khrushchev and Mr. Nixon debated with strong words and forceful arguments. But their talk was straightforward and there was no hint of ill feeling in their fast and furious interchanges.

Nothing like the Nixon–Khrushchev exchange has occurred within the memory of the gray-haired member[s] of the Moscow or Washington press corps. Most of the talk was conducted with dozens of photographers recording every gesture. Newsmen sat at the feet of the Vice President and the Premier taking down each word.

Even to correspondents familiar with Mr. Khrushchev's capacity for catch-as-catch-can conversation and Mr. Nixon's ability to field rhetorical line drives, the day seemed more like an event dreamed up by a Hollywood script writer than a confrontation of two of the world's leading statesmen.

The high point occurred after the two men, accompanied by most of the members of the Soviet Presidium, had started a hectic tour of inspection of the American Exhibition.

Mr. Nixon had started the frank talk with some remarks earlier in Mr. Khrushchev's offices. They had a further exchange before the color cameras of the television studio of the exposition.

Argument in the Kitchen

But the climax came when they went into the model American home – the home that *Pravda* had criticized as not representative and too expensive for the average American worker.

The two statesmen, a little exhausted after battling through hundreds of camera men, newsmen and Russian and American workers, were walking rather swiftly through the house when Mr. Nixon halted Mr. Khrushchev.

He drew him over to the model kitchen. Here Mr. Nixon said: 'You had a very nice house in your exhibition in New York. My wife and I saw and enjoyed it very much. I want to show you this kitchen. It is like those of our houses in California.'

Mr. Nixon showed Mr. Khrushchev a built-in panel washing machine.

'We have such things,' Mr. Khrushchev said.

'This is the newest model,' Mr. Nixon replied. 'This is the kind which is built in thousands of units for direct installation in the houses.'

Mr. Nixon added a word about the interest of Americans in making the life of their women easier. Mr. Khrushchev rejoined that in the Soviet Union they did not have what he called 'the capitalist attitude toward women,' apparently meaning that discrimination and exploitation of women did not occur under communism.

'I think that this attitude toward women is universal,' Mr. Nixon said. 'What we want to do is to make more easy the life of our housewives.'

Housing Prices Discussed

Mr. Nixon explained that the model house could be built for $14,000 and that most United States veterans of World War II had bought houses in the bracket of $10,000 to $15,000.

'Let me give you an example you can appreciate,' Mr. Nixon said. 'Our steel workers, as you know, are now on strike. But any steel worker could buy this house. They earn $3 an hour. This house costs about $100 a month to buy on a contract, running twenty-five to thirty years.'

'We have steel workers and we have peasants who also can afford to spend $14,000 for a house,' Mr. Khrushchev said.

He said American houses were built to last only twenty years, so that the builders could sell new houses at the end of that time.

'We build firmly,' Mr. Khrushchev said. 'We build for our children and grandchildren.'

Mr. Nixon said he thought American houses would last more than twenty years, but even so, after twenty years many Americans want a new house or a new kitchen. Their kitchen is obsolete by that time, he said. The American system is designed to take advantage of new inventions and new techniques, he explained.

'This theory does not hold water,' Mr. Khrushchev rejoined. He said some things never get out of date – houses, for instance[;] furniture and furnishings, perhaps, but not houses.

Mr. Khrushchev said he had read much that Americans had written about their houses and did not think it was all strictly accurate.

Mr. Khrushchev said he hoped he had not offended Mr. Nixon.

'I have been insulted by experts,' Mr. Nixon said, laughing. 'Everything we say is in good humor. Always speak frankly.'

Mr. Khrushchev said in reply:

'The Americans have created their own image of the Soviet man and think that he is as you want him to be. But he is not as you think. You think the Russian people will be dumbfounded to see these things, but the fact is that newly built Russian houses have all this equipment right now.'

Moreover, Mr. Khrushchev said, 'In Russia all you have to do to get a house is to be born in the Soviet Union. You are entitled to housing.'

'I was born in the Soviet Union,' he continued, 'so I have a right to a house. In America, if you don't have a dollar you don't have the right to choose between sleeping in a house or on the pavement. Yet you say that we are the slave of communism.'

'I appreciate that you are very articulate and energetic,' Mr. Nixon said.

'Energetic is not the same as wise,' Mr. Khrushchev said with a laugh.

'If you were in our Senate,' the Vice President said, 'we would call you a filibuster. You do all the talking and don't let anyone else talk.'

Mr. Nixon said the American exhibition was designed not to astound but to interest – just as was the Soviet exhibition in New York.

'Diversity, the right to choose, the fact that we have 1,000 builders building 1,000 different houses is the most important thing,' Mr. Nixon said.

'We don't have one decision made at the top by one government official. This is the difference.'

'On political problems,' the Soviet Premier said, 'we will never agree with you. For instance, Mikoyan likes very peppery soup. I do not. But this does not mean that we do not get along.'

'You can learn from us, and we can learn from you,' Mr. Nixon said. 'There must be a free exchange. Let the people choose the kind of house, the kind of soup, the kind of ideas that they want.'

And so it went on the opening day of the American National Exhibition in Moscow.

(*New York Times* website)

EXERCISE

After reading the report, I should like you to reflect on the following questions.

1   While neither Khrushchev nor Nixon made explicit reference to political ideology, they used the the 'Kitchen debate' to emphasize differing attitudes on the part of the state to the provision of housing. How would you characterize their views?

2   Although Nixon was later keen to play down this confrontation as political improvisation, the fact that one of the memorable skirmishes of the cold war was ignited by a kitchen seems important. Why might the home be an important symbol for both sides?

3   Nixon's rhetoric and the evidence of the displays in the American National Exhibition suggest that the home was the subject of processes of modernization, understood in technical and material terms. While it seems unproblematic to think about the modernization of housing, how might we reflect on the notion of the modernization of the *home?*

DISCUSSION

1   I'll reflect on Nixon's picture of American housing first. Above all, the American vice-president stressed consumer sovereignty in the housing market. According to this view the individual has the right and the ability to determine the kind of home that he or she occupies, and the housing developer, under the pressure of competition, has to satisfy his or her needs and preferences. Housing reflected, in a sense stressed by Nixon, the interests and tastes of individual purchasers. He emphasized the capacity of private business to build and sell houses at a price which might be afforded by the working classes (embodied by Nixon in the symbol of a steelworker, an important figure in Soviet iconography). Capitalism and American democracy were expressed by him in terms of personal choices in marrying, having children, buying a home and gaining access to a cornucopia of consumer goods.

To strongly emphasize the commodity character of the American house, Nixon endorsed the way that it had become subject to the mechanism of fashion. The 'American system', as he characterized it, was built on the obsolescence of its products. Obsolescence – whether functional (i.e. that things ceased to work as well), qualitative (i.e. that things were superseded by other better things) or psychological (i.e. that things fell out of fashion) – was widely claimed to be a key factor in a 'virtuous circle' which kept demand and economic growth high. Before America had slipped into recession in 1958, there had been much discussion of the need to keep the national economy growing at a time when most markets seemed to be saturated. Commentators used terms such as 'post-scarcity' to describe the extent of American affluence. Obsolescence was promoted by economists, designers and manufacturers of commodities like automobiles as the solution to the so-called problem of under-consumption and to stave off recession. George Nelson, the designer responsible for the interiors of the pavilions at the American National Exhibition, had written an article in 1956 in which he claimed that obsolescence was not only the 'American way of design' but also 'the future': 'As other societies reach a comparable level [of consuming], similar attitudes will emerge' (Nelson, 1956, p. 82).

It is perhaps not surprising, then, that the housing industry began to adopt some of the marketing strategies and design techniques of automobile manufacturers. Housing developers, sometimes building entire suburbs, sought to drive down costs by using mass-production techniques while maximizing the appeal of their homes to the customer. New gimmicks were introduced, such as free, built-in appliances, and houses were promoted through 'annual model changes'. Vance Packard, an American consumer rights activist, was exercised by the ways in which kitchen appliance manufacturers and housing developers emphasized the fashionability rather than the utility of their products. In his 1960 book, *The Waste Makers*, he observed that

> Home builders [are] talking excitedly about the House of Tomorrow, which will come in sections, and all or part of the house can be traded in for a new model. The kitchen of tomorrow is to be bought as a unit, with annual model changes available for the discontented.

> (Packard, 1960, p. 121)

What of Khrushchev's view of housing? To counter Nixon, the Russian premier stressed three characteristics of Soviet housing policy: first, that Soviet housing, like socialism itself, was connected with long-term goals and, as such, was not a matter of individual property but a social resource; secondly (and unconvincingly), that Russian homes were as well equipped as American ones; and thirdly (and most important), that shelter was a right in a socialist society.

It is no coincidence that Khrushchev wanted to emphasize housing at his meeting with Nixon, for he had made a particular ideological investment – after some initial hesitation – in this aspect of the Soviet economy. Housing lay at the heart of attempts to garner support for his renewed vision of socialism (Ruble, 1993). He had set in motion an enormous building programme which aimed to meet sensational promises made at the twentieth Communist party congress in 1956 that each Soviet family would be housed in its own apartment. Soviet housing conditions were at that time appalling: during the campaigns in the 1930s to collectivize agriculture and industrialize the country countless thousands of peasants had been driven into towns and cities ill prepared to house them, while wartime devastation had left numerous cities like Minsk and Kiev extensively damaged and countless people homeless.

The proposed solution to this problem was the construction of a new domestic landscape of squat, five-storey apartment buildings in the 1950s and high-rise tower-blocks (the so-called *novostroiki*) in the 1960s. To meet the housing needs of even a small proportion of the population, it was imperative to build quickly and cheaply. As a consequence, Soviet authorities turned to standardization and the prefabrication of building elements. For instance, in an unexpected echo of American ideas about modular kitchens installed into the home as units, specialists investigated the possibilities of prefabricating building panels with integrated windows and plumbing elements. However, important differences underlay this apparent coincidence. Standardization was adopted as a key concept in industrialized housing and, by extension, in socialist economics which prioritized needs over choices. Why offer five different types of washing machines or, as Khrushchev asked on another occasion, thirty-eight designs for schools? 'Soviet' standardization and 'American' obsolescence occupied inverse positions in relation to the question of consumer choice.

2 The drama of the cold war – enacted by scientists working to design the first intercontinental ballistic missile while sputniks tracked invisibly overhead and secret agents searched for the 'enemy within' – may well have seemed rather distant from the everyday concerns of Americans and Russians in the 1950s. By contrast, the 'Kitchen debate' brought the conflict into a more familiar and yet more dramatic setting. In Karal Ann Marling's words,

> the kitchen raised the temperature of the debate by reminding those who saw the photos (of Khrushchev and Nixon) that what was at stake in an era of atomic bombs was existence – home, hearth, all the most basic human functions.
>
> (Marling, 1994, p. 278)

The display emphasized the belief that marriage, the family and all the emotional and material comforts of home were private freedoms and at the same time public emblems, essential to the existence and image of the USA.

America's claim to have responded positively to Khrushchev's call for 'peaceful coexistence' seemed to be supported by the kinds of technology on show in the 1959 exhibition. The labour-saving devices in the kitchen, or the colour television, seemed to be almost effortless triumphs of American technical ingenuity.

As such, it seems to me that the home and its contents cannot be considered ideologically neutral, as somehow separate from political matters. The USIA and the American agencies responsible for the exhibit had anticipated that the display of American domesticity would have great impact on the Russian visitor. Living in cramped conditions, often sharing a communal apartment with a number of other families, or even squatting in dingy cellars and ruins left from the war, the Russians were encouraged to compare their material world with that on display in Moscow. Would any other exhibition strategy have provoked envy? And after the exhibition closed, in a mood of self-congratulation, American diplomats in Moscow claimed that it had heightened demand for more and better consumer goods among the Russian populace, as well as 'conscious imitation in several fields', from 'the blond streaks in the hair-dos of fashion models' to 'the projected modernisation of refrigerator and washing machine design' (quoted in Hixson, 1997, p. 211). The failure of the system to satisfy the appetite to consume would, it was believed, speed its downfall. In the 1990s the unsatisfied arousal of consuming desires was again invoked, often controversially, as an important factor in the collapse of eastern bloc socialism. Katherine Verdery, an anthropologist, has written:

> Even as the regimes prevented the people from consuming by not making goods available, they insisted that, under socialism, the standard of living would constantly improve. This stimulated consumer appetites, perhaps with an eye to fostering increased effort and tying people into the system. Moreover, socialist ideology presented consumption as a 'right'.

> (Verdery, 1996, p. 28)

3   I doubt that a comprehensive answer to this question is possible. It requires reflection on differences between the relatively uncomplicated word 'house', and the more suggestive and symbolic 'home'. Nevertheless, we can map some broad contours of the term.

The word 'home' indicates not only a sense of physical place but also a 'state of being' (Rybczynski, 1987, p. 62). Making a home has been closely connected to the practice of personalizing space by an individual or a closely tied group such as a family. In a context like Britain today, to be 'at home' is to feel comfortable in the intimate presence of others within that circle, surrounded by one's possessions. This has not always been the case. It is generally accepted that this modern, 'bourgeois' conception of the home – based on domesticity, intimacy, privacy and the family – emerged in Europe in the seventeenth century (Kumar, 1997, pp. 210–11). In fact such conceptions have often stressed the role of the home as a place of sanctuary, a place to escape from a changing and often threatening world (Bryden and Flood, 1999). The 'private domain [was] the only place where a person could legitimately escape the inquisitive stare of industrial society' (Phillipe Ariès quoted in Kumar, 1997, p. 210). I am sure that you can already see problems with this definition, but I hope that you'll agree that it has had and continues to hold some currency.

So what does it mean to modernize the home? If we accept the close connection between the home and the self, modernization implies some sense of social reorganization, or even improvement of the individual. I find it hard to imagine how the home might be modernized 'from within'. The stimulus to change must come from without, whether in the form of ideals or from more direct social pressures. Let's take a familiar example. Despite the autonomy suggested by its name, 'do-it-yourself', the home-improvement phenomenon which first took hold in the 1950s, was hardly a form of individualism. In stressing the virtues of masculine work 'at home' or in stripping the home of dark and panelled Victorian decoration (at least in mid-century Britain), this 'movement' directed social judgements or pressures on the householder.

There has been a long history of institutional campaigns of housing reform since the nineteenth century. Sometimes undertaken by the state and at other times by reforming social agencies such as the church, the objectives of these crusades was the 'improvement' of social attitudes and behaviours. As such, they sought not just to modernize the fabric of the house, but to improve the 'state of being' at home. (It is worth pausing here to see if you can you think of examples of this kind of reform.) The 'private' state of the modernized home is therefore only private in some ways, in that (to adapt Ariès's phrase) it is the 'legitimate' subject of 'the inquisitive stare' of the reformer.

Let me illustrate this point with an example from Russia in the 1920s. A connection between the home and the self was made in that country after the October Revolution. The 'bourgeois' conception of home as private – both socially and spatially – was rejected in a series of decrees issued in 1918 nationalizing land and abolishing the private ownership of property. In effect, the private realm was to be subsumed into the collective sphere. Collective modes of housing were not only adopted as a matter of exigency, but proclaimed as the democratization of space (Bliznakov, 1993). Grand pre-revolutionary apartments, each once inhabited by an aristocratic family and its servants, were subdivided to provide homes for a number of working-class and peasant families (these communal apartments were known as *komunalki*).

Some social theorists and members of the architectural avant-garde declared that new ways of organizing the home would produce new social relations which, in turn, would produce a new consciousness. This thinking underscored the most revolutionary housing schemes of the 1920s. The Stroikom group of architects, for instance, designed a *dom-komuna* (house-commune) for 1,000 adults and 680 children (see Figure 6.3). In this collective home, food was to be prepared in a single public kitchen and consumed in a shared canteen, while children would live away from their families, attending a 'boarding school' on site. Reflecting a contemporary revolutionary critique of bourgeois gender relations, architecture was to be used to liberate women from domesticity. Minimal allowances of private space were provided in the design, in order to foster the kind of communalism lauded by

Figure 6.3 Axionometric projection of a *dom-komuna* designed by the Stroikom group, USSR, late 1920s

communist ideologues and inhibit the private possession of things. In fact the desire for such things was expected to disappear when all human needs were satisfied by the perfect environment. The architects argued the case for their scheme thus:

> The widespread housing types today, in bourgeois countries and in ours, are all, without exception, individual apartments preserving the family as an economically independent unit ... All so called 'worker's dwellings' created by the bourgeois society are either simple barracks without any conveniences, or huts and cottages where a decent and cultured life is unthinkable.

> The new socialist community needs correspondingly new housing types, responsive to the new way of life, and the new economic and cultural needs of the population ... Public services for workers' families (food preparation, cleaning, laundry), for their children (education, care and supervision), and for the cultural and recreational needs of the workers and their children could and should be socialized. Therefore, all spaces serving the entire collective ... should be well-equipped public rooms for dining, rest, reading, exercise and for children's needs. Only bedrooms and rooms for individual rest and study should be recognized as private individual spaces.

> (Quoted in Bliznakov, 1993, p. 115)

These buildings were to exploit the kind of openness that modern building materials and techniques such as glass curtain walls could provide. Privacy, a condition then associated with an antiquated social form – that of the family – was to be inhibited by design. This scheme, like others, expressed the idea that the environment could determine behaviour. In other words, Soviet citizens could be 'improved' by their environment. Few schemes of this kind were built (Buchli, 1999), though many people lived in communal environments occupied by a number of families where their actions were circumscribed because they were visible to others (Gerasimova, 2002) – another, rather different form of environmental determinism.

Modernizing the socialist home

To explore the connection made between the modernization of society and the modernization of the home in the eastern bloc, I'd now like to reflect on the period before the Khrushchev reforms. For the next reading I have selected what seems to me a typical article published in the people's republics during the period of postwar reconstruction. It appeared in a Polish journal, *Stolica* ('capital city'), in 1953. Poland, like all the new states absorbed into the Soviet 'sphere', was remodelled as a socialist society in a matter of a few furious years after the Second World War. Stefan Staszewski, a leading Communist party propagandist, recalled this process in a candid interview during the mid 1980s.

> [T]he sights were set on the view from the East. Nationalize all economic life, destroy co-operatives and private trade and bring everything under the state monopoly. And if you have the administration, the money, and all the material means under your control, it's not difficult to nationalize society as well.

(Quoted in Torańska, 1987, p. 138)

Just as in the Soviet Union, housing in Poland was a key aspect of state activities. The wholesale destruction of cities such as Warsaw provided a major opportunity to demonstrate the strength of the command economy and the principles of Marxism–Leninism in reshaping Polish society.

Stolica was a fortnightly illustrated magazine dedicated to the theme of reconstruction and the cultural life of Warsaw. Read throughout the country, it appears to have been a relatively popular magazine (with an average circulation of 40,000 copies in the early 1950s). In 1953 the editors introduced an occasional feature which ran under the title of 'How to furnish a new flat'. It is an extract from the first article in this series, written by Stanisław Komornicki, that is reproduced below. It is important to remember that this piece, like all material published in the Polish press, was subject to censorship. While Komornicki is critical of the design and provision of furniture in Poland, he is keen to demonstrate his political *bona fides* in the paragraphs that open and close the piece.

Stanisław Komornicki, 'How to furnish a new flat'

In its concern for the worker, the People's Republic has attached the greatest importance to building housing. The expression of these concerns is the colossal number of apartments that will be realized in the Six-Year Plan (1949–55). The estates which have already been completed have been given to workers and the 'working intelligentsia' who, before 1939, were cooped up in great numbers in damp, mouldy basements like underground barracks and, in the best cases, in the unlit corners of rented tenements lacking even basic sanitation.

The new, bright and comfortable apartment has become not only a site of rest for the worker, but also a place where one can work on self-improvement – a place where one may think through many of the rationalizing ideas that can arise in the course of professional work.

Unfortunately a certain 'but' exists. In my opinion, in the present age there is a growing problem connected to the aesthetic, comfortable and practical furnishing of the modern interior. It often seems that after buying furniture, one's flat is not attractively or comfortably arranged.

Why does such a difference exist between the pleasing furnishings of local clubs, houses of culture and cafés and that of the average worker's home? It is because the deciding voice in the furnishing of these places is that of the specialist – the interior designer.

Instead, the worker or member of the 'working intelligentsia' is left to his own devices when furnishing a flat. It is clear that the architect cannot be responsible for each new flat in every district, but why cannot he help, even if only to advise? ... An example of this problem was even found at the Interior Design Exhibition ... Not one of the interiors of workers' flats was tastefully arranged with mass-produced furniture from CHPD [Central Furniture Manufacturer]. The kind of furniture which we admired at the

[An interior of an apartment in an old 'style' without the advice of an interior architect]

exhibition is never to be found on sale. That is why a look around the exhibition was like taking a tour of a museum.

Currently CHPD sells constantly in its shops the same patterns of ensembles and pieces of furniture. Tasteful designs – for which there are many willing purchasers – are produced in very small numbers. Why in recent years have they produced tasteless and commonplace furniture? In present conditions most purchasers buy everything that CHPD 'palms off' on them. A feeling of regret arises after arranging these pieces in the home ... if only CHPD would put into mass production some designs with high aesthetic standards such as the prototypes produced by the 'Harmony' design group (Ład). I am certain that close cooperation between these two institutions would lead to good results, both in terms of high artistic standards and inexpensive production ...

We must not forget that the new, aesthetically furnished apartments have to eradicate old and bad customs and habits, to become one of the 'elevators' of the new culture, taking full account of the rights and obligations of the citizen.

How very characteristic is the phenomenon of discontent among some workers' families in their new apartments equipped with relatively small kitchens. Accustomed to having a 'black room', they revive this bad memory of past, sad times. Soot, like all bygone things of this sort, should become a memory, never to return.

There is still another reason why the new occupier may not manage to furnish their apartment. It is his own furniture.

There must be differences in the furnishing of a three-room flat in the new housing blocks in the city centre, the one-person 'kawalerka' [bachelor flat] in the green suburb, and another in the flat in the historic buildings of the 'Old Town' [of Warsaw].

The mistakes that new occupants make are well known: they remove historic 'stoves' [tall ovens decorated with ceramic tiles traditionally used to heat middle class homes] in apartments in the Old Town because they do not have enough room for a huge cabinet or chest of drawers! Naturally, it is more difficult when new occupants have furniture that is already old. However, this problem still occurs when a new householder buys furniture for his empty apartment. Once again, we will avoid these many and frequent nuisances as well as the destruction of the new apartment (such as in the case of this stove) if, at the right moment, we listen to the voice of the specialist – the interior architect ...

> The realization of this problem will be proof of the elevation of national culture in the battle for a better, more beautiful and successful future of the working people.
> (Komornicki, 1953, transl. David Crowley)

EXERCISE

1 In which ways do the 'positive' and 'negative' qualities of homes and home-making practices described by Komornicki represent values rather than practical considerations?

2 What is the nature of the 'problem' as described by Komornicki?

DISCUSSION

1 In one way, Komornicki comes close to expressing what would seem to be a contemporary view, which is that the home is in some sense a reflection or an expression of the attitudes and culture of the person who lives there. The home is an image of the self. However, this is not the narcissistic or heightened individualistic sense of domestic self promoted by the glossy magazines and Sunday supplements in Britain today, or in other words the idea that the home is an expression of individuality or personality. Home in Komornicki's conception is more like an expression of 'good character' rather than personality. (Take a moment to think about the differences between these two terms.)

I think that this is expressed by Komornicki when he says at the outset that the comfortable and well-designed home would allow its occupants to continue their labours after the day's work through 'self-improvement'. Moreover, in his view the new home will not support antiquated or reactionary ways of living. The 'black room' invoked by Komornicki was traditionally a multifunctional room in the peasant home. Organized around the hearth, it was the place where household labour was conducted and meals consumed. By contrast, the 'white room' in the peasant home was reserved for displays of precious belongings and for receiving important guests such as the village priest. The reproduction of peasant domesticity in the socialist metropolis was often, as in this case, the subject of disapproving comment: a form of atavism which stood in the way of progress.

In Poland during the 1950s the notion of having 'good character' might have been expressed as being 'cultured' (*kulturalny*). This attribute or virtue had acquired a political premium in the Soviet Union in the 1930s under Stalin's leadership (described as *kul'turnost'* in Russian) and migrated to the new people's republics in the late 1940s (Naimark, 1995, pp. 398–434; Crowley, 2000, pp. 33–4). *Kul'turnost'* describes the process of 'civilization' or improvement of the individual (Kelly and Volkov, 1998, p. 295). In the 1930s Russian peasants and workers had new and sudden opportunities to advance through the party or industry, joining the new administrative elite. The idea of *kul'turnost'* sought to shape their behaviour in accordance with cultured norms drawn from high levels of education and a traditional notion of social and moral conduct. These two attributes were connected, in that the individual was expected to be knowledgeable about culture and to draw from it lessons for the conduct of life.

Kul'turnost' also legitimated the ownership of what had once been decried as bourgeois possessions that detracted from the ascetic values of the revolution (Hessler, 2000). Everyday things had an important role in the practices related to *kul'turnost'*. Modest objects like fringed lamps and white lace tablecloths were interpreted as instruments through which habits and attitudes could be changed and, as such, were highly symbolic possessions (Kettering, 1997). Catriona Kelly and Vadim Volkov single out curtains in the Soviet Union in the 1930s as the 'universal symbol' of *kul'turnost'*: clean, they signalled domestic order; hung in a shared space such as the communal apartment or workers' barracks, they suggested a degree of privacy and decency. Not only did such things represent a high level of *kul'turnost'*, they also constituted part of 'a material infrastructure' which 'contained an implicit concept of its user, including the user's practical skills, rhythms of activity, level of self-discipline, and basic habits' (Kelly and Volkov, 1998, p. 300). Conversely, the lack of *kul'turnost'* was a threat to order: 'everyday misconduct [was elevated] into a political crime' (Boym, 1994, p. 289).

Could Komornicki's emphasis on the ceramic 'stove' in old Warsaw apartments, even if a redundant thing in practical terms, be to do with its capacity to serve as a measure of culturedness?

2   Komornicki is clearly unhappy about the quality and availability of things needed to furnish a home in Warsaw in 1953. A lobbyist for the design profession, this is for him a matter of establishing good contacts between occupants of apartments and architects, or inventive designers such as members of the Harmony cooperative he mentions. In one sense he is right. If one were to judge the material culture of countries like Poland or East Germany on the prototypes and models in domestic design exhibited at home and abroad during the 1950s, most observers would be hard pressed

to distinguish between east and west. I have reproduced here an image of an interior designed by Harmony designer Marian Sigmund, an expressive and self-consciously modern group of objects in the modish 'contemporary style'. But new designs such as this were rarely put into production.

The reasons for this lie in the strategies for managing the economy in the eastern bloc at this time. In general terms (and with some local variation), socialist states operated what Polish economist Oscar Lange has called '*sui generis* a war economy', based on massive investment in heavy industry; full nationalization entailing the closure of many small enterprises to channel resources and labour into larger, 'more efficient' industrial concerns; the imposition of a new financial system controlled by a central bank, thereby keeping all investment in state hands; and, most important, the establishment of central-planning mechanisms which would manage demand according to a 'Five-Year Plan'. As in the USSR in the 1930s, the postwar period in central/eastern Europe saw enormous emphasis placed on rapid industrial growth in the iron and steel industries as well as in engineering. Official ideology claimed that only intervention into the organization of the resources of an economy could raise standards of living for all. In reality, however, domestic consumption was a very low political priority during the late 1940s and early 1950s. The shops were empty.

Figure 6.4   Interior designed by Marian Sigmund for a national design exhibition, Poland, 1958. Photo: *Stolica*

Central control over the economy was total. Enacting policies adumbrated by the ruling party, each national economy had at its heart a central planning office which drew up detailed plans for every manufacturing concern. Copious calculations determined investment levels, the supply of raw materials and other resources, and the range of different products to be made. This was understood as a politically determined system. Competition, profit and market prices were eliminated. The price paid by consumers, whether for basic foodstuffs or for scarce consumer durables, did not result from an assessment of real relative costs but from a judgement about the 'correct' relationship between the value of things. High demand and low levels of production, as well as an artificial pricing regime, meant that this was a producer's market in which the consumer had relatively little sway over the things that reached the shops. In fact, the volume of production and the quality of goods were shaped not by demand but by state command. Managers in industry were under strong pressure to meet often impractical and inflated targets. As Ivan T. Berend has noted, central planning in its classic Stalinist form was based on fear (Berend, 1996, p. 7). Consequently production returns were often falsified and quality thresholds slipped. As plan culture was built on quantitative markers rather than measures of quality, there was little incentive to introduce flexibility or new technology into industrial production. Thus while, for example, millions of chairs or spoons may have been made to order, the plan had little to say about the quality or design of those products. To emphasize the need for economic reform, Khrushchev produced a vivid illustration of the failings of rigid central planning in the design of items such as over-large sofas and ponderous chandeliers.

> It became the tradition to produce not only beautiful chandeliers to adorn the house, but the heaviest possible. This was because the heavier the chandeliers a factory produces, the more it gets, as its output is calculated by the ton. So factories make chandeliers weighing hundreds of pounds and fulfill the plan. But who needs such a plan?
>
> (Khrushchev, 1961, p. 395)

In this context, the role of product innovation and design was generally passed over to official agencies and offices attached to government ministries (like the Harmony cooperative). These bureaucracies often lacked formal connection with industry, so many new designs remained 'on the shelf'. At the same time most managers in industry, fearful of not achieving production targets set at the centre, kept 'successful' designs from the capitalist era (the period before 1917 in Russia or before 1945 in central/

eastern Europe) in production. The material culture of the eastern bloc, particularly in its early phases, was shaped by aesthetic conservatism and an economy of fear.

The thaw at home

When a new generation of communist leaders such as Khrushchev in the Soviet Union took power in the mid 1950s during the period known as 'the thaw', they set about reforming many aspects of society and the economy. 'Destalinization', as it was called in the west, touched many, if not all, aspects of life in the eastern bloc, but I'll concentrate here on its promises of privacy and consumerism. Although 'the thaw' has tended to be measured by a decrease in fear, or by the freedoms extended to more or less esoteric realms of high culture such as abstract art, one could argue that its impact on ordinary people was largely felt in terms of consumption – whether in the restoration of once denigrated forms of culture like jazz (Stites, 1992, pp. 123–47) or in the spread of appliances in the mechanized household.

After revealing the corruption and terror of Stalin's autocratic rule, Khrushchev and his allies set about rejuvenating the socialist project in order to repair the damaged authority of the Communist party. Seeking to distance themselves from their Stalinist predecessors, the new authorities wished to be seen as a modernizing and, in some respects, liberalizing influence on society. At least initially, they tolerated a degree of free speech and allowed a relaxation of censorship. While the party-state did not abandon its interest in ideology, it espoused a 'technocratic' view of progress (Nove, 1975, p. 142). For instance, the ubiquitous tower block, constructed with industrial materials and increasingly prefabricated elements, was adopted as a quintessentially modern development throughout the eastern bloc and, as such, one which the communists were 'compelled' to introduce. Speaking to a gathering of Soviet architects in 1954, Khrushchev urged them to abandon their pretensions to art by competing to produce the best designs for new housing using industrial materials and standardized, prefabricated parts (Khrushchev [1954] 1993, p. 185). By the same measure, Stalinism was now represented as kitsch and bad taste (Reid, 1997). Architecture under Stalin – epitomized by the grandiose 'decorated cake' towers planned for Moscow in the late 1940s – had, it was now claimed, been distorted by ideology. Decorous possessions such as lamps and lace which had previously been invested with the power to inculcate *kul'turnost'* were now cast as signs of 'petit-bourgeois' consciousness.

The prevailing model of housing, adopted by all eastern bloc states, was the single family apartment. It was inscribed in the new programme of the CPSU in 1961: 'Each family, including newly-weds, will have a well appointed flat in accordance with the requirements of hygiene and cultured living' (quoted in Gerchuk, 2000, p. 88). For many people, the great appeal of these new apartments, despite their mean allowances of space and poor construction, was that they offered the possibility of privacy. New social relations could be made in homes which were not subject to the surveillance of neighbours in the *komunalka* (communal apartment). Svetlana Boym describes the significance of the small kitchen in Moscow's high-rises in expansive terms.

> In the 1960s an alternative 'kitchen culture' emerged. The members of the Moscow intelligentsia who happened to live in their own separate flats started to have unofficial kitchen gatherings in their homes ... The kitchen provided a perfect informal setting for the subtle, casual but friendly intimacy that became a signature of that generation.
>
> (Boym, 1994, p. 148)

Increased privacy may not have been an aim of 'the thaw' but it may have been one of its consequences. In fact Boym has argued that the assertion of privacy was 'a way of carving out an alternative space, a way of personalizing and de-ideologizing the official maps of everyday life' (Boym, 1996, p. 165). Writing in the final years of the Soviet Union, Sally Laird has gone further, arguing that privacy was not grasped as an opportunity for sanctuary but as a matter of 'defiance'.

> Everything about the *Novostroiki* [the high-rise blocks of the 1960s and 1970s] – their location on the city's edge, their sameness, the sameness of their tawdry furnishings – proclaims that the private life of Moscovites is marginal, an afterthought, a coda to their 'real' lives as Soviet citizens and workers. Privacy and individuality must be created and celebrated despite this spacelessness, in defiance of it.
>
> (Laird, 1989, p. 5)

Destalinization also brought significant changes to the way that the west in general and the USA in particular could be represented (though some echoes of Soviet enthusiasm for American engineering and technology before the purges of the 1930s can be found; see Scott, 1942). At the height of the cold war in the early 1950s, leading eastern bloc ideologues such as the Russian Andrei Zhdanov represented the USA as a culturally bankrupt society entirely enthralled by venal consumerism. And in 1952 an exhibition entitled 'This is America' toured the satellite states displaying products from 'the gutter of capitalist culture', including American intelligence and military equipment, *Brother Karamazov* cartoon books, cheap plastic toys and risqué publications (Potocki, 1994, p. 278). During 'the thaw', when the Soviet leadership sought 'quieter' relations with the west, subtle but significant changes in the representation of the USA and American lifestyles occurred. While the USA continued to be represented as a society which deprived its minorities of their civil rights and held menacing 'imperialist' intentions in the world, American materialism was no longer viewed entirely negatively. US technological achievements could not be ignored or overshadowed by exaggerating the significance of minor Soviet scientists. It became possible for commentators throughout the bloc to refer to American achievements *as achievements*: for instance, architects writing in a Polish magazine on the 'problems' of kitchen design in the year of the American National Exhibition in Moscow referred to the situation in the USA because, they claimed, a little disingenuously, the greatest problem that both countries shared was that of providing mass housing (Maas and Referowska, 1959, pp. 28–9). The fact that the ideological and economic orientation of the two countries was polarized was less important than the usefulness of the technical knowledge which could be obtained from the American building industry. Specialists – such as architects and designers – were increasingly encouraged to look westwards, whether that meant to the USA or even, in the case of the Soviet Union, to Poland and Czechoslovakia (Gerchuk, 2000, p. 82).

More important, American standards of living were adopted as benchmarks by which socialist societies were supposed to judge their achievements. As early as July 1954 Khrushchev, campaigning to build his authority after Stalin's death, had predicted with characteristic bluff that by the 1970s the USSR would outstrip the USA in terms of the provision of consumer goods (Breslauer, 1982, p. 36). Such promises were lent gravity by projections in the Seven-Year Plan announced at the twenty-first CPSU congress in 1959: typical was the promise of a sixfold increase in the manufacture of refrigerators (Khrushchev, 1961, p. 442). The party made the attainment of high living standards for all a precondition of the impending passage to full communism (Reid, 1997, p. 188). (Khrushchev even went so far as to paint in the details of the picture of this material utopia when he promised that by 1980 the citizens of the Soviet Union would enjoy some consumer goods for free: this was the threshold of a new world of common things rather than personal possessions – see Nove, 1975).

Many such pledges were made in the eastern bloc after 1956. The renewal of the material world was generally characterized in terms of extending the supply and quality of consumer goods to be consumed as private property rather than, say, extending the communal facilities available for public use. The inflated promises of party leaders were just one of a number of images of demotic abundance which characterized the 1960s. The eastern bloc seemed set on creating an attractive consumer culture: American-style supermarkets occupied city streets (Crowley, 2000); home decorating magazines were on the news-stands; product packaging became more colourful and enticing; and the 'socialist advertisements' designed by newly founded state agencies appeared on billboards and on the pages of magazines (Neumann, 1992; Hanson, 1974). Where the 1950s had been a period of rationing and production targets for the majority, the years that followed were ones of excitement and promise (or 'arousal', as Verdery suggests; see the discussion above following the first reading).

The extent to which the supply and range of consumer goods actually improved varied from country to country and was often exaggerated. While maintaining the orthodoxy of central planning, some reform-orientated states like Poland and Hungary introduced a partial market economy with the intention of increasing the production of consumer goods. Greater flexibility and decentralization in industrial production had the effect of encouraging manufacturers to compete with one another. Reform economists even argued in favour of profit – once regarded as a wretched offence against the working class – as the measure by which productivity should be gauged. The effects were tangible. In Hungary, where consumerism advanced most strongly, ownership of items such as televisions, vacuum cleaners, washing machines and fridges grew from minuscule levels at the end of the 1950s; within a decade they were to be found in the majority of homes (Ferge, 1979, pp. 300–1). By contrast, attempts to improve the supply of consumer goods in the USSR were more cautious and were largely a matter of altering the priorities within the central plan. Here, as elsewhere, the effects of the new consumer orientation of the economy were mixed. Although the production of consumer goods increased by 60 per cent during the Seven-Year Plan which came into effect in 1959, one observer noted that the pressure to increase production did not mean better quality things, while increased choice meant that many shoddy items now remained on shop shelves (Nove, 1969, p. 356).

In the 1960s the combination of new patterns of domesticity and the paraphernalia of consumerism (even if sometimes only as images and promises) might seem to suggest a kind of ideological retreat. Some contemporary commentators did see it in these terms. In János

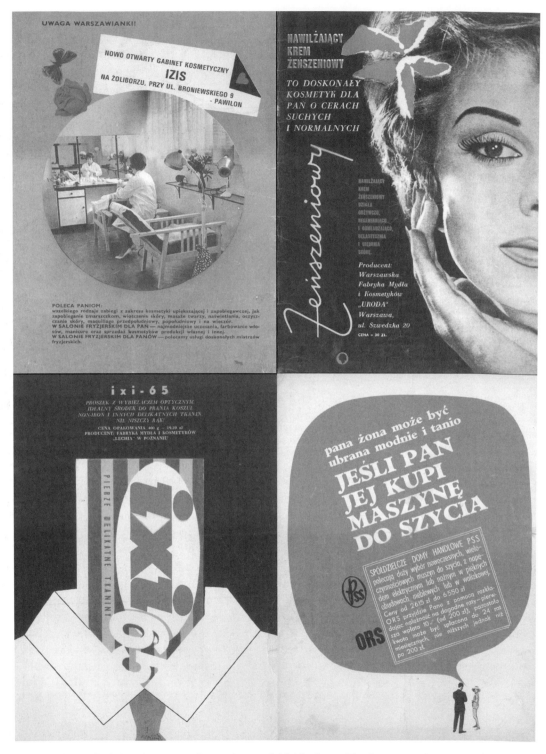

Figure 6.5 Polish advertising from the mid 1960s from *Ty i Ja*, a popular general interest magazine

Kádár's Hungary – where the process of creating a consumer society went furthest of all – some 'idealists' lamented the consumer orientation of the new Five-Year Plan announced in 1960. It was said that western-style 'gadgets' would only produce a bourgeois mentality, anti-social individualism and 'technical fetishism', while fashionable commodities would (in an echo of Marx) ultimately demoralize their owners by arousing, yet not satisfying, 'false needs' (Gömöri, 1963, pp. 64–6). After further economic reforms in the late 1960s, the growth in the provision of consumer goods in Hungarian society increased still more and, like a reflex, commentators periodically lamented their 'anti-social' effects (Ferge, 1979, pp. 305–7; Berend, 1996, p. 216).

Expressed as social critique in Hungary, this viewpoint is visible in campaigns to reform the furnishings of the home in the Soviet Union too. The final reading in this chapter is an extract from an article by Victor Buchli, describing this crusade. Strikingly, he characterizes 'the thaw' after 1956 *not* in terms of the promise of privacy, ideological 'moderation' and consumerism – as I have depicted it above – but as an attempt to control or regulate consumption and instil 'ascetic' attitudes. His argument challenges the conventional view that this was a period of liberalization after Stalinist 'totalitarianism'.

Khrushchev, Modernism, and the Fight against *Petit-bourgeois* Consciousness in the Soviet Home

Byt, Dizain, and Socialist Ethics

Buchli notes: 'The term *byt*, loosely translated as daily life, is an ethnographic term relating to the totality of quotidian behaviour. It refers to every aspect of daily-life from food, clothing, domestic material culture and family life. It can also be understood as the English word "lifestyle" with the additional sense of the ideological underpinnings of quotidian behaviour and material culture.'

While *byt* re-emerged as a problem – almost indistinguishable in rhetorical form from its roots in the late-1920s – the field was by no means the same. The retreat from the regulation of the domestic realm under Stalin left its impact. An entire generation was raised in expectation of the joys of domesticity under terms of locally empowered action which as in other realms of social and political life characterized and assisted Stalinist state legitimacy.[1] In a recovering and re-building post-war society, these joys could not easily be denied – neither could the idea of the individual independent Stalinist agent functioning arbitrarily and locally outside objectivized Modernist norms.[2] The rhetoric of reformers

[1] Buchli, 'The Narkomfin Communal House, Moscow', 1996, pp. 198–208.

[2] Ibid., pp. 199–208. Modernist norms here refers to the body of understandings characteristic of the Modern Movement in architecture, design, and social and city planning in industrialized societies which attempt to regulate human behaviour according to unitary, utilitarian, and rationalistic norms.

often echoed the hostile tones of earlier ones from the late 1920s, often in direct contradiction with Party and government policy. An irreconcilable tension was in place between the 'on the ground', that is the 'as built' situation and the 'as legislated' directives of Party and government. The discourses of *byt* reform relied upon *byt* reformist objectives of the first cultural revolution as the only remaining legitimating socialist discourse on the domestic realm in the wake of Stalin's death and the dismantling of the cult of personality. *Byt* theory and *byt* practice were at loggerheads. The only remaining legitimating discourse on domestic practices, which in the 1920s aimed to obliterate the domestic sphere, was in direct confrontation with the expectations and aspirations towards domesticity of most Soviet citizens.

This tension was alleviated in two ways – first by understanding that Soviet society was experiencing 'high-socialism'; that it was on its penultimate phase before attaining full-blown Communism. In the 1960s that was expected to occur around 1988. Consequently Soviet society was seen to be in a transitional phase; therefore it was necessary to accommodate existing conditions. This allowed reformers to understand behaviour not corresponding to *byt* reformist ideals as temporary, regardless of how strongly individuals may have felt about their behaviour. It was simply part of an ontological phase towards full-blown Communism where domesticity would eventually become irrelevant. Secondly, normative understandings of taste began to perform an important role in regulating pre-existing patterns of domestic behaviour which flourished under Stalin and were now increasingly perceived as *petit-bourgeois*. Taste encouraged more acceptable socialist behaviour that would conform with socialist ontology. Consequently, taste and its arbiters could safely diffuse these contradictions through its regulatory functions. That is, the pursuit of domesticity could be accommodated if it followed certain rules that acknowledged this ultimate socialist ontology. Arbiters of taste could pick up those strivings for domesticity and redirect them in a manner that would eventually see them wither away as full-blown Communism was reached and the domestic 'hearth' completely obliterated. Much of the rhetoric therefore revolved around the rationalization of what *byt* theoreticians referred to as 'irrational consumer behaviour'.[3] Thus Stalinist excess could be adequately contained by means of this disciplining regime of taste.

[3] See I. Z. Zarinskaia, 'Sotsial'nye i esteticheskie aspekty formirovaniia zhiloi predmetnoi sredy', Candidate's dissertation, VNIITE, 1987.

Needless to say, in strict terms of design, minimalism was the operative word in the arbitration of taste. This minimalism was very reminiscent of the Nordic Modernism of the West in the 1950s and 1960s – a point many Western scholars maintain, insisting that Soviet *dizain* (design) was derivative. That copying occurred was without question but for the majority of Soviet citizens outside of Moscow these trends were certainly perceived as indigenous and thoroughly Soviet. However, if Soviet designers – both industrial and architectural as well as other arbiters of taste – looked at Modernist Western trends (they certainly were not looking at other non-Modernist trends in Western design), they were simultaneously looking at those same Modernist elements that emerged from the Cultural Revolution of the 1920s. It was no accident that theoreticians such as Khan-Magomedov began to re-evaluate the accomplishments of the pre-Stalinist generation of Soviet designers.[4] In any case, the superficial appropriation of certain Western principles by Soviet designers does not diminish the unique and socially significant manner in which these appropriations were deployed within the Soviet context.

Between 1956 and 1962, a number of institutions responsible for the socialist rationalization of the domestic realm was steadily built up. The physical infrastructure within which to realize *byt* reform was established by the foundation of *Gosstroi* in 1955 and subsequent directives of the Twentieth (1956) and Twenty-First (1959) Congresses on *byt* and the housing drive. The *tabula rasa* was established upon which the first flank of the domestic front was fought. In 1962 a Soviet of Ministers of the USSR directive entitled 'Concerning quality improvement of the production of machines and consumer goods through the inculcation of methods of artistic construction' called for the rationalization of the industrial process and co-ordination of various professional and industrial concerns in order to create a rationalizing and centralized process of *dizain* over the material goods produced by the Soviet economy.[5] The culmination of the rationalization of the infrastructure of *byt* reform was achieved with the foundation in 1962 of the All Union Scientific-Research Institute for Technical Aesthetics (VNIITE). Its mandate was to provide the rationalizing expertise of architects, industrial designers, planners, sociologists and historians for institutions such as *Gosstroi* and other sectors of

[4] See S. O. Khan-Magomedov *et al.*, 'Traditsii i istoki otechestvennovo dizaina', *Tekhnicheskaia estetika*, no. 21, 1979; 'Nekotorye problemy razvitiia otechestvennovo dizaina', *Tekhnicheskaia estetika*, no. 41, 1983.

[5] Kosheleva, *Rabotnista*, p. 25.

the productive economy responsible for the production of consumer goods.

The second flank of the domestic front, that dealt with pre-existing practices and the housing stock, realized *byt* reform through the arbitration of taste. Those involved revived literature on household advice and produced numerous books and pamphlets culminating in the Great Soviet Encyclopaedia's popular *Entsiklopedia Domashnevo Khoziaistva* (*Encyclopaedia of Household Economy*) first published in 1958 and continuously republished until the collapse of the Soviet Union in 1992. This literature was complemented by the journal *Dekorativnoe Iskusstvo,* and various professional journals such as *Tekhnicheskaia Estetika* by VNIITE. The concerns of *byt* reformers were given frequent coverage in popular women's journals such as *Rabotnitsa* and *Krestianka* as well as other popular media.

To shore this flank on the domestic front further, the pre-Stalinist institution of the *domkom* (housing committee) was revived with a vigour that could have only been dreamt of by earlier *byt* reformers at the time of the first Cultural Revolution. In its new form the *domkom* became the vehicle through which Party members of a particular community could actualize *byt* reformist principles at the most immediate point of contact on the domestic front, at the level of the individual household. Altogether the rationalization of *byt* on the infrastructural level and in the sphere of taste served to regulate the domestic sphere on every imaginable front. With the establishment of the VNIITE in 1962, this assault was given its final co-ordinated form which through the 1960s and early 1970s attempted to obliterate the domestic realm and vestiges of *petit-bourgeois* consciousness, towards the ontological realization of full-blown Communism ...

Soviet Interiors

Eliminating the *stolovaia*: Mono-functional Versus Multi-functional Interior Plans

One of the most significant innovations of the housing boom was the reintroduction of open plans in apartment layout. There was a considerable degree of innovation in the generation of various sorts of standard plans that could accommodate the greatest degree of family variation. These attempts were very similar to earlier Constructivist ones emphasizing flexibility and other Modernist schemes from the 1920s in Western Europe.

One of the most significant aspects of these revived open plans was the reintroduction of multi-functional zone planning. Stalinist-era apartment plans were characterized by inwardly focused, mono-functional and spatially discreet rooms, reminiscent of pre-Modernist pre-revolutionary housing. In the 1920s such plans, categorically decried as *petit-bourgeois*, were designed to accommodate the inwardly focused, segregated, and politically reactionary bourgeois nuclear family. Though such planning was not rejected in the late 1950s and early 1960s by *byt* reformers for the same reasons, the old mono-functional layout was none the less rejected. The old apportionment of space characteristic of the Stalin era and *petit-bourgeois* interiors had furniture centripetally

[Figure 1] An 'old fashioned' and 'petit-bourgeois' interior from the Stalin era unfavourably compared with a post-Stalinist 'modern' and 'socialist' interior (Photo: Eto Nuzhno Novoseltsam, Moscow: Ekonomika, 1966)

8. Комната с традиционной расстановкой мебели

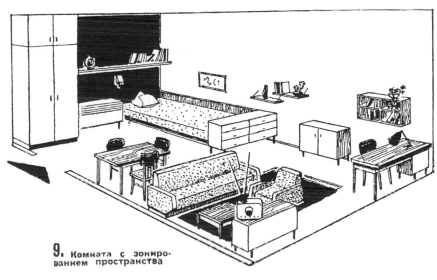

9. Комната с зониро-ванием пространства

arranged around the perimeter of the room, focusing on the family dining table or *stolovaia* at the centre. This was illuminated by the room's only light source, usually a large silken lampshade. Such configurations were summarily rejected as 'old-fashioned' as can be seen in [Figure 1]. Here we can see how the 'traditional' arrangement above gives way to the zoned 'modern' arrangement below. The centrality in which nuclear familial relations were expressed by the Stalinist/*petit-bourgeois* layout, was now exploded into a space divided up into rationalized functional zones as this figure shows.

Most significant in this explosion of the old layout was the elimination of the dining area or *stolovaia* in its entirety. New apartment schemes accommodated dining in the kitchen, thereby relegating the family ritual of taking meals together to the

[Figure 2]   Khrushchev-era kitchen with fold-away furniture (Photo: *Entiklopedia Damaslmego Khoziastvo*, 1962)

'mechanical' regions of the apartment where food was prepared and waste eliminated.[6] The *stolovaia* in effect lost its former spatial and ceremonial centrality in domestic life. If a kitchen was too small for dining, then the furniture for accommodating family meals took the form of a folding table that was stored and pulled out only when necessary [Figure 2] Permanently standing furniture was placed along a wall; forming a separate functional zone with no particular spatial or symbolic emphasis (refer to lower image in Figure 1).

Transformable Furniture: Accommodating Contradiction

One of the significant innovations in the material culture of the interior was the development of transformable furniture. This had importance in two ways for the *byt* reformist interior of the 1960s. First, it physically minimized the number of artefacts (i.e. furniture) to be found in the domestic sphere, by using one piece of furniture to serve functions that two or three separate pieces might have in the past. In many respects this was part of the general process later *byt* reformers in the late 1970s referred to as *razveshchestvleniia* (the de-artefactualization) of the domestic sphere.[7] This was the intentional and gradual evanescence of physical objects supporting the domestic sphere that like the state would wither away with the realization of full Communism.

Second, transformable furniture served to mask functions that were considered inappropriate and secondary to the primary uses of certain rooms and furniture. For example, this ensured that a 'common room' appeared as one with its appropriate functional zones. The primary appearance and use of transformable furniture always corresponded to the correct representation of a common room as a place where members of the family gathered in the evening or received guests. The secondary and tertiary uses of transformable furniture always referred to functions that were not normally considered appropriate to the common room (a couch or bookshelf could convert into a bed, a cabinet into a child's bed and desk, a buffet into a study or a combination stereo/commode into a dressing-table) ... Most significantly, the dining table could just simply disappear. Thus a single room apartment could give the appearance of an integrated and spare common room, such that

---

[6] See Ellen Lupton & J. Abbott Miller, *The Bathroom, The Kitchen and the Aesthetics of Waste: A Process of Elimination*, MIT Press, 1992 for an excellent discussion of these processes in a Western context.

[7] See N. Travin, *Material'no-veshchnaia sreda i sotsialisticheskii obraz zhizni*, Nauka, 1979.

the visitor might assume that the children's room and parent's bedroom were simply off the corridor somewhere by the toilet ... In fact these functions that were visually factored out into imaginary other spaces could all be accommodated in one space.

It is clear from the production of such transformable furniture, and the insistence of *byt* reformers on their use, that a very particular image of the common room was anxiously desired. Why this image was sought above others is difficult to say precisely. On one hand, it allowed anyone with a one-room apartment to feel as though most of the time they were living in an apartment with at least two other rooms. In this respect one might be witnessing an accommodation to individual material aspirations. On the other hand, in the spirit of Khrushchev's peaceful competition with the capitalist West, such images demonstrated that Soviet consumers aspired to similar images of domestic life and prosperity. Images of Western conditions would filter through the popular press, certainly amongst design professionals and more specifically though large competitive international exhibitions such as those staged periodically at the VDNKh exhibition grounds. At quick glance such rooms appear spacious, comfortable, and well appointed. The fact that they were designed in such a way as to

[Figure 3]   A mechanic's family at home, Ust'-Kamengorsk, 1966 (Photo: Tsentral'nyi Gosudarstvenyi Arkhiv Kinofotodokumentov, SSSR, Nos: 185729)

accommodate three generations of a single family eating, sleeping, procreating, and working all together in one room is never readily apparent from these images ...

Elimination

The next step was actually to streamline the number of items of material culture within the apartment. The slogan of 1920s *byt* reformers *nichego lishnego* (nothing superfluous) was constantly reinvoked in the 1960s. The aim was to eliminate as many items of material culture as possible associated with the *petit-bourgeois* and Stalinist domestic realm. All but the most essential of items was to be eliminated. This applied to furniture, particularly buffet cabinets. Oft-cited artefacts to be rid of included embroidered napkins, wall rugs, figurines, and various other knick-knacks. In particular *sloniki* were singled out. These rows of seven little white elephants proliferated in Stalinist interiors and served as a metonymic gloss for Stalinist *petit-bourgeois* consciousness. These elephants ... were the focus of heated attacks by arbiters of taste in popular magazines and newspaper editorials.

In many cases, some items of furniture one simply could not do without. People needed beds; they needed places to sit. Household advisers instructed owners to physically alter individual pieces of furniture so that they conformed to *byt* reformist practices. Large beds were to be either cut down with their posts removed or feet lowered. Frames could be eliminated leaving just the mattress. Advisers advocated mounting them on a low platform. Similarly divans were to have their high backs hacked off leaving no surface to support embroidery and figurines, such as the seven little elephants. All that should remain was a low-cushioned platform for sitting.

Having exploded the centripetal plan and lowered the furniture to create the desired horizontality, the next step was to change the walls, floors, and window treatments. These manipulations required material inputs and were additive rather than subtractive (although their effect was more subtractive in appearance). However, the production of paints and wallpaper designed in accord with new *byt* reformist aesthetics was sufficient such that they were both available and cheap in price. The elaborate, ubiquitous, and unofficial *alfreinaia rabota* (or *trompe-l'oeil*) of Stalinist interiors was actively discouraged ... Instead, uniform and light surfaces were promoted ... Appropriate wallpaper and paint products ensured that these schemes were realized.

The manipulation of wallpapering and paint radically reconfigured interior architectural space. This achieved the most effect with the least amount of material and labour input. As the maintenance of wall surfaces was considered part of the tenant's responsibilities, the cost of this most impressive of manipulations of interior architectural space was borne directly by the tenant and not the city council or state enterprise. In addition, inspections by members of the *domkom* often addressed themselves to the need for constant interior painting and wallpapering. Guides for *domkom* party members suggested that walls be resurfaced every spring, ensuring the single most spatially significant alteration of domestic space by the inhabitants on a regular basis. These injunctions to redecorate were timed to coincide with Communist holidays such as May Day, and the anniversary of the October Revolution of 1917. Thus the seemingly banal activity of regular wallpapering and painting served at once to reaffirm the pursuit of domestic pleasures by a household and to give concrete expression to the construction of socialism and the legitimacy of the state.

(Buchli, 1997, pp. 163–4, 166–8, 170–1)

EXERCISE

After reading the extract, reflect on the extent to which Buchli describes socialist things and spaces or socialist discourses about things.

DISCUSSION

I think it is important to recognize that Buchli presents the case of the reformers rather than the attitudes and practices of actual householders. While there would seem to be good evidence that modern design was genuinely popular (Gerchuk, 2000), possession of an apartment in the contemporary style (no doubt a rare thing) did not necessarily signal commitment to the revival of a revolutionary bolshevik spirit. Moreover, as Buchli indicates, the spatial benefits and cultural associations of tasteful, compact modern design had other, positive connotations: not least the suggestion of spaciousness and an allegiance with 'foreign' style. It is worth recalling here that the open-plan home was an innovation in American housing at this time too. This seems to me to beg questions about different kinds of research into actual consuming processes and practices, as well as the circulation of knowledge about things. The kind of generalized householder imagined by the *byt* activists would have to be much more sharply defined to take into account some of the cultural dimensions of age, ethnicity, class and gender. Similarly, inherited possessions like heirlooms or memory objects like souvenirs – under threat of what Buchli describes as 'elimination' – carry both general and highly particular meanings. The call for their elimination might be general, but their removal will always be highly specific.

What Buchli's argument suggests is that although discourse about the home and its furnishings had a particular character that reflected the political or ideological concerns of the Khrushchev era, in forms and design or in their instrumental qualities these things did not display a particular or uniquely 'socialist' character in any ideal sense. This is a pattern which seems to run throughout the history of socialism in eastern Europe (with the possible exception of some experiments in the 1920s). It is hard to see in which ways any of these cupboards, kitchen utensils or floor-plans differed from their equivalents in western Europe. The heightened east–west discourse that took place in the late 1950s, to a certain extent symbolized by the American National Exhibition of 1959, ensured that the material culture of the eastern bloc could no longer be the kind of self-sufficient system that it had once claimed to be (Merkel, 1998, p. 282).

Conclusion

Raymond Stokes has pursued the question of the 'socialist thing' in the field of technology in the GDR (Stokes, 1997). He has come to similar conclusions to those that I have drawn in this chapter: that the 'socialist thing' appeared and disappeared like some kind of immaterial mirage. Yet, in an aside, Stokes makes an interesting if controversial observation when he suggests that it was often the material failures of the socialist economy which might allow us to identify a distinct material culture:

> although the idea of the 'socialist artefact' never really bore fruit, a recognisably 'eastern bloc technological style' did emerge ... Influenced by centralized planning and its consequences, the ... eastern-bloc countries produced both consumer and producer goods which were frequently disappointing in design and/or quality.
>
> (Stokes, 1997, p. 239)

In other words, it was the often-remarked-upon failure of things to perform or their lumpen qualities which lent the socialist societies a particular, undesired material identity. The ubiquitous high-rise *novostroiki* are a case in point. Ruble calls them 'superficially modern' buildings in that they might be distinguished by the deficiencies in their design (such as 'blind' kitchens without natural daylight) or performance (for instance, upper-storey windows that shatter for no apparent reason on a calm day) (Ruble, 1993, p. 234). Similarly, Milena Veenis describes the material reality of the GDR as 'hard couches, bending staples and the need to use ten matches to light a candle' (Veenis, 1999, p. 92). It would seem that many of the items produced in the eastern bloc aroused modest expectations which they were ill equipped to realize (in fact at some time in the 1960s a new word entered Polish speech to describe these things: *brakorobstwo* – meaning new and yet already faulty products).

However, should we ascribe the significance of the material culture of the eastern bloc to its failings? I mentioned at the outset of this chapter that the domestic landscape of the eastern bloc of the 1960s has become enveloped in nostalgia since the collapse of the system. But I doubt whether one is likely to maintain a long-term affection for such flawed things. Along with a number of other commentators, it seems to me that we have to focus our attention elsewhere (see Merkel, 1998; Betts, 2000). While Khrushchev and the reformist party leaderships elsewhere in the bloc sought to be seen as modernizers of the socialist project, another, not unrelated, kind of modernization took place. The relative and new affluence of the period meant that this was when people bought their first electric kitchen appliances or purchased that miraculous box, the television. Nostalgia for these things may well be to do with recapturing an irrevocable excitement dating from that time: something that is not quite the same as political ideology. In this respect at least, 'modern' consumption of this kind may be a pan-European phenomenon, happening sooner here and later there, but constituting a common experience nevertheless. It was, rather, the discourses about consumption and the home rather than about actual things which reflected the ideological contest that divided Europe for much of the period after the Second World War.

References

Abercrombie, Stanley (1995) *George Nelson: the Design of Modern Design*, Cambridge, MA, MIT Press.

Arvatov, B. [1925] (1997) 'Everyday life and the culture of the thing: toward the formulation of the question', *October*, 81, pp. 119–28.

Berend, Ivan T. (1996) *Central and Eastern Europe 1944–1993: Detour from the Periphery to the Periphery*, Cambridge, Cambridge University Press.

Betts, Paul (2000) 'The twilight of the idols: East German memory and material culture', *Journal of Modern History*, vol. 72, pp. 731–65.

Bliznakov, Milka (1993) 'Soviet housing during the experimental years, 1918 to 1933', in William Craft Brumfield and Blair A. Ruble (eds), *Russian Housing in the Modern Age: Design and Social History*, Cambridge, Woodrow Wilson Center/Cambridge University Press.

Boym, S. (1994) *Commonplaces: Mythologies of Everyday Life in Russia*, Cambridge, MA, Harvard University Press.

Boym, S. (1996) 'Everyday culture', in Dimitri Shalin (ed.), *Russian Culture at the Crossroads*, Boulder, CO, Westview.

Breslauer, George W. (1982) *Khrushchev and Brezhnev as Leaders*, London, Allen & Unwin.

Bryden, Inga and Floyd, Janet (1999) (eds) *Domestic Space: Reading the Nineteenth-Century Interior*, Manchester, Manchester University Press.

Buchli, Victor (1997) 'Khrushchev, Modernism, and the fight against *petit-bourgeois* consciousness in the Soviet home', *Journal of Design History*, vol. 10, no. 2, pp. 161–76.

Buchli, Victor (1999) *An Archaeology of Socialism*, Oxford/New York, Berg.

Crowley, David (1999) '"Beauty, everyday and for all": the social vision of design in Stalinist Poland', in J. Attfield (ed.), *Utility Reassessed*, Manchester, Manchester University Press.

Crowley, David (2000) 'Shopping with Stalin', in David Crowley and Susan E. Reid (eds), *Style and Socialism: Modernity and Material Culture in Post-War Eastern Europe*, Oxford, Berg.

Ferge, Zsusza (1979) *A Society in the Making*, Harmondsworth, Penguin.

Garcelon, Marc (1997) 'The shadow of the leviathan: public and private in communist and post-communist Society', in Jeff Weintraub and Krishan Kumar (eds), *Public and Private in Thought and Practice*, Chicago, University of Chicago Press.

Gerchuk, Yuri (2000) 'The aesthetics of everyday life during the Khrushchev thaw in the USSR (1954–64)', in David Crowley and Susan E. Reid (eds), *Style and Socialism: Modernity and Material Culture in Post-War Eastern Europe*, Oxford, Berg.

Gerasimova, Katerina (2002) 'Privacy in the soviet communal apartment', in David Crowley and Susan E. Reid (eds), *Socialist Spaces: Sites of Everyday Life in the Eastern Bloc*, Oxford/London, Berg.

Gerö, András, and Petö, Iván (1999) *Unfinished Socialism: Pictures from the Kádár Era*, transl. James Patterson, Budapest, Central European University Press.

Gömöri, G. (1963) 'Consumerism in Hungary', *Problems of Communism*, vol. 12, no. 1, pp. 64–6.

Hanson, Phillip (1974) *Advertising and Socialism: the Nature and Extent of Consumer Advertising in the Soviet Union, Poland, Hungary and Yugoslavia*, London/Basingstoke, Macmillan.

Hessler, Julie (2000) 'Cultured trade: the Stalinist turn towards consumerism', in Sheila Fitzpatrick (ed.), *Stalinism: New Directions*, London, Routledge.

Hixson, Walter L. (1997) *Parting the Curtain: Propaganda, Culture and the Cold War, 1945–1961*, London/Basingstoke, Macmillan.

Jackson, Lesley (1994) *'Contemporary': Architecture and Interiors of the 1950s*, London, Phaidon.

Kelly, Catriona and Volkov, Vadim (1998) 'Directed desires: *kul'turnost'* and consumption', in C. Kelly and D. Shepherd (eds), *Constructing Russian Culture in the Age of Revolution 1881–1940*, Oxford, Oxford University Press.

Kettering, Karen (1997) '"Ever more cosy and comfortable": Stalinism and the soviet domestic interior, 1928–1938', *Journal of Design History*, vol. 10, no. 2, pp. 119–36.

Khrushchev, Nikita [1954](1993) 'Remove shortcomings in design, improve the work of architects', in Joan Ockman (ed.), *Architecture Culture 1943–1968: a Documentary Anthology*, Columbia Books of Architecture, New York, Rizzoli.

Khrushchev, Nikita (1961) *Conquest without War*, New York, Simon & Schuster.

Komornicki, Stanisław (1953) 'Jak urządzić nowe mieszkanie: artykuł dyskusyjny', *Stolica*, 1 March, p. 7.

Kumar, Krishan (1997) 'Home: the promise and predicament of private life at the end of the twentieth century', in Jeff Weintraub and Krishan Kumar (eds), *Public and Private in Thought and Practice*, Chicago, University of Chicago Press.

Laird, S. (1989) *Novostroika*, London, ICA.

Ludwig A. and Stumpfe, M. (1995) *Alltagskultur der DDR: Begleitbuch zur Austellung Tempolinsen und P2*, Berlin, be.bra verlag.

Maas, Jan and Referowska, Maria (1959) 'Kuchnia', *Architektura*, 2, pp. 28–9.

Marling, Karal Ann (1994) *As Seen on TV: the Visual Culture of Everyday Life in the 1950s*, Cambridge, MA, Harvard University Press.

Marx, Karl [1867] (1992) *Capital*, London, Lawrence & Wishart.

Merkel, Ina (1998) 'Consumer culture in the GDR, or how the struggle for antimodernity was lost on the battleground of consumer culture', in Susan Strasser, Charles McGovern and Matthias Judt (eds), *Getting and Spending: European and American Consumer Societies in the Twentieth Century*, Cambridge/Washington DC, Cambridge

University Press/German Historical Institute.

Naimark, Norman M. (1995) *The Russians in Germany: a History of the Soviet Zone of Occupation, 1945–1949*, Cambridge, MA, London, Belknap Press of Harvard University Press.

Nelson, G. (1956) 'Obsolesence', *Industrial Design*, pp. 84–6.

Neumann, E. (1992) 'The planned economy in search of the world standard: reflections on design and advertising in the DDR', *Design Issues*, vol. 8, no. 2, spring.

New York Times website: http://www.nytimes.com/learning/general/ onthisday/big/0724.html

Nove, Alec (1969) *An Economic History of the USSR*, Allen Lane, London.

Nove, Alec (1975) *Stalinism and After*, London, Allen & Unwin.

Packard, Vance (1960) *The Waste Makers*, London, Longman.

Potocki, Rodger (1994) 'The life and times of Poland's "bikini boys"', *Polish Review*, no. 3, pp. 259–90.

Reid, Susan E. (1997) 'Destalinization and taste, 1953–1963', *Journal of Design History*, vol. 10, no. 2, pp. 177–202.

Ruble, Blair (1993) 'From khrushcheby to korobki', in William Craft Brumfield and Blair A. Ruble (eds), *Russian Houseing in the Modern Age: Design and Social History*, Cambridge, Woodrow Wilson Center/ Cambridge University Press.

Rybczynski, Witold (1987) *Home: a Short History of an Idea*, Harmondsworth, Penguin.

Scott, John (1942) *Behind the Urals: an American Worker in Russia's City of Steel*, London, Secker & Warburg.

Stites, R. (1992) *Russian Popular Culture: Entertainment and Society since 1900*, Cambridge, Cambridge University Press.

Stokes, Raymond (1997) 'In search of the socialist artefact: technology and ideology in East Germany, 1945–1962', *German History*, vol. 15, no. 2, pp. 221–39.

Toranska, T. (1987) *Oni*, London, Collins Harvill.

Veenis, Milena (1999) 'Consumption in East Germany: the seduction and betrayal of things', *Journal of Material Culture*, vol. 4, no. 1, pp. 79–112.

Verdery, Katherine (1996) *What Was Socialism and What Comes Next?* Princeton, NJ, Princeton University Press.

Wright, Gwendolyn (1980) *Moralism and the Modern Home: Domestic Architecture and Cultural Conflict*, London/Chicago, University of Chicago Press.

Acknowledgements

Grateful acknowledgement is made to the following sources for permission to reproduce material in this book:

Chapter 1

Bodnar, J. (2001) 'Globalizing art and consumption: art movies and shopping malls', *Fin de Millenaire Budapest: Metamorphoses of Urban Life*, University of Minnesota Press. Copyright 2001 by the Regents of the University of Minnesota.

Humphrey, C. (2002) 'An ethnography of consumption in Moscow, 1993', *The Unmaking of Soviet Life: Everyday Economies After Socialism*, Cornell University Press. By kind permission of Taylor & Francis/ Routledge.

Mintz, Sidney W. 'Introduction', *Sweetness and Power.* Copyright © 1985 by Sidney W. Mintz. Used by permission of Viking Penguin, a division of Penguin Group (USA) Inc.

Samuel, R. (1994) 'Resurrectionism', *Theatres of Memory*, Volume 1, *Past and Present in Contemporary Culture*, Verso.

Chapter 2

Council of Europe, 'Preamble and Articles 1–14', *The European Convention on Human Rights*, Rome, 4, November 1950. Copyright © 1995–2002 HR-Net (Hellenic Resources Network). An HRI Project. All Rights Reserved.

Chapter 3

James, S. (1999) 'Standard histories: assumptions, limitations and objections', *The Atlantic Celts: Ancient People or Modern Invention*, British Museum Press.

Chapman, M. (1992) 'A branch of Indo-European', *The Celts: The Construction of a Myth*, MacMillan Press. By permission of Palgrave Publishers Ltd.

Loffler, M. (1988) 'The Celtic Congress of Caernarfon 1904', *A Book of Mad Celts*, Gomer Press.

Figures

p. 111: Megaw M. R. and Megaw, J. V. S. (1989) 'Area of birth of the La Tene art style', *Celtic Art from its Beginnings to the Book of Kells*, Thames & Hudson Ltd.

p.139 and 144: Copyright © The National Library of Wales.

p.141: Copyright © Gwynedd Archives Service.

Chapter 5

Zatlin, J. R. (1997), 'The vehicle of desire: the trabant, the wartburg, and the end of the GDR', *German History*, vol. 15.3, Hodder and Stoughton Educational.

Figures

p.234: Courtesy of *Eulenspiegel*, 51 (1988), 7.

Chapter 6

Salisbury, H. E. (1959) 'Nixon and Khrushchev argue in public as US Exhibit opens: accuse each other of threats', *The New York Times*, Copyright © 1959 by The New York Times Co. Reprinted with permission.

Komornicki, S. (1953) 'Jak Urzadzic Nowe Mieszkanie' in trans. Artykul dyskusyjny', *Stolica*, Prasa.

Buchli, V. (1997) 'Khrushchev, modernism and the fight against petit-bourgeois consciousness in the Soviet home', *Journal of Design History*, vol. 10, no. 2, The Design History Society. By permission of Oxford University Press.

Every effort has been made to trace all the copyright owners, but if any has been inadvertently overlooked, the publishers will be pleased to make the necessary arrangements at the first opportunity.

Index

296